Christine Melville Kenworthy is the author of 'The Nut Shop'.
She was born in Newcastle upon Tyne and lives on the North East coast with her
husband, daughters and cats.

Visit Christine's website at www.christinemelvillekenworthy.com

"The Nut Shop is a very human story about neighbours, friends and family and
how they work together through the shop's good times and bad times. It is a joy to
read out loud, with a smile, if not a laugh, on every page. Even through the bad
times the love at the heart of the book shines through."

"What a marvellously funny, warm real story."

"A charming, witty and warming book. Once started it was impossible to put down
– thought provoking mixed with laugh-out-loud funny!"

"It made me laugh and cry and by the end I felt as if I knew the characters
personally."

"A funny and fabulous book which I read in one sitting. Move over James Herriot
– Christine has stolen your crown!"

"A fantastic light-hearted, funny read. I couldn't put it down!"

"If you liked Maeve Binchy then this is for you. A great book with a definite feel-
good factor to it. Funny in places but thought-provoking at times."

"An amazing book full of loveable characters and a series of hilarious situations
that make this book impossible to put down. Would recommend to anyone who
loves a comedy!"

Dedicated to my sister, best friend and fellow Nutlady

Lorraine Melville Bewick
Love you sis

Thank you to everyone who read the first draft of Gathering Nuts and gave feedback and encouragement:
Pam Bell, Heather Burton, Alison Brown, Ebun Culwin, Janet Douglass, Simon Fawcett, Juliet Freel, Phil Hughes, Sally Jackson, Anna Kenworthy, Rose Kenworthy, Audrey McIntyre, Michael Ohajuru.
Many thanks to David Close and Michael Ohajuru for website advice.
Cover design by Simon Fawcett.

GATHERING NUTS

BY
CHRISTINE
MELVILLE KENWORTHY

Christine Kenworthy

CHAPTER ONE

I pushed my sleeve against the steamed-up shop window to clear a circular patch, and gazed out at the slow procession of drivers peering through their frosted windscreens as they edged along. An endless snake of traffic crawled along Station Road as commuters trundled into town, emitting great clouds of exhaust fumes that mingled with the icy mist. The frost had given everything a shimmering coating and had chilled the air until it was almost too painful to breathe.

'Looks like the Arctic out there,' I said to Lorraine who had lit the gas rings and was rubbing her hands together over them.

'It's like the Arctic in here,' she said. 'I'm bloody freezing.'

The kettle boiled and she made lemon and ginger tea. I wrapped my fingers around the warm mug and sipped the scalding liquid. Lorraine looked perished. Her face was pale and her lips blue although she was bundled in layers of clothes and had not yet removed her coat and hat. She sat hunched on a stool behind the counter sipping her tea.

'What time is Rick coming with that heater?' she asked.

'He said first thing this morning. He'll probably be here soon.'

Rick worked in the tool hire centre at the bottom of the bank and had offered us free loan of a Calor gas heater.

'Come on, we'd better get started,' I said, putting down my mug and moving towards the kitchen. Lorraine didn't move.

'It's too cold. I can't function.'

'It's one extreme or the other in here,' I said remembering the problems we'd had in the summer when the shop had been so hot we'd all felt permanently exhausted and our big display fridge had broken down with the strain of trying to maintain a steady temperature. Trying to sell health foods in an environment like a hot house had not been ideal.

Lorraine followed me into the kitchen, removed her gloves, and after washing her hands at the sink, replaced them with a fingerless pair and began chopping onions and carrots to make soup.

'You can't cook like that,' I said laughing. 'You look like Fagin frying up sausages for the gang.'

5

'Wanna bet? I'm not taking anything off. I'm freezing.'

Personally I wasn't too bad. I was wearing thick tights beneath my trousers and two tee-shirts as well as a jumper and could bear to take off my coat and hat. At six months pregnant I felt like I had my own little internal central heating system. It was just my fingers and toes that were cold.

Our part time assistant, Nadine, arrived cheerfully complaining about the cold.

'What do you look like?' she said, laughing, when she saw Lorraine swaddled in her many layers of clothing, scraping carrots with a scarf tied around her face.

'Yes, you may well mock,' Lorraine said good-naturedly. 'But I'm actually the only one doing any work.' We took the hint and went to help with the day's preparation, making sandwich fillings and chopping salad while Lorraine made soup.

This was the beginning of our second year in business. Our first year had been fraught with a whole diversity of problems ranging from an infestation of moths, having our window smashed by a deckchair wielding drunk, and an arson attack on the gym upstairs which then spread to our premises. However, with the help of family and friends, we had survived and I felt very optimistic and excited about the coming months and especially about our baby who was due to arrive at the end of March.

Rick arrived with the Calor gas heater.

'There you are, hinny. That should warm you up a bit. There's about half a bottle of gas left to start you off. When you're ready for a new one give me a shout and I'll give you a discount off the next one.'

'That's great, thanks Rick,' I said and Lorraine gave him a carton of soup and a couple of bread rolls. When he'd gone I pondered on where to put the heater.

'Do you think we should have it in the shop front for the customers or in the kitchen for us?'

'In the kitchen for us,' Lorraine and Nadine said together and we pushed it through the gap between the counter and the big fridge into the kitchen. We were sitting in front of it waiting for the kettle to boil again when Nige our postman arrived.

'Morning campers,' he said depositing a pile of letters on the counter. He looked at Lorraine in her bundle of clothes and laughed. 'Look at the state of you. Nanouk of the North! Looks like you've been overdoing it a bit with the whale blubber darlin'.'

'You want to see yourself,' she told Nige, who wore a Davy Crockett hat with earflaps and imitation beaver tail along with his favourite green and pink hand knitted scarf that was wound around his oversized raincoat. 'And if you think I'm making you a cup of coffee after that remark you can think again.'

'I'll get it,' Nadine said laughing, and as she got up to fill the kettle the door opened and Georgina arrived.

'By, it's cold enough to freeze the goolies off a brass monkey,' Georgina said as she put her shopping basket down.

'Coffee or lemon and ginger tea?' Nadine asked her.

'Ooh, lemon and ginger please.'

Nige and Georgina visited us every morning and we would start the day with a hot drink and the local gossip. Georgina was an artist and scraped together a living selling handmade pottery and jewellery and doing face-painting at fairs and parties. She therefore had plenty of spare time and spent quite a lot of it with us in the shop. Nige however, did not have plenty of spare time, yet managed to fit in time for a coffee and a gossip every morning. I often wondered if his bosses at Royal Mail had any idea of how much time he spent skiving and how little work he seemed to do.

'How's bump?' Georgina asked.

'Fine,' I said, patting my stomach. 'Getting bigger every day.'

'Have you been to Barbara's yoga classes yet?'

'No not yet.'

'You really should go, you'd enjoy it and it would do you the world of good.'

Barbara was a high-spending customer who shopped with us every Friday. A committed vegetarian and passionate about the local community she refused to shop in supermarkets preferring to support local businesses. She ran yoga classes at her home, to which Georgina was a frequent participant. Barbara had suggested I go along and had promised to show me exercises that would strengthen my abdomen and therefore make giving birth easier. I knew I should give it a go, not only for my benefit and the baby's, but to show support to Barbara who was such a loyal customer. But memories of past experiences of formal exercise put me off.

I'd never been one for exercise classes. I'd been to an aerobics class with a friend and hated it. I'd jumped about, frantically trying to keep up with the woman at the front who was barking directions, but no matter how hard I tried I couldn't seem to move in the same direction as the rest of the class. As my embarrassment increased, so did my lack of co-ordination, until I'd completely lost the ability to distinguish left from right and became a whirlwind of flinging arms and legs. My friend thought it was the funniest thing she'd ever seen and was disappointed when I vowed never to repeat the experience.

I was the same at the gym. I would cling to the hand bars of a treadmill as my feet were constantly swept from beneath me, struggling to keep my balance as I fought to keep my legs striding, aware of others next to me jogging along rhythmically as they watched the overhead television screens.

I couldn't see the point of the television screens. I mean, how were you supposed to keep up with Coronation Street when your ears were pounding and a red haze had descended in front of your eyes? The weight of my bottom bobbing up and down was very uncomfortable and I wondered if others were suffering in the same way. Hanging on tightly I'd turned my head to sneak a look at the women next to me. They didn't seem to be having the same problems at all. For a start they were upright and running at a steady pace. There were no sweaty red faces, just a lot of make-up and swishy blond hair. And none of them had buttocks big enough to wobble never mind bounce.

'Why not come with me tomorrow?' Georgina suggested. 'There's a class at six. You could come to mine after closing and we'll go from there.'

I hesitated.

'Exercise classes aren't really my thing. I prefer keeping fit by walking or riding my bike.'

'It'll be good for the baby.'

'I think you should go,' Lorraine said and Nadine agreed with her.

'You'll enjoy it, it'll be a laugh.'

'You mean it'll be a laugh for you when Georgina tells you how rubbish I am at it,' I said.

'Eeh, I can just imagine you having to be carried out with your legs tied in a knot around your neck,' Nige laughed.

'Thanks for that Nige,' I said. 'Oh all right I'll go. But just once. Just to say I've been. It's not going to be a regular thing.'

Business was quiet during the morning but surprisingly busy at lunchtime. I'd thought it would be too cold for people to leave their offices to come in search of a take-away lunch, but the rush began as usual just after twelve. Our hot food was popular; luckily we had plenty of home-made soup in the freezer as it seemed to be selling by the gallon. Having the cooker on for most of the morning as well as the Calor gas heater had raised the temperature in the shop quite considerably. Lorraine was able to remove a few layers of clothing and now looked closer to her usual size.

'Another four vegeburgers please,' she called from the counter and Nadine added them to the pan. I felt my stomach rumble, they smelled delicious. I made a mental note to have one for lunch.

Lorraine and Nadine often teased me that I must be carrying a baby elephant judging by the amount of food I put away but I couldn't help it. I felt hungry all the time and working with food all day was just too tempting.

The vegeburgers were my biggest weakness. We served them in the most deliciously soft sesame seed rolls with crisp salad and creamy mayonnaise. Or you could add mushrooms or grated cheese or coleslaw. Or if you were a greedy pregnant woman you could add all of these and a fried egg on top too.

The lunchtime rush always stopped at two o'clock as dramatically as it had started when we would sit and eat our lunch, taking turns to get up and serve customers.

I went to put the kettle on to make our hot drinks and Nadine went to the kitchen to see what was left in the tubs, clearing the empty ones to the sink.

'What are you having?' she asked. 'There's plenty of egg mayo left and cream cheese.'

'Egg mayo'll do for me thanks,' Lorraine said.

'Egg mayo and salad all round?' Nadine said, then seeing my face said, 'Or do you want one of your usual egg-mushroom-cheese-salad-coleslaw-mayo-burgers?'

'Oh go on then, I'll force myself,' I said. 'I'll cook it.'

'No I'll do it,' Nadine said. 'You go and get your cup of tea darlin' and I'll make you one.'

As she was piling it all into a huge wholemeal stottie, a girl entered the shop wearing paint spattered jeans and a sweatshirt.

'God it's freezing out there,' she said, then seeing Nadine piling mushrooms on top of my towering burger said, 'Mmm, that looks nice. Could you make me one?'

The girl told us her name was Janice and that she was busy painting walls in a flat she'd just moved into further down the bank with her five children, who ranged in age from eight months to seven years.

'Five kids!' Nadine said. 'You'll have your work cut out!'

'I can handle the five kids,' Janice said. 'It's the five fathers that cause the problems.'

She went to look around the shelves and selected some packets of biscuits, organic chocolate bars, cartons of fruit juice and a family-sized carrot cake.

'A few treats for the kids,' she said as she handed over a twenty-pound note. Nadine packed the purchases in a carrier bag and handed over change and Janice left whistling cheerfully.

'Five men,' Nadine grumbled as she watched Janice strut cockily down the street. 'One would do me.'

CHAPTER TWO

Janice was back first thing next morning while Lorraine was counting the float into the till. I was unpacking the bread delivery and Nadine was collecting dishes and utensils together, ready for preparing the sandwich fillings.

'Could you do me another one of those huge burgers? It was gorgeous,' she said.

'No problem,' Nadine told her. 'Just give me a minute to get sorted out and I'll stick one in the pan for you.'

'Actually I'll take some for the kids too,' Janice said 'Do me six all together.'

'Six of the huge ones?' Nadine said. 'Will the kids be able to eat all that or shall I do you smaller ones for them?'

'Nah, just make them all the same.'

'Are you sure? What about the little ones? I mean the baby won't eat one will he?'

'So what?' Janice said. 'If they don't get eaten they'll go in the bin. It's not really a problem is it?'

Nadine shrugged and put the vegeburgers into the hot pan. Janice collected a pack of fair trade ground coffee, a pat of organic butter, a bottle of orange juice, a box of muesli and a bottle of organic milk. I rang them in the till and packed them in a couple of bags for her.

'Anything else?' I asked.

'Yeah, actually I think I'll have some of that bread, it smells great.'

She indicated to the fresh bread I'd just stacked on the shelves behind the counter. She chose six poppyseed knots, six rye baps and a sunflower seed loaf and I added them to her bill. She paid with a fifty pound note and Nadine handed her the six huge vegeburgers that she'd wrapped and put in a bag.

'See ya later,' Janice said as she left loaded down with carrier bags.

'Seems to have plenty of money,' Nadine said. 'Do you think she's on benefits or do you think she gets loads of maintenance from the five dads?'

'I don't think she has a job,' put in Lorraine. 'She wouldn't really have time would she, not with five kids.'

'Don't know,' I said. 'It's none of our business really. As long as she spends it here I don't really care!'

'That's true,' Lorraine said. 'She's only been in here twice and she's spent nearly sixty quid. Let's hope she keeps it up.'

The morning's task was to change the window display. We'd just received a delivery of books called 'De-tox your Body Naturally' and I arranged some of them in the window along with bottles of carrot and beetroot juice, herbal teas, exfoliating body brushes, essential oils and Dead Sea bath salts.

De-toxing was extremely fashionable at that time. Many celebrities were extolling the benefits of a regular de-tox and one in particular had devised her own de-tox diet and exercise programme which was currently very popular.

De-toxing can have very beneficial effects on the body and can be used as a powerful healing tool. However, as always there were those who were taking the whole thing to extremes and were using it as a form of rapid weight-loss programme. Nadine was influenced to try it by the stick-thin actresses and models that were advocating it at every opportunity.

'I'm going to start my de-tox tomorrow,' she told Georgina and Nige as she demolished a cheese savoury stottie the size of a dustbin lid.

'That's what you said yesterday,' Georgina said.

'Yes, I know but it's not something you can rush into. I want to do it properly. I'm determined to follow the plan word for word then by the end of next week I'll look like Carol Vordeman. It says in the book you have to de-tox your mind too and take a few days to get yourself into the right mental state.'

'You're already in a right mental state if you think drinking cucumber juice for a couple of days will make you look like Carol Vordeman,' Nige said.

Nadine ignored him but if she was hoping for support from Georgina she didn't get it.

'De-tox is a right load of tosh,' Georgina said. 'If you eat proper healthy food in the first place you shouldn't need to de-tox.

It's just another load of marketing hype to make money out of gullible people.'

I said nothing. Although I could see the benefits, I'd never been on any kind of diet plan in my life and didn't want to change the habit. But I had to admit we were making a lot of money from customers following de-tox plans. As well as herbs, juices and skin cleansing products they were also buying artichoke and milkthistle preparations to cleanse the liver, aloe vera and psyllium husks for the bowels, kelp to stimulate the metabolism and an assortment of essential oils to combat cellulite and skin problems.

Later that afternoon, during a quiet spell, Lorraine and I sat in front of the heater drinking organic hot chocolate and eating a box of cranberry and ginger cookies that a sales rep had left as a free sample. The afternoon light was beginning to fade and the shop was cosy and fragrant with the smell of hot food. We listened to a radio play, and afterwards the local news, which foretold of snow.

'I hope it doesn't snow for the sponsored walk,' Lorraine said. 'It will be awful if we have to walk in a snowstorm. You hadn't forgotten about it had you?'

'No,' I lied. 'Anyway we have a couple of weeks yet, anything could happen with the weather by then.'

'Oh I was thinking it was next weekend,' Lorraine said.

'No. Week after. So there's time for snow to arrive and disappear again before then.'

Nadine, Georgina, Nige, Peter and Lorraine and I had agreed to take part in a sponsored walk in remembrance of Josie, a friend of ours, who had died of cancer the previous year. A local cancer charity had announced it was holding a fund-raising walk so we'd sent off for details and they'd sent us an information pack with sponsor forms.

'These forms are filling up nicely,' I said, looking at the pile of sponsor forms we'd left on the counter. 'People are being very generous.' I read the amounts on the sheet. 'Five pounds, twenty pounds, ten…another ten…there's a pledge of fifty pounds here from Mrs Forbes-Williamson.'

'Josie was well-liked,' Lorraine said. 'Customers have been more than happy to donate in her name.'

Our peace was shattered by the telephone ringing. Lorraine went off to answer it and I took the opportunity to help myself to another cookie.

'That was Julie Bradley,' Lorraine said when she'd hung up. Julie was a reporter from our local newspaper, the Daily Echo, and had published a couple of articles about us in the past, both of which were filled with inaccuracies.

'She's writing a piece on the current craze of de-toxing and she's asked if we can give her some facts.'

'Is she coming in to speak to us?'

'No, she said she's really busy at the moment so I said we'd ring her back with the information. She said if we give her details of some of the products we sell she'd include them in the feature. Might get us more sales. I've made a few notes, have a look and see if you can think of anything else we need to tell her.'

I took the pages from Lorraine and scanned them. They contained information about the benefits of detoxing, how to choose a detox programme and details of useful foods and supplements stocked at Nutmeg.

'Yeah, looks fine to me,' I said as I handed them back to her. 'The only other thing I'd mention are the possible side effects.'

Sometimes, detox followers experience what is known as a 'cleaning crisis' when the body works to expel toxins from its system. For a short period a toxic overload can occur with symptoms such as bad breath, flatulence, headaches and an increase in perspiration. These effects are usually short lasting and are taken as a sign that the detox is working.

'I don't think that's a very good idea,' Lorraine said. 'We're trying to sell these things, who's going to come in to buy stuff that's going to give you B.O. and make you fart?'

'Very true. But it's probably better to be honest about it then they'll know what to expect.'

'Oh all right,' Lorraine said and she reluctantly scribbled a couple of lines on her list before going to call Julie with the information. She was back minutes later.

'That was quick.'

'She was busy,' Lorraine said. 'She took a few notes but said she would look up some facts later to pad out her article. She's going to write it as though she's interviewed me about my detox plan.'

'But you haven't got a detox plan. You've never done one.'

'I know, I know. But she said it would sound better written as an interview than just a list of facts so she's going to make it up. She'll write it as though she's asked me about my experiences of my detox plan.'

'You're brave,' I said, thinking of the disastrous articles Julie had written about us in the past; articles with incorrect quotes and ambiguous wording that had made us look foolish.

'Aren't you worried she writes something you wouldn't say that will embarrass you?'

'No, not really. I mean it's all just facts about detox. What could go wrong with that?'

At ten past five Lorraine went to post some letters so I took advantage of business being quiet to start cashing up and processing the day's delivery notes and invoices. I wanted to get closed up quickly so that I could get changed for my first yoga class at Barbara's. As I sat behind the counter writing the day's cheques into the banking book, the doorbell jangled and I looked up to see an elderly woman enter with the aid of a stick.

'Afternoon,' I said.

As she approached the counter wheezing and panting, I was surprised to notice that she was much younger than I'd first thought her to be. I judged her to be probably in her early fifties. Her tightly permed grey hair covered her head like coiled springs and her dowdy clothes and stiffness of movement all contrived to add more years.

'Can I help?' I asked.

'I only wish you could dear,' she said as she settled herself on a stool in front of the counter. 'I've got so many problems I don't know where to start. You would not believe the things I suffer from.'

My heart sank. Some customers loved to come in to talk about their health problems and on many occasions, Lorraine, Nadine or myself had found ourselves slowly withering into a stupor, as some hypochondriac spent a happy hour or so relating their tales of woe. This was just the kind of customer I did not need if I were to get away on time. Anticipating that she would not leave

15

without some sort of treatment or remedy, I mentally planned to cut short the conversation as quickly as possible and sell her something harmless like a bottle of vitamin pills. I forced a smile and rearranged my features into what I hoped was a sympathetic listening face.

The woman, who told me her name was Val, explained that she had suffered from poor health for as long as she could remember. She reeled off a huge list of ailments she'd suffered over the years and I felt a pang of guilt. I'd always been lucky with my health and apart from the occasional cold very rarely ailed anything.

Poor woman, I thought. She's come here for advice and help and here am I, healthy and young and so caught up in my own life that I begrudge spending a bit of time to help someone in need. I resolved to do my best to help her and not to be so selfish. So what if I was a bit late for the yoga class? Would it matter compared to helping another human being?

Twenty-five minutes later, Lorraine returned to find me slumped behind the counter, eyes glazed, having journeyed through irritable bowel syndrome, menstrual problems, arthritis, dandruff, flatulence, indigestion, allergies, various sprains, bruises and broken bones.

'Sorry to interrupt,' Lorraine said abruptly, 'but we're closed.'

She helped Val to her feet and gently but firmly guided her to the door.

'But I haven't finished,' Val said indignantly. 'I'm only up to nineteen-eighty-four.'

Slowly regaining consciousness, the present came back into focus and I became aware that Lorraine was pushing a resistant Val towards the door.

'Lorraine!' I hissed.

How rude of her, I thought. She was practically dragging the poor woman out.

'Call back tomorrow, we'll see you then,' Lorraine said pleasantly as she nudged Val out of the door.

'But I was going to show you my varicose vein,' Val said as Lorraine closed the door and turned the sign to 'closed'.

'I can't believe you did that!' I said to Lorraine. 'The poor woman.'

'Poor woman my arse. Sorry like, but I've no patience with people like that. She comes in every Wednesday morning when you're at the ante-natal clinic and Nadine and I have to listen to her whinging on for hours.'

'Lorraine! She's really ill, she told me all about it, how can you be so hard?'

'How can you be so soft?' Lorraine said. 'There are loads of people who come in here with genuine health problems who deserve your sympathy but all she's got is a severe case of whingy-itis.'

She closed the blinds as she spoke and I pulled my yoga clothes from my bag and began to change.

'I can't be bothered with people who don't try to help themselves,' Lorraine said, still on her soapbox. 'There's nothing wrong with her that a good kick up the backside wouldn't put right. I'd like to do it for her myself.'

Although I was a bit shocked at Lorraine's attitude, I had to laugh. Because she was so robust herself and never made a fuss when she was ill, she had no patience with self-pitiers. She was still chuntering about it as we assembled our layers of jumpers and coats and put on hats and scarves.

'I'd love to just tell her to shut up and bugger off,' she ranted. 'I mean, she wants to think about people who are really ill, people who just get on with it instead of whinging and complaining.'

'I just think you need to be a bit more sensitive sometimes,' I said. 'The woman is in poor health.'

'I'll save my sensitivity for those who need it.' Lorraine said as she turned off the lights. 'Honestly you're far too soft.'

She opened the door then immediately screamed and jumped back in shock as a figure emerged from the shadows to grab her arm.

'Did I ever tell you about the time I had pernicious anaemia?'

'Val!' Lorraine said. 'What are you doing jumping out on people like that? You nearly gave me a heart attack.'

She hustled Val away from the doorway and locking the door behind us, we went into the street, the icy wind stinging our faces and stealing our breath.

'Don't talk to me about heart attacks,' Val said. 'I had a suspected heart-attack only last year.'

'You shouldn't be hanging about out here, it's freezing, you'll catch your death.' Lorraine said sternly.

'I know and with this ice I could fall and break my legs as well.'

Lorraine looked at me and raised her eyes then bent to unlock the car door. Val took a step towards the road and wobbled elaborately, waving her stick as she gave a badly acted performance of someone almost falling over. Lorraine looked at me, her face stiff with exasperation.

'Get in,' she said ungraciously to Val. 'I'll give you a lift home.'

She took Val's stick from her and threw it on the back seat then helped Val into the passenger seat.

'Actually, I was going to get a taxi to my brother's house in the West End,' Val said. 'Could you just drop me off there?' Lorraine hesitated.

'Ok, no problem,' she said through gritted teeth and she began to scrape ice from the car windows.

'Excuse me,' whined Val from inside the car, 'do you think you could do that with the doors closed? It's very draughty in here; I don't want to get a chill in my kidneys.'

Lorraine stopped scraping and closed the doors none too gently, irritation showing on her face.

'Aren't you getting in?' she said to me, resuming her ice scraping.

'No thanks, I'll walk,' I said laughing. 'It's just along the road.'

I pulled up my hood and as I started towards Georgina's, Val wound down the car window a couple of inches and I heard her call to Lorraine.

'Could you come and adjust this seat? It's at the wrong angle for my back and I don't want to put it out again. The last time I had trouble with my back I was in bed for months.'

I turned back to face Lorraine and saw her jaw tighten as Val wound up the window.

'So when are you going to tell her to shut up and bugger off and give her that kick up the backside?' I asked and Lorraine scowled at me.

'You know your problem?' I said over my shoulder as I started to walk along the street. 'You're too soft.'

CHAPTER THREE

By the time I'd walked the short journey to Georgina's, my ears were stinging and my face was numb.

'Come in, take off your coat,' Georgina said. 'We've just got time for a drink before we go. Hot chocolate ok?'

'Mmm, lovely,' I said and I sank into a huge armchair feeling the warmth of the open fire envelop me. I rested my head against the cushions and looked around. Thick velvet curtains were drawn against the early evening gloom, and several small table lamps, along with the glow of the coals, gave the room a warm radiance.

Georgina was a regular visitor to the Narly Neh, an antique-come-junk shop at the foot of the bank, and had furnished her home in her own eclectic style. Lorraine and I often took turns to visit the shop during quiet times. It had originally been called The Nearly New Shop but as several of the letters that made up the sign had fallen away years ago and had never been replaced it was known locally by the name that the remaining letters spelled.

Many treasures had been discovered there. I'd bought a set of Edwardian crystal glasses for much less than the price of a new set and my husband Peter had brought home a pine bookcase for the baby's room to house the children's books we'd started collecting as soon as we knew we were to be parents. Lorraine had found an ebony table with carved elephants that now stood in her hall holding a huge table lamp.

Georgina's artistic talent was very apparent; the mix of pieces from different eras and styles could very easily have resulted in a jumble of clutter, however the result was very effective.

I looked at the art deco sofa, the inlaid wooden bookcase stuffed with books, the brass fender, the bamboo table holding a Victorian jug filled with lilies, and the warm colours of the rugs and cushions. A row of 1950s vases were displayed on the mantelpiece and at the side of the hearth, two cats lay snuggled together in a basket lined with a patchwork quilt. The only thing that seemed out of place was the television set, too modern and garish for this peaceful and timeless room.

Georgina returned with the hot drinks and we sat companionably, listening to her huge 1940s wireless. The combination of the hot chocolatey milk and the cosy ambience of the room seeped through me and I felt my eyes beginning to close. One of the cats yawned and stretched, turning onto its back to warm its stomach from the fire. I too yawned.

'Can't we just stay here?' I asked. The last thing on earth I felt like doing was to go to a yoga class to force my body into strange shapes.

'No way,' she said collecting the empty mugs. 'You're not getting out of it now.'

We bundled ourselves up in our outdoor things and the cats looked up at me sleepily as I bent to stroke their warm fur.

'Lucky little buggers,' I said to them as they cuddled together in front of the glowing embers and Georgina and I went out into the freezing street.

Barbara was pleased to see us. She led us up three flights of stairs to her attic where a group of around ten women were sitting on folded blankets discussing the news that Charles and Diana were planning to divorce.

'That poor girl has been very badly treated,' one of the women said. 'He should never have married her.'

'Well I think she went into it with her eyes open. She only has herself to blame,' said another.

There was a chorus of disapproval at this as the other women defended Diana and slated Charles. One of the women turned to me.

'What do you think about it?' she asked and before I could speak Georgina sprang into a rant about the drawbacks of having a monarchy and the shortcomings of Prince Charles. Luckily Barbara interrupted the tirade before Georgina could launch into her well-worn sermon about the evils of the male as a species, and introduced us to the women. I huffed and puffed my hellos still recovering from the ascent.

'Help yourself to a blanket from the cupboard,' Barbara said pointing to a pine cupboard beneath the eaves at the far side of the attic. 'There's a money box on top to put your fee into, thank you.'

I followed Georgina and took a blanket after dropping my three pound coins into the wooden box.

'Find yourself a space and remove your shoes,' Barbara instructed and the women shuffled about to create room. Georgina laid her blanket on the floor and indicated for me to do the same next to her but I had spotted a space near a long wall mirror and made my way towards it. I preferred to be at the back where I could hide. I placed my blanket on the floor and sat on it, as everyone else was doing.

I looked around at the other women. I seemed to be the youngest there, I guessed the others to be mostly in their forties and fifties. One looked positively ancient. Poor old dear, I thought. I wonder if she has any idea what she's let herself in for. I was glad to see there was not a hint of lycra anywhere. Everyone was dressed in loose baggy clothes and I relaxed about my outfit.

The only jogging bottoms I'd been able to find in the house that would accommodate my bump were a pair of Peter's old running pants that he'd worn to paint the hall ceiling and were speckled with white emulsion. The elastic in the ankles had either snapped or perished with age and as the legs were far too long anyway, I had tucked them into my socks which I'd pulled up to mid-calf.

Barbara switched on a cassette player and the air was filled with the most beautifully soothing music as she spoke to us. Her voice was calm and gentle.

'Right, everyone. I will start as usual with The Salute to the Sun.'

She stood in the centre of the room, placed her hands together in front of her chest and breathed deeply. I watched in anticipation. She stood with eyes closed, breathing deeply.

I waited. Is that it? I thought.

Eventually she began to move, gradually stretching her arms oh-so-slowly above her head. When she was at full stretch she again kept the position whilst breathing deeply. Barbara continued her slow and controlled movements, changing from pose to pose, stopping to breathe deeply as each position was accomplished.

I sat cross-legged on my blanket watching in awe. Is this what I was going to have to do? Was I supposed to be memorising this routine? I was amazed at this different Barbara I was watching. Lithe and supple, her movements smooth and controlled; she showed no resemblance to the middle-aged housewife who shopped with us weekly. I watched apprehensively. There was no way I'd be able to get my body into those shapes.

Barbara came to the end of her demonstration. She looked around slowly as if returning to the present moment from a distant place in her mind.

'And now it's your turn,' she said quietly and everyone rose and began to emulate what they'd just been shown. I watched the others surreptitiously, trying to follow them. Everyone seemed to know what they were doing except me. Moving and stretching, totally engrossed in the moment. I caught Georgina's eye and she smiled encouragingly. The old dear, who'd told me her name was Olivia, was holding a position that if I hadn't seen with my own eyes would have sworn was physically impossible.

I tucked my over-sized tee-shirt into Peter's jogging pants to keep it out of the way as I shuffled about trying to keep up with the others. As I stretched my arms above my head, copying the woman closest to me, I caught sight of my reflection in the wall mirror and for a moment did not recognise myself. Peter's jogging pants were at full stretch over my bump with my top tucked into them and my trouser legs tucked into my socks. I realised with a start that this Tweedle-Dee figure staring back at me was my reflection. I looked like a barrel with clothes on.

Barbara moved noiselessly toward me.

'How are you doing?' she asked quietly.

'Not too well,' I admitted pulling my top out from the elastic of my trousers in the hope of looking slightly less Humpty-Dumptyish.

'Don't worry,' she said. 'It takes a while to get the hang of it. I'll go through it with you.'

She talked me through The Salute to the Sun movements and I practised alongside her.

'I think I've got it!' I said as I suddenly realised that I was remembering the sequence of positions. Barbara left me to it and I noticed that I was actually enjoying the smooth flow of movements. The stretches seemed to release tensions in my body that I hadn't known existed and concentrating on my breathing as well as getting the movements right left no room in my mind to think about anything else. As someone with the kind of chaotic mind filled with random thoughts constantly whizzing around, I found this very liberating.

Barbara took us through other sequences, amending some of the positions that were unsuitable for pregnancy and I practised my own, usually easier, versions.

As the session progressed, I felt my body become more energised and my mind become clearer and less cluttered.

This is amazing, I thought. Usually exercise left me feeling exhausted and aching. The time flew past and I was disappointed when Barbara announced the end of the session.

'We will end as usual with a relaxation and visualisation exercise,' she said and as everyone straightened their blankets and lay down, I did the same.

'Imagine yourself in a place of nature,' Barbara said in a sing-song voice, once everyone had ceased shuffling about on blankets. 'See it,' she breathed. 'Feel it. Smell it. Be there.'

Place of nature, I thought. Place of nature. Like what sort of place of nature? A beach? A forest? My mind flicked rapidly through scenes of woodlands and meadows and sandy beaches.

'And take a deep breath, and let go,' Barbara said. When she said 'go' she exhaled loudly like she was letting the air out of a tyre. Hisses of breath echoed around me as the others deflated their tyres.

I still hadn't got my place of nature sorted. A beach, I thought frantically. A beach with white shining sand and lapping waves. I saw it clearly, an expanse of shimmering white sand reflecting the sunlight and a turquoise blue sea. It was deserted, I was the only one there and I lay back absorbing the peace and slowly released my breath.

'And let go,' repeated Barbara with another hiss. I exhaled heavily and relaxed and as I did, an elderly woman on a mobility scooter drove right across my beach in front of me.

Excuse me, I said silently. This is a private beach. This is my tranquil place. Go away.

The woman on the scooter came to a halt in front of me.

Get off my beach, I told her. But the more I tried to imagine the beach without the woman on her scooter, the more firmly the vision seemed to plant itself in my imagination, becoming more distinct until I could clearly see the woman's face. I saw suddenly her mournful eyes and expression of gloom and I realised it was Val.

I opened my eyes in shock, then reminding myself that it was just my imagination settled down again. Once more I visualised my beautiful beach and once more Val appeared on her scooter. I frowned trying to erase her from my vision but the harder I concentrated, more details came into focus.

'And relax,' breathed Barbara. Relax, relax I chanted and Val dismounted her scooter, huffing and wheezing as she shuffled across the sand towards me

Startled, I opened my eyes and shook the picture from my mind. Start again, I thought. I settled into my blanket and closed my eyes.

A field of wild flowers? Yes that's it. Long grass, poppies, the drone of a bee toiling close by. In and out of flowers. I breathed in deeply and relaxed. Tranquil and beautiful. At least it was until Val appeared, trundling through the grass on her scooter.

Try again. What about a garden? Yes. A beautiful, planted garden.

The walled garden of Wallington suddenly came into focus and my tensions began to slip away as I melted into the vision. I saw the flower-filled borders, the clipped hedges and the lichen covered stone figures. I moved effortlessly through the conservatory, through a spectrum of colour, ingesting the myriad of delicious scents. I bent to admire the tiny ballerina flowers of a fuchsia and as I did a familiar face appeared over the terracotta tub, her face long and woeful.

I imagined I was at the top of a mountain, looking down on rolling valleys and patchwork fields and there she was, hovering in the sky, slowly making her way towards me.

I imagined a woodland, filtered with dappled light and drops of shining dew, and she appeared gradually like the Cheshire cat, but with a pair of slowly appearing doleful eyes rather than a grin.

I was aware of Barbara talking the others through a relaxation sequence, but I was still struggling to find my place of nature.

Oh to hell with it I thought. I give up. I lay back, prepared to lie it out until Barbara had finished her exercise.

'Feel the tension evaporate from your body...' she was saying. 'You are as light as air. You are floating in peace and tranquillity.' And in spite of myself, I found I was floating into a semi-dream world…

'…And come slowly back to the present moment. Become aware of your surroundings and *breathe*.'

Barbara's voice pulled me back from a balmy summer's day at Wallington's Portico Walk where I sat amongst buttercups and daisies watching baby rabbits at play, to the dimly lit attic and I opened my eyes to find that thirty minutes had passed.

'You were trying too hard,' Georgina said later when I told her about the appearance of Val. 'Don't you see that as soon as you stopped trying and relaxed it was ok and you got into it? When you try *not* to visualise something, the picture just becomes clearer in your mind.' She laughed. 'When I first went to meditation classes, every time I tried to empty my mind, all I could see was this enormous chicken. The more I tried to eliminate it from my mind, the more firmly planted it would become. Sometimes there was a whole row of giant bloody chickens. It took me ages to get rid of them. You see I had sort of trained my mind to see them. I was *expecting* to see them every time I tried to relax.'

'Why giant chickens?' I asked, laughing.

'Who knows? Why giant chickens? Why Val?' She sighed thoughtfully. 'The mind is a complex and mysterious enigma.'

CHAPTER FOUR

I told Lorraine and Nadine all about the class the next morning.

'My body feels really supple and energised,' I said. 'I had a great night's sleep after the class and I feel so calm and balanced and at peace with the world.'

'Get lost,' Lorraine said scathingly. 'People do yoga for years to get those sort of results, not one session.'

'I don't think you should be ridiculing something you know nothing about,' I said in a superior tone. 'I think you should try it.'

'The tree,' Lorraine said, standing on one leg and holding up her arms, fingers splayed. Nadine laughed and put one hand on her hip and the other in the air.

'The teapot.'

Lorraine laughed and stuck out her bum and flapped her elbows.

'The chicken,' she said.

'The giant chicken,' Nadine said and they both collapsed, laughing hysterically.

'Very funny,' I said, wishing I hadn't given them so much detail and anticipating what was coming next.

'The Val,' Lorraine said, pulling a long sullen face and wobbling about pretending to hold a stick.

'I should have known you'd just take the mick, you ignoramuses,' I said as they continued to laugh. 'Actually, the yoga class has given me an idea. I think we should learn about alternative therapies and practices. It would complement our natural remedies if we could recommend therapies to our customers.'

Lorraine wiped her eyes and looked at me. I looked from her to Nadine and let them have my fantastic idea.

'I think we should convert the office into a therapy room and offer treatments.'

'Treatments? What sort of treatments?'

'All sorts of things,' I said struggling to think of a natural therapy. It was a subject I didn't really know much about.

'Reflexology,' I said at last. 'Stuff like that.'

'Reflexology?' repeated Nadine. 'Isn't that when they massage your feet?'

'Hang on a minute,' Lorraine said. 'I'm not sitting in the office twiddling some strange bloke's toes.'

'I might, if they're nice,' Nadine said.

'I'm not talking about us doing the treatments,' I said. 'We're not trained. I mean getting therapists in. We'd get appointments for them and charge a percentage of whatever they charge the customers.'

'Actually I think you might have something there,' Lorraine said. 'There was a bloke in the other day asking if we knew of a local hypnotherapist.'

'Hypnotherapist?' said Nadine. 'I saw a hypnotist once at the City Hall. He had people running about doing really stupid things. He made this bloke think he was a tortoise and he kept crawling around the floor with his jumper pulled over his head. Ridiculous it was.'

'That's a different kind of thing altogether,' Lorraine said. 'Hypnosis can be used to help things like stress and pain control.'

'By making people think they're tortoises?' Nadine said.

'By reprogramming their minds,' Lorraine said.

'Reprogramming their minds! Is that possible? Can you do that?' Nadine asked incredulously.

'Of course,' Lorraine said. 'A good hypnotherapist can access your mind and change your thinking patterns, get rid of phobias and bad habits, stuff like that.'

'That's amazing,' Nadine said. 'I wonder if it could make me thin?'

'It's a possibility,' I said and I remembered Georgina's words. I gave a deep sigh and attempted to look intelligent. 'After all, the mind is a complex and mysterious enigma.'

Business was hectic that day, lunchtime trade was brisk and our detox products continued to sell well.

A feature on a popular lifestyle television programme had added more fuel to the already enormously popular craze by interviewing a selection of gorgeous celebrities who swore detox was the secret to their svelte bodies and glowing skin.

Lorraine made a mini display at the side of the counter, which enticed customers as they queued for sandwiches.

'Just wait till my feature is published in the Daily Echo,' she said, pleased that her display idea had worked so well. 'Sales will rocket when they read that!'

Janice spent nearly sixty pounds on detox books, herbs, supplements and essential oils despite Lorraine's advice that a smaller selection would suffice.

'Oh if I'm going to do something I like to do it properly,' she said, so Lorraine shrugged and took her money. She also pledged twenty pounds to our sponsored walk.

'Twenty pounds? Are you sure?' I asked her. 'A couple of pounds would do.'

'Hey, I can afford it, I'm loaded,' she said, so I thanked her and gave her the sponsor sheet to record her details.

It seemed that every other customer was trying a detox of some sort and we became proficient in answering questions about suitable products.

A woman who called to ask Lorraine about colon cleansing herbs looked vaguely familiar and I was trying to remember where I'd seen her when it suddenly came to me.

'Hello there, I saw you at Barbara's yoga class didn't I?' I said.

'Yes,' she said, 'that's right. I love my yogy-yogy class. I'm Fiona. I run the nursery up the road and I've meant to pop in here so many times and now I've finally got round to it.' She gave us each a beaming smile.

'I'm Christine and this is my sister Lorraine. We run the shop together.'

'I've seen you at yogy-yogy too haven't I?' Fiona said, turning to Georgina. Georgina looked at Fiona with a look of distaste.

'I thought you looked familiar. Yes, I go to Barbara's *yoga* too.'

Fiona giggled.

'Oh that's just my little name for it. I always call it yogy-yogy class.' She giggled again.

'How very amusing,' Georgina said. 'I always call it yoga.' Fiona looked a little hurt but laughed politely.

'Well I'm very pleased to meet you properly and you can call me Fee,' she said smiling at Georgina.

'I'm Georgina,' Georgina said gruffly, 'and you can call me Georgina.'

'What can we do for you Fee?' I asked, sensing Georgina's irritation.

'Oh,' Fee blushed. 'I've been having a bit of trouble with my...*poos*,' she whispered. 'I thought some of your herbs might help. I'm afraid I've had a visit from...*Running Mr Brown*.'

Georgina rolled her eyes and I gave her a warning look. I led Fiona to the supplements shelves as I heard Georgina mutter to Lorraine,

'You know me, I like to call a spade a spade and the shits the shits.'

It didn't take a great deal of intuition to know that Georgina and Fee were never going to be great friends.

The next morning we awoke to a pure white world. Despite the freezing temperature and the fact that I knew there would be traffic delays all the way to work, I couldn't help feeling a thrill at the beauty of it all.

I pulled on a pair of wellies and as Peter worked at de-icing the car I had a quick stroll around the garden, looking at the snow laden branches and noticing snowdrops pushing their tiny green spikes through the white carpeted lawn. As I had always loved to do as a child, I took delight in making the first footprints in the snow. I ran my hand over my bump smiling to myself at the thought of a much smaller pair of wellies making prints next to mine.

Lorraine was clearing snow from the pavement in front of the shop when I arrived. Her face was red from exertion and she was panting great clouds of mist. She paused from her shovelling when she saw me approach.

'Get the kettle on, I'll be in shortly,' she said.

The temperature inside the shop was the same, if not lower than that outside. A thin layer of icy swirls covered the inside of the windows like delicate lace curtains. Lorraine had left the gas rings burning and the Calor gas heater was hissing out its maximum heat but they had made little difference and I shivered as I filled the kettle and took the mugs from their hooks.

'Bbrrrrrr! Is that tea ready?' Lorraine burst through the door, still carrying her shovel. I handed her a drink.

'Took me ages to get the car started this morning,' she said as she warmed her hands over the gas rings. 'I think it's on its last legs. I've got the deliveries to do tonight and I'm not sure if the car will make it, especially if this snow continues.'

We ran a weekly delivery service and each Friday afternoon we loaded Lorraine's old Renault 5 with boxes for her to deliver while I manned the shop.

'The brakes are going too,' she said. 'I really need to get them seen to. In fact I could do with getting a new car.'

'Don't worry,' I said. 'If the worst comes to the worst we can ask Peter to take the deliveries tomorrow morning.'

'Do you think the sponsored walk will be still be on if it's snowing?'

'I think so,' I said. 'It did say to meet at Tynemouth Priory whatever the weather.' Part of me was hoping for a cancellation as a legitimate way to get out of doing it.

'Good, I'm really looking forward to it.'

'Yeah,' I said. 'Me too.'

A snow-sprinkled Georgina arrived, cursing as she stamped the snow from her Doc Martens.

'It's lethal out there,' she said. 'I've just nearly skidded on me backside. What daft sod cleared the path?'

'I did,' Lorraine said. 'To make it easier for customers to get in.'

'You've made it worse man, it's freezing out there, it's iced over all ready. It's like a skating rink.'

'Well pardon me,' Lorraine said. 'I was only trying to help. Do you want this drink or not?'

Georgina took the mug of hot apple and cinnamon tea and as she edged herself onto a stool near the counter the door burst open and Nige staggered in.

'Holy polony,' he said. 'I've just nearly went me length. I slipped on that ice. One leg went one way and one leg went the other way.' He bent over and held his groin. 'I've pulled a muscle I didn't even know I had.'

'Stop doing that and sit down,' Lorraine said, putting his drink on the counter. 'I was just trying to help. I'll sort it.'

'There's a big pack of sea salt in the back,' I told her. Why don't you sprinkle it over the pavement?'

Lorraine went into the office to look for the salt and hearing a scream from the direction of the window I turned in time to see Fee crash to the ground.

'Blimey, there's another one gone down,' Nige said as I hurried out to help her up.

'Oh dear,' Fee said as she limped into the shop. 'What a fright I got.'

'You all right darlin'?' Nige asked. 'I've just done the same thing myself.'

Fee gave a weak smile.

'I feel such a silly-billy,' she said. 'Some of the nursery parents saw me. I fell right on my bottom in front of somebody's daddy.'

'Hurry up with that salt Lorraine!' Georgina yelled. 'Fiona's just gone arse ower tit.'

CHAPTER FIVE

The snow continued to fall, silently forming a thick blanket that muffled the day and emptied the streets of traffic and people.

Lunchtime was quiet; we'd sent Nadine home early in anticipation of disruption on the Metro system and there were so few customers that Lorraine and I were able to sit and eat lunch undisturbed. I poured us each a bowl of steaming hot leek and potato soup that we ate with great hunks of cheese-and-olive bread.

'I think I'll start the delivery round as soon as I've finished this,' Lorraine said. 'I'm a bit worried about the car in this weather. It's temperamental at the best of times.'

'Yeah, you're probably right,' I said. 'We'll get the orders boxed up and you can get it done before the weather gets much worse.'

I cleared away the bowls and Lorraine went to fetch some cardboard boxes to pack the orders into. Reading from the order book we gathered items and packed them into the boxes.

Lorraine put on her outdoor things and went off to de-ice the car whilst I wrote out the invoices. Once I'd finished, I rang the totals through the till. Lorraine had not returned. She seemed to have been ages. I walked to the window and cleared a space in the condensation and peered out.

The bonnet of the car was open and Lorraine was huddled over the engine, seemingly twisting something or other with a piece of rag. I watched as she climbed into the car to turn on the ignition and after a few spluttering coughs the engine suddenly burst into life.

Jumping out of the car she quickly slammed down the bonnet and rushed into the shop.

'Quick, it's running,' she panted as she picked up one of the boxes and balanced it on top of another. 'Let's get this stuff loaded before it packs in again.'

She cautiously picked her way across the pavement to her car where she balanced the boxes against her bent knee as she opened the tailgate then pushed them in. Back inside she stooped to lift another two boxes, straining as she carried them to the door.

'Bring me that big one next,' she said, then as she saw me bend to pick it up immediately yelled,

'STOP! No! Sorry, forgot about bump. Leave them I'll do it.'

Feeling guilty at not being able to help. I managed to shuffle the boxes nearer the door by pushing them along with my feet. I watched as she loaded them into the back of her Renault and set off, cautiously nosing her way into the stream of traffic.

After mooching around the empty shop for a while, straightening a packet here and a jar there, I decided it would be an ideal time to get on with some cleaning jobs. I filled a plastic bowl with hot soapy water, turned on the radio, donned a pair of rubber gloves and began systematically stripping and scrubbing the wooden shelves.

Usually this was a job I hated but curiously as my pregnancy advanced I found myself enjoying more and more the process of cleaning and tidying and gained great satisfaction in seeing the transformation I could create around me.

Nadine and Lorraine would watch and nod knowingly, murmuring 'nesting-instinct' when they witnessed this, teasing me that I was driven by my hormones to get a nest ready for my chick. I denied this vehemently but secretly had to acknowledge that this frenzied cleaning obsession was the antithesis of my pre-pregnancy personality.

Running a shop involved more cleaning and maintenance jobs than most people probably realised. Every afternoon Nadine tackled the huge pile of dishes, pans and utensils that accumulated in the sink during lunchtime and although we often promised to get her a dishwasher we never did as any money earmarked for the purpose was invariably used for yet more stock. The kitchen, including surfaces, cooker, floor and fridges had to be cleaned daily. The office and shop floors were swept and mopped every evening and also by Nadine at regular intervals throughout the day. We took turns to clean the toilet and to take home hand towels and tea towels to launder. The stock gathered dust at an amazing rate and shelf cleaning was like painting the Forth Bridge. There was also the job of checking the fridge temperatures. At the request of Edward Reeves, our local Environmental Health Officer, we kept a note of all the fridge and freezer temperatures at regular intervals throughout the day. This was a time-consuming task and we often forgot, so most of the temperatures in the book were made up.

The stock itself took a lot of nurturing. As well as ordering, unpacking, checking, pricing and displaying it, we had to make a note of use-by dates and remove goods or reduce prices before expiry.

Because Peter hated to serve behind the counter and was not much help in the kitchen, he was press-ganged into being the stock checker. Each week he'd check every item on the shelves noting in the huge shop diary any items that were close to expiry. Wherever possible we used these in our cooking as soup or sandwich ingredients or in a dish for our 'daily specials'. Each morning before starting to cook we scanned the diary to check for Peter's lists that he scrawled in red marker pen to make sure they weren't overlooked.

He headed his lists with the letters 'O.O.D', an acronym for 'out of date' which earned him the title of The Ood Dude.

I was happily scrubbing away at a sticky patch on the honey shelf when the telephone rang. It was Lorraine.

'I'm in the phone box on the corner of Woodburn Grove,' she panted. 'The car's buggered again. I've left it on the High Street. Luckily I was driving to Mrs Bunting's with the last delivery. I had to carry the boxes up The High Street, along Hunter's Road, past the park and about two miles down Birchwood Avenue. I'm knackered, I had to make three journeys.' She stopped to take a breath.

'But there's a howling snowstorm out there!' I said. 'You must be frozen.'

'I am! And exhausted.'

'Why didn't you ring from Mrs Bunting's? You could have waited there and I'd have rung Peter to come and get you.'

'Wait at Mrs Bunting's? You're J-O-K-I-N-G!'

Mrs Bunting was one of our best delivery customers but also one of the most awkward. Every week she telephoned with her order, her voice booming down the phone as she announced,

'This is Mrs Bunting. B-U-N-T-I-N-G' and then proceeded to yell her list at me, spelling out words as she went to make sure I understood. Although well into her eighties she lived life to the full and had caused quite a stir at our Christmas evening with her wild dancing.

'Didn't she ask you in to warm up?'

'No she did not. She answered the door in a bikini. She seemed surprised to see the snow.'

'A bikini?'

'Yes. She said, 'Oh gracious me, look at the weather. I had no idea. I've been using my sunlamp you see.' Then she looked me up and down and said, 'Dear, dear, how dishevelled you are. You may stand on my D-O-O-R-M-A-T while I fetch your cheque,' and she slammed the door and left me standing in the blizzard. I couldn't even see the doormat never mind stand on it.'

'How are you going to get back? Do you want me to ring Peter to see if he can pick you up when he's finished work?'

'No, he doesn't finish for another half an hour and anyway it'll take him ages to get through the traffic. I'll just have to leave the car where it is and walk back.'

'Ok, see you soon. I'll put some soup on to heat,' I said as Lorraine's money ran out and the pips sounded.

'What did you say?'

'I said I'll heat you some soup!' I shouted. 'S-O-U-P!'

The next morning I arrived at the shop later than usual as I'd been to the antenatal clinic for my routine check-up. I always came back from the appointments feeling cheerful, having been reassured that all was well. When I reported at the reception I would be handed my maternity medical card that had been filled in by hand by one of the midwives. Her handwriting was not the best. Most of the details on the card were practically illegible. At the bottom of the card she had written 'Father is a twin' which actually looked like 'Father is a twit,' as though written there to warn other midwives about Peter. This never failed to make me laugh and I giggled my way through the consultation.

'Morning!' I called as I walked in. Nadine, who was making hot drinks gave me a warning look and nodded towards Lorraine but before I had a chance to ask what was up Lorraine stormed over and slammed a newspaper on the counter.

'Look at that!' she yelled. 'That woman has done it again. I'm a bloody laughing stock.'

I pulled the paper towards me and saw that Lorraine was referring to Julie Bradley's article about her detox.

'Here, drink that,' Nadine said to Lorraine as she gave both of us a mug of tea. 'Honestly, it's not that bad…' she said, then seeing Lorraine's face turn purple with rage she faltered and continued '…well, yes it's bad, but it could have been worse…well possibly…and people won't know it's you anyway and…'

'Listen to this!' Lorraine yelled and she read from the article.

'Lorraine Melville, owner of Nutmeg Wholefoods in Station Road, Fordham is a detox enthusiast. She said 'Regular detox makes my skin glow and makes me radiate energy and vitality.' Lorraine, 24, detoxes twice a year by sticking to a diet of fresh foods, cutting out sugar, fats, alcohol and additives and supplementing her diet with herbs and natural tonics.'

'That's not too bad,' I said. 'I mean it's a pack of lies but it certainly doesn't make you look a laughing stock.'

Nadine nudged me.

'It's the next bit she doesn't like.'

Lorraine glared at her then continued reading.

'When asked about the side effects of detox Lorraine admitted that she does suffer from problems such as increased flatulence, bad breath, greasy hair, excessive sweating and bouts of diarrhoea but added 'I feel this is a small price to pay in comparison with the benefits.'

I avoided looking at Nadine as I struggled to keep my laughter under control.

'I've a good mind to sue! I didn't say any of that! Reporting lies and making people look ridiculous!'

Lorraine flung the paper into the bin. I heard a stifled snigger from Nadine and I could hold back no longer. I scuttled into the office and pretended to check some invoices until I could compose myself.

'I know you're laughing in there.'

'Sorry Lorraine,' I said 'but you've got to see the funny side.'

'Eeh, sorry darlin',' Nadine said, wiping her eyes. 'But it is funny isn't it?'

'No it's not, actually,' Lorraine snapped. 'I know for a fact that if those things had been written about one of you two it would have been a different story. And if that wasn't bad enough, I've now got to go and collect my car.'

'How are you going to get it to the garage?' I asked.

'I rang Dad this morning. He's going to take me to collect it tonight and tow it over there.'

'Well at least that will save you from having to pay the garage to move it,' Nadine said cheerfully but was answered with a 'harrumph' from Lorraine.

By the time we'd drank our tea and prepared the sandwich fillings Lorraine had calmed down and I thought it was best not to mention the subject of detox again. I decided it was a good time to tell her the latest developments in my therapy room project.

'I forgot to tell you, I've arranged for a couple of therapists to come in to see us on Friday regarding hiring the therapy room,' I said.

'Therapy room?' Nadine said. 'Don't you mean junk room?'

'Great,' Lorraine said. 'What therapies do they practise?'

'One is a Reflexologist and the other does some sort of massage I think,' I said. 'I'm not too clear about it really. I thought we could find out more when they come in.'

'But where are they going to see people?' Nadine asked. There's not room to swing a hamster in there.'

'I have plans!' I said. 'Peter is going to build a partition to divide the office. There will be a small space here...' I demonstrated by holding out my arms to divide the space '...and then this area at the back will be enclosed. It should be just big enough for a therapy couch, a couple of chairs and a small table.'

'Sounds good,' said Nadine, then spotting Nige and Georgina arriving said, 'I'll just go and put the kettle on.'

'Morning everyone, 'Georgina said.

'Morning sexy, how's the diarrhoea?' Nige said to Lorraine.

'Nige!' I said. It had taken ages for Nadine and I to coax Lorraine out of her fettle and I didn't want to start it all off again.

'Shut up Nige,' Lorraine said. 'I didn't say those things. It's a pack of lies and I'm not happy about it.'

'I'm not surprised, I wouldn't want everyone knowing I had bad breath and flatulence.'

'Give it a rest Nige,' I said. 'She's upset about it.'

'It was funny though,' Georgina said. 'You've got to laugh.' Nige and Georgina sniggered together.

'You are so predictable,' Lorraine said. 'I knew it would appeal to your childish sense of humour. How immature.'

Nadine placed a tray of drinks on the counter.

'There we are,' she said, then tried to change the subject. 'Weather's a bit brighter today. It's stopped snowing.'

'I'll just sit upwind of you if you don't mind,' Nige said to Lorraine, moving a stool further along the counter as he took his mug. Lorraine gave him her special look-that-could-kill and stormed off into the kitchen.

I told Nige and Georgina my plans for the therapy room as Lorraine crashed saucepans around in the kitchen.

'We're going to let the room by the hour to therapists and we'll advertise their services to our customers and take appointments for them. What do you think?'

'Sounds great,' Georgina said. 'I know a good homeopath. She may be interested. I'll give you her number.'

'Oh, it all sounds a bit dodgy to me,' Nige said shaking his head. 'People sneaking in to a back room to pay for personal services…'

'That's just the kind of stupid attitude we're trying to change,' Lorraine said, banging down the pan she was holding. 'Natural therapies are a valuable aid to an overstretched National Health system. They can help people to cope with less serious ailments and eliminate stress.'

'Eeh well why don't you try it yourself?' Nige said and Georgina slapped him. 'You seem like you could do with a bit of stress therapy yourself today.'

Nige never knew when to quit.

'Shut up Nige,' Georgina said. 'Joke's over. Just leave it like a good boy. '

'Yes, shut up Nige,' I said to him seriously. 'Lorraine's not having a good day. As well as the article, her car broke down yesterday and she had to leave it in a parking bay on the High Street.'

'You left it overnight on the High Street? Gawd, it'll have probably been wrecked by vandals by now,' Nige said. 'Either that or it'll have been clamped.'

'Come on Nige,' Georgina said. 'Time to go. I'll walk down the bank with you.'

She took his coffee cup from him and pulled him towards the door.

'See you tomorrow.'

'See you,' said Nige. 'Let me know what therapies you're going to be offering. If there're any dodgy ones I might be interested.'

Georgina gave him an extra push towards the door.

'Let me know if you find a therapist who can cure foot-in-mouth disease and I'll bring him back,' she said as they left.

CHAPTER SIX

'Are you sure this is a good idea?' Lorraine asked as we pulled down the shop blinds.

'Shouldn't we wait until the snow has gone?'

Dad had arrived to help Lorraine collect her car from where she'd abandoned it on the High Street. The plan was for them to drive to the High Street in Dad's car and tow Lorraine's car to the garage she used in Byker, where she would leave it for the mechanic to look at in the morning.

'No, we'll be fine, it's not too bad out there, let's go,' Dad said and he opened the shop door.

One of the endearing but sometimes worrying things about our father was his invariable ability to see everything with a childlike sense of adventure often with little concern for possible pitfalls.

The snow was around eight inches deep, and a lot higher beneath the shop window where it had drifted. The roads were now silent; most people had driven home early, leaving only the deep furrows marks of their tyres as evidence of their presence. The traffic-lights changed, allowing access to the non-existent traffic, their colours reflecting on the compact snow.

Peter locked the shop door and pulled down the shutter as Dad roughly scraped his windscreen with the sleeve of his coat and opened the car door.

'Jump in,' Dad said and Lorraine climbed into the passenger seat.

'See you tomorrow…hopefully,' she said.

'Actually, I think we'll follow behind,' Peter said as we climbed into our car.

'What for?' I asked. I didn't fancy hanging about in the snow for any longer than necessary. I was looking forward to a hot bath, my jarmies and dinner in front of the television.

'Just in case we're needed,' Peter replied and I grumbled as I fastened my seatbelt, pulling my scarf further up around my ears.

The drive to the High Street was slow and treacherous. Periodically the car would skid slightly, causing me to instinctively wrap my arms protectively around my bump.

There were few cars on the roads, those drivers that we did encounter edged carefully past us as we engaged in a slow dance, passing each other in a series of calculated movements, aware that a wrong move could cause us to slide into each other.

'Bloody hell,' Peter said as we watched Dad's car suddenly veer across the road in front of us, just missing a lamppost. Dad gained control and returned the car to its previous position, continuing as though nothing had happened. 'Do you think they're ok?'

'He'll be loving it. Lorraine's probably not though,' I said as we watched his car glide swiftly to the left then straighten up and continue.

'If it's like this next weekend you won't be able to do the sponsored walk,' Peter said.

'Why not?' I asked, argumentatively.

'Because I don't think it's a good idea for you to go walking along the seafront in icy weather in your condition.'

'In my condition! I'm pregnant not decrepit.' I folded my arms across my chest.

'Well ok, in your pregnant condition.'

'Hmm, we'll see,' I said.

It was one thing me not wanting to go, but quite another being told I couldn't.

The High Street was deserted. The snow shimmered with colour reflected from the illuminated signs of the shuttered shops. Even the street's many pubs were silent, the usual chatter and music replaced by the eerie creaking of a wooden pub sign swinging on its chains.

'There it is,' I said pointing at the snow-laden Renault standing forlornly at the side of the road. We pulled up behind it and by the time we had climbed out of the car, Dad had unpacked a towrope and was tying it to his tow bar. I got out of the car and pulled the hood of my coat over my head.

'Are you sure that will hold?' I asked.

'Once I tie this knot, nothing will be able to pull it off,' he said as he enthusiastically threw the rope around itself.

'Just make sure it's safe,' Lorraine said as he demonstrated his knot tying technique while he secured the rope to his towbar.

'Yes, yes, just get on with it, we're all freezing here.'

Lorraine stamped her feet and shivered then went off to clear the windscreen of her car.

'Are you sure this is tight enough?' I asked, pulling the rope at the end tied to the tow bar. 'You'll have to drive really carefully, her brakes are a bit dodgy. Are you really sure about this rope?'

Peter took my arm and guided me towards our car.

'Come on, stop fussing, your Dad knows what he's doing,' he said and Lorraine and I threw each other a look.

Peter hadn't known him as long as we had. He'd once glued himself to the floor under a bench with Evostick when fitting flooring in Lorraine's kitchen. His shoes had made an unusual feature in her new kitchen; they were there for days until he managed to work out how to remove them.

He'd also once managed to jam his ear in the cover of a ticket machine he'd been repairing in a carpark in Newcastle City Centre, much to the amusement of the drivers waiting to purchase tickets. So we'd be forgiven for having misgivings about his knot-tying abilities.

'Right. All done, off we go,' Dad said as he jumped into the front of his car and waved to Lorraine who was waiting in hers. Peter started the engine and we set off, Dad in front towing Lorraine and us following.

'He's going a bit fast,' Peter said as we watched Lorraine's car career around a corner on the end of its towrope.

'I hope that knot holds,' I said.

'I hope the brakes hold,' Peter said.

We followed the Renault through the deserted streets to Heward Road where the two cars charged towards the roundabout. Dad signalled right and as he turned off the roundabout to head towards Byker, Lorraine shot across the roundabout and continued straight ahead down Mellow Bank.

'Oh my God!' I yelled. 'The rope's snapped. I knew it! She's gone down Mellow Bank.'

Peter, who had immediately brought the car to a halt at the side of the road said,

'Don't worry, she's a pretty good driver, she'll brake and pull in.'

He opened the door and climbed out.

'If her brakes hold out,' I said panicking. 'And if they don't, that bank heads straight down to the river.'

We were both out of the car now; Peter took off down Mellow Bank, half running and half sliding and I followed, struggling in the snow, trying to catch up.

The little Renault meandered precariously down the bank, seeming to diminish in size as it headed away from us towards the horizon. We stopped running for a few seconds and watched, panting for breath as it disappeared around the final bend in the road. Hearing a voice behind us I turned to see my Dad slithering down the bank towards us.

'Is she ok?' he called.

'She's gone round the bend,' Peter called which in other circumstances may have got a laugh. He set off again hurtling through the snow and we stumbled after him.

'I knew that rope wouldn't hold,' I panted in the best 'told-you-so' manner I could manage while struggling downhill through deep snow accompanied by my bump.

'Oh it wasn't the rope,' Dad said in a fairly cheerful voice considering the circumstances. 'No, it was her bumper. It came off. It's still tied to the rope, the knot held firm.'

'You tied it to the bumper?' Peter shouted from further down the bank and we scurried around the bend afraid of what we would find.

'She's ok,' I heard Peter shout and I heaved a sigh of relief as I saw Lorraine standing beside her beloved Renault that was now wedged against a lamppost. The bonnet was buckled and part of the front grill lay amongst broken headlamp glass and pieces of number plate. Lorraine, as could be expected, did not look happy.

'You daft bugger,' she yelled as she picked up pieces of debris from her car. 'I could have ended up in the Tyne. And look at the state of my car! You've finished it off!'

'Never mind the car, are you all right?' Dad asked calmly. 'That's the important thing.'

'I'm all right, it's my car that isn't,' yelled Lorraine. 'Look at it! It's wrecked! It's knackered!'

She flung the pieces of number plate and metal she'd picked up to the ground. We looked at the shattered front of her car, Peter and I still out of breath and not really knowing what to say.

Dad however, remained optimistic as always.

'Good knot though,' he said. 'Told you it would hold. That's lucky. '

CHAPTER SEVEN

I couldn't wait to get started transforming the office into our new therapy room.

Peter had cleverly partitioned the stockroom/office, ingeniously condensing our storage area by building floor-to-ceiling shelving with an integral desk area. The remaining space was to be used as the therapy room.

We toyed with various ideas for colour schemes and furnishings but as it was a tiny space choice was limited. The room was just large enough to house a therapy bed, two small chairs and a tiny coffee table.

'I want the room to look comfortable but uncluttered,' I said as Lorraine and I discussed colour schemes. 'It has to look like a proper consultation room, not too homely.'

'We need a pale colour because it's such a small room,' Lorraine said. 'Anything too bright or dark will make it claustrophobic.'

After rejecting most colours of the spectrum for a variety of reasons (cream boring, pink too girlie, green too obvious, yellow bilious, red too bright, orange overpowering, purple hippyish, brown don't even go there) we finally decided on pale shades of lilac and blue.

As Nadine and Lorraine prepared fillings and salads, I changed into old clothes and went off to start painting walls.

'Leave the high bits,' Lorraine said. 'I don't want you falling off the ladder. I'll do them later.'

'Ok,' I said, intending to ignore her. I turned up the radio and got to work transforming the room.

It didn't take long to complete the first coat, high bits included, and I stopped to have a break with Nadine and Lorraine.

'When are those two therapists coming in? Nadine asked as she handed us mugs of tea.

'Tomorrow afternoon,' I said. 'We have a Reflexologist coming at 2 o'clock and a woman who does Indian Head Massage at three. They've both said they will give a demonstration of their work.'

'Don't forget the Karma delivery is due tomorrow afternoon too,' Lorraine said. 'So they can't take up too much of our time.'

Our main supplier delivered stock to us every Friday afternoon and it was the biggest job of the week unpacking and checking off the goods before pricing and displaying them.

'And we have the delivery orders to set up and take out,' Lorraine added.

'Well I thought you could get on with that while I speak to the therapists,' I suggested. 'Unless you want to swap.'

'No chance,' Lorraine said. 'I'm not having me feet fiddled about with. Or an Indian Head Massage, whatever that is. I'll sort the Karma, just try not to take too long.'

'Ooh, I wouldn't mind a free treatment,' Nadine said. 'Sounds lovely.'

'Well stay around. The first therapist's coming at two so your shift will be finished,' I told her.

By lunchtime I had finished the second coat of paint and after tidying up and changing my clothes, sat down to have a sandwich with Nadine and Lorraine.

'It looks really good,' Lorraine said as she inspected my work. 'It's hard to believe this was our tatty old storeroom a few days ago.'

'Let's get it set up, I can't wait to see it properly finished,' I said.

'Shouldn't you wait for the paint to dry?' Nadine asked. But we were too impatient.

'No,' Lorraine said. 'It'll be fine, come and give me a hand with this therapy bed.' They carried the folded couch into the room and succeeded in assembling it without getting any paint on it although Nadine managed to leave an imprint of her bottom on the wall as she bent down.

'Careful!' I said, with the irritation of someone desperate to do the job but not able to. I hated having to stand by and watch other people do tasks that my bump would not allow, especially when I was so certain I could do them so much better.

Lorraine and Nadine carried in the two small tub chairs and coffee table; there was just enough space for them to fit snuggly in the corner. We had bought two cream shaded lamps - we had asked

Peter to remove the overhead fluorescent light feeling it was too harsh - so we plugged them in and laid down a woven rug that Lorraine had brought from her spare room. A couple of framed prints and some scented candles finished the room. We were all really pleased with our efforts and spent the afternoon congratulating ourselves and inviting customers to come through and take a look.

Janice called and was shown around, along with three of her children who rushed in noisily and threw themselves on the therapy couch.

'Careful you don't hurt yourselves,' I said pointedly as I caught a candle that was kicked flying, hoping that Janice would tell them to get off but she didn't.

'Oh it's fab!' she said as her offspring trampolined on the couch, screeching and trying to push each other off. 'I'll have to come in for a treatment. Book me in for one of everything.'

'One of everything…? Em, well we have Reflexology and Indian Head Massage lined up but we are hoping to have some more therapists signed up soon,' I told her.

The smallest child fell from the bed, hitting her head against the floor and began crying angrily.

'Just book me in for an appointment with each one as you sign them up,' Janice said, 'I'm really into all this weird stuff.'

'It's not really weird,' I said with a forced laugh. 'We're trying to dispel that sort of image and encourage people to try some new treatments…' My voice grew louder as I competed with the bellowing child who had grabbed her brother by the neck and was desperately trying to strangle him.

'Of course we're not trying to suggest that people try these treatments instead of visiting their doctor…' I continued as the strangled brother joined his sister in a raucous wailing competition.

The third child laughed hysterically, rolling on the bed holding his sides. I gave up trying to be heard, as Janice seemed to suddenly become aware of them and slapped them in turn.

'Pack it in,' she screeched and I excused myself and returned to the shop front leaving the three children screaming hysterically as Janice yelled at them 'Shut yer whinging faces or I'll bliddy shut them for you.'

'What on earth…?' Lorraine said. Janice appeared dragging her offspring with her, still yelling and fighting.

'Better get this lot home,' she said. 'Little buggers. See you later. Don't forget my appointments. Bye!'

I went back into the therapy room to straighten the couch and rearrange the cushions that the children had thrown askew.

'Those kids are horrors,' Lorraine said. 'She needs to take a firm hand with them. Our Mam would never have let us get away with that.'

That was true. Our mother was very strict about our behaviour in public, and that wasn't just restricted to our childhood. She was also quite blunt in her comments if she was unhappy about anything we were doing.

Even though we were in our late twenties she disapproved of us wearing anything that would draw attention to ourselves. If our clothes were too bright they were 'bobby-dazzlers', too avant-garde and we looked like 'somebody not right.' Any tight fitting clothes would incite her well-worn saying, 'you look like three pound of tripe in a one pound bag.'

When we'd had our ears pierced we'd been told that if God had meant us to have holes in our earlobes He'd have put them there.

I was not looking forward to the day she discovered Lorraine had a tattoo on her bum.

'We wouldn't have dared!' I said. 'Anyway, they're just kids. She was very hard on them slapping them like that. That was uncalled for. After all there was no real harm done.' I bent to pick up a cushion and my eye caught sight of one of our new cream lamps lying shattered on the floor next to its squashed shade.

'Look at that!' I said as I picked up the pieces of china. 'They need a good walloping, the little sods.'

Later that afternoon, Lorraine went off to collect her car from the garage. Dad had been forgiven after suggesting he sorted the repairs and had taken it to the garage to have it fixed and the bodywork patched up.

I was kept busy with customers and I told everyone who came in about the new therapy room, hoping that they would spread the word.

I made the mistake of mentioning the new therapy room to Val.

'Will I be able to have treatments on the National Health then?' she asked.

'No, I'm afraid not,' I told her.

'How much will it cost?

'I'm not sure, it depends on the therapist. But I would imagine between twenty-five and forty pounds a session depending on the length of the session and the treatment given.' I'd discovered this was the going rate at present for these types of treatments at other clinics.

'What!' Val said faintly. 'Oh dear, I need to sit down.' I quickly carried a chair to the front of the counter and she collapsed upon it.

'Oh my goodness,' she said. 'I can't afford that. What will I do?'

Err, don't have any treatments? I thought, but did not say.

'How about I test out the therapists for you?' she asked hopefully. 'I wouldn't charge you, I'll just book an appointment like one of those secret-shoppers and let you know what goes on. I could try each therapist for my different problems.'

'Well, thank you for the offer, but really, these are qualified therapists, they don't need testing out,' I said, wishing I had never started this conversation. Val seem to think for a while then she said,

'What would happen if I was in here shopping like usual and just say, suddenly I had a funny turn, would one of the therapists treat me then?'

'NO! No, they wouldn't. They couldn't because it would be…unethical and against the law,' I said hoping I sounded convincing.

There was no way I was having Val coming in acting out one of her 'funny turns' every time she fancied a free session with a therapist.

'Well what about a buy one get one free offer for regular customers,' she persisted.

Honestly, I was beginning to see what Lorraine meant now. The woman was a pain in the arse.

'I'll see what I can do,' I told her. 'Now if you don't mind I have to close for a few minutes to make a very important phone call…?'

'Oh don't bother closing,' she said. 'I'll sit here and watch the shop for you.'

So I had no choice but to go into the office and have a pretend, one-sided conversation with an imaginary person about some very important matter while she sat in front of the counter telling customers about her health until Lorraine came back and shooed her out.

CHAPTER EIGHT

The next morning we showed off the therapy room to Georgina and Nige. Georgina seemed impressed but Nige was more interested in asking our opinion about a Valentine card he'd bought for Gus.

'Do you think it looks tacky?' he asked, showing us a huge card covered in pink glitter and ribbons.

'Gawd that's hideous!' Georgina said and Lorraine and I nudged her as Nige's face fell.

'It's what Gus will think that matters,' Lorraine said diplomatically. 'Is it his sort of thing?'

'No, not really.' Nige looked crestfallen. 'It's more my taste really.'

'Then he'll love it,' I said. 'It will remind him of you. Georgina smirked.

'Heap of shite anyway, Valentine's day,' she said. 'Just a commercial scam invented to make money and put pressure on women to feel unloved and rejected if some man doesn't present them with an odious card carrying an insincere, over-sentimental message. Pathetic.'

'Take it you never get one then?' Nige asked.

'That's irrelevant,' she said, as Lorraine and I laughed. 'The one thing guaranteed to put me straight off a bloke would be if he were feeble enough to buy into all that crap and send me a card.'

'Well I love getting them,' Nadine said. 'It makes me feel special.'

'Exactly my point!' Georgina told her. 'What is wrong with you that you need a man's approval to feel special? Honestly, I sometimes wonder why my generation fought so hard for equality when the next generations are bent on taking us back to where we were. Men have had it easy for too long, I tell you, if I had my way…'

'Anyone for a cuppa?' I interrupted, trying to distract Georgina from starting on one of her 'All Men Are Bastards' rants.

Don't get me wrong, I'm all for equality and I know there are some obnoxious men out there. Maybe I've been lucky but the men in my life have always been reliable and straightforward and I have often found women to be of a more devious nature.

I hurried into the kitchen to put the kettle on leaving the others to listen to her theory of forced castration for straying husbands.

When I returned, the subject had been changed by the arrival of a sales rep who was unloading samples of organic chocolate.

It didn't take much effort on his part to persuade us to place an order for several cases of different varieties, and he left unaware that he'd made it onto our list of favourite reps.

The sales reps who visited our shop were a mixed bunch. Many of them were condescending and insincere, unwilling to listen to our requirements as they launched into hard-sell mode. Others were passionate about their products and took into account our customer base when advising us about which of their products to stock. Some we looked forward to seeing and would invite them to join us for a cuppa and a chat, like Jim Dixon from Herbfirst.

Jim was a lovely man, genuine and kindly and treated us in a very fatherly way. He never tried to push us to order stock that we didn't want, and helped us whenever he could with free samples and display materials.

'Are you going to attend the Health Show at Brighton in the autumn?' he'd asked on his last visit. 'The company are giving a free case of Echinacea with every order taken at the show.'

'We hadn't really thought about it,' I said. 'It would be nice to go, I guess.'

'It's always a fantastic event,' Jim said. 'There'll be loads of stands with all manner of products, and most companies have special offers and deals just for the duration of the show.'

'Sounds good,' Lorraine said. 'We'll try to sort something out.'

'Yeah, we'll look into it,' I said.

'The hotel has a great deal on for visitors. If you book tickets, ask if they have any of the special offer rooms left, although you'll have to be fast, they always go quickly because it's such a great deal.'

'That sounds good. We'd have to stay over and neither of us know Brighton at all so that would be ideal.'

'Well if you make it, come and say hello. And if you don't manage to get there, I'll put your next order through with the ones from the show so you'll get your free case of Echinacea.'

Oh if only all the reps were like Jim!

Some of reps just didn't seem to have what it took at all.

I was alone in the shop one Tuesday morning when a short man in a belted raincoat, carrying a briefcase entered.

He reminded me of an insect. If a human-being slowly began to turn into a bee, this man would be what the first stages of metamorphism would look like. A yellowish fuzz covered his spherical head, his face was round, as were his glasses and his eyes. He appeared to have little or no neck as his head emerged straight from the top of his raincoat. His arms and legs were short and he wore highly-polished black round-toed shoes that looked like black beetles. He stood next to the honey shelves near the front door, a fixed smile on his face.

'Hello,' I said, but he just nodded and held out an arm towards a waiting customer, his gesture suggesting I should serve the customer first.

I began to worry that he was perhaps a flasher waiting for the shop to empty so that my undivided attention would enable him to enjoy the full force of my shock.

I didn't know much about men with a penchant for exposing themselves in public, but I'd heard that they did it because they relished the reaction of their victim, and also that they tended to wear long raincoats, so I braced myself ready to be completely unresponsive.

'Hello,' he said, when the customer had closed the door behind her.

I narrowed my eyes and grimaced, giving him a look that I hoped said *don't mess with me pal* but which more likely said *I've got bad indigestion.*

'Would you. Like anything. Today?'

He spoke in a hesitant way, pronouncing his words carefully.

'No thank you.'

He dipped his head, if he'd been wearing a cap I think he would have doffed it, and left.

From then on, he'd arrive each Tuesday morning, same raincoat, same carefully placed smile. He'd wait patiently until the shop emptied of customers - which could sometimes be a long time - then he would say,

'Would you. Like anything. Today?'

After being informed that we didn't, he'd buzz off.

Lorraine and I became used to seeing his raincoated figure lingering near the honey shelves, waiting. We named him Mr Bumble because of resemblance to a huge bee and also because of his tendency to hover around honey.

Over the months, the mystery of his intention intrigued us until eventually, one Tuesday, when he asked,

'Would you. Like anything. Today,' I finally just asked outright.

'What do you mean? Why do you keep coming here? What do you want? Are you selling something?'

He blushed with excitement and rushed to the counter where he opened his briefcase to show us samples of his paper and packaging products.

We placed a substantial order for paper bags, recycled carriers, cardboard food trays, soup cups, bread paper, till rolls and stickers and he buzzed off, like a bee that had got the pollen. If only he'd made himself clear earlier he could have made a lot more money – and saved us a lot too. He became one of our regular suppliers although never sat with us to chat and drink tea. In fact, ten years later he was still coming in to wait by the honey shelves (which were no longer the honey shelves but the tea shelves) to say,

'Would you. Like anything. Today?'

Another salesman who visited was so shy and unsure of himself that he would stand sweating and taking great gulps as he spoke to us.

Bless him, he was only about seventeen, still with the spots of puberty on his face. He was tall and gangly with a rather large Adam's apple that bobbed alarmingly as he swallowed. He represented Bishop's Herbal Remedies, a reputable company who produced a range of remedies in rather attractive packaging for common ailments such as period pains, sore throats and the like. They were very popular, and filled a whole shelf with their colourful boxes.

To try to put him at his ease, I would chat and joke but his discomfort was contagious and the more he sweated and swallowed, the higher pitched my voice became, my words faster and my nervous laugh louder, until I became like some sort of manic puppet from a children's television program. This would make him more uncomfortable and we would enter into a spiralling cycle of sweating, swallowing, gabbling and giggling.

Once, he arrived at a very busy time so I suggested he check the shelf for me and fill in an order sheet of the products we needed. I thought it might boost his confidence and I prepared to show delight at whatever he had ticked on his order form and thank him for being such a fantastic help. He stood at the shelf, counting and re-counting the boxes then took a deep breath and returned to the counter. He consulted his order pad and gulped then said,

'Right. I see you have piles, flatulence and diarrhoea...' at which Peter immediately began to guffaw with laughter.

'Well excuse me!' I said, laughing. At last here was a joke to break the ice and have a good chuckle about. Unfortunately he was horrified and his Adam's apple went into overdrive.

'Sss...sorry,' he stammered. 'I'm so sorry. I just meant...' He was so embarrassed he could hardly speak.

'Don't worry, it's ok,' I said. 'I was just teasing. I knew what you meant.'

Unable to carry on, he rubbed his sweating palms on his trousers then pushed the list across the counter for me to read and sign, and without looking at it, I took a pen and wrote my name at the bottom whilst telling him that it was wonderful, fantastic, amazing, tremendous and superb, like I was reading a list of synonyms.

Unfortunately, Peter's funny bone had been well and truly tickled and he was still falling about.

'Look!' he roared, pointing at the shelf. 'She has spots and boils too! Ha ha ha!'

I gave him a warning look, but he was off on one.

'Hee, hee! And dandruff! You've got that too. And warts, ha ha ha!'

The young lad hurriedly tore off the top copy of his order pad and placed it on the counter. He stuttered his apologies for any offence caused and took his leave, while I tried desperately to reassure him and Peter held his sides, gurgling like a drain and shouting,

'You've even got erectile dysfunction!'

He left the company very soon after. I think his visit to us may have been his last straw.

One of my least favourite reps was a hawk-nosed, beady-eyed man who came to take orders for home-made flapjacks and biscuits. He had a habit of standing just within the boundary of a person's personal space, putting his face close to theirs, so when he spoke to me, I would subconsciously take a step back. He would then take a step closer, I would take a step away from him and off we would go.

If it were a long conversation we could circle the shop three or four times. Once he backed me towards the shop door and we danced along the pavement to the greengrocers, around an A-board advertising 'local home-grown spuds' and back into the shop.

Lorraine and I either loved a visit from a new sales person or hated it depending upon the rep.

The quality of their products had little to do with our decision on whether or not to place an order. Reps who were patronising or condescending in any way were disposed of quickly, however interesting their products or amazing their offers. If we liked the rep, they were plied with tea and biscuits while we compiled an order, regardless of what they were selling.

All manner of products were purchased during these sessions and a lot of them were absolute rubbish. At the time, carried away at the excitement of new stock we would convince each other of how revolutionary/unique/useful the products were, setting ourselves up for disappointment when they arrived and subsequently remained on our shelves unsold.

This irritated the life out of Peter and he would make his disapproval obvious.

'What the heck have you two bought now?' he asked as we unpacked a consignment of 'easy to use accurate body-fat indicators'. I was already doubting our purchase as we unpacked them but I said,

'They're the latest must-have in diet and fitness. Body-fat indicators. They measure how much excess body-fat you have.'

Lorraine opened one of the boxes to reveal a large pair of plastic tweezers with numbers printed along their length.

'What did you call them? Body fat what?' Peter asked. 'They look like those things you use to pick sausages off a barbeque.'

Lorraine was reading the instruction leaflet.

'Body-fat indicators, she said. 'You open them like this and grip any excess fat around your stomach with them and then you read the scale to find out how much fat you have to lose.'

She demonstrated by pinching her arm with them.

'I see,' Peter said. 'And how much did you pay for those?'

'Can't remember,' I said. 'About a fiver each.'

It was more than that, but as the product seemed to become more ridiculous by the minute I didn't want to admit we'd paid eight pounds a unit for a case of fifty units.

'But they retail at £19.99,' Lorraine added. 'It's a good mark-up.'

'Well it is if you sell them,' Peter said. 'But who's going to pay twenty quid for a pair of sausage-grabbers to nip their fat bits with?'

Even our super-dieter Nadine was unimpressed.

'You know how gullible I am for diet fads and slimming aids,' she said to us. 'But even I can see those are utter rubbish. Eeh, I can't believe you think people will buy them. I'm sorry like, but twenty quid to squeeze me belly-fat that I already know is there? I don't think so. It's not even like it's going to help shrink it or at least disguise it, like a pair of elastic knickers or something. It just nips it and leaves it there.'

The more the 'easy to use body-fat indicators' were discussed, the more absurd they became. They became known as the 'sausage grabbers' and Georgina and Nige would regularly count the boxes to see if any had sold. They also suggested we hold a competition to find the most imaginative function for them.

'They have a function,' I told them. 'They are very popular at the moment, a favourite diet tool.' At that point Lorraine and I were still trying to save face about our purchase.

'So how many have you sold then?' Nige asked.

'Lots of celebrity couples use them,' Lorraine said, ignoring his question.

'I say, ding dong!' said Nige. 'Celebrity sausage grabbing.'

Georgina took a pair from the shelf every morning and announced the 'use of the day' which included eyebrow pluckers for yetis, big toe measurers, and a tool for nipping a snoring partner's nose.

The sausage-grabbers stayed on our shelves, their price periodically reduced until months later we sold a pair to a very gullible customer for £2.99 and the rest ended up thrown in the back of the stock room.

Another of our bad buys was a sack of Carlin peas, sold to us by an enthusiastic rep who told us that they had been eaten on Carlin Sunday - the fifth Sunday of Lent - since 1644. Apparently they were very popular soaked, boiled and then fried with sugar and vinegar and sometimes, rum.

'They are also known as pigeon peas,' the rep said, as we signed his order for a 25kg sack. 'They are especially popular in the north east.'

Perhaps he meant in the north east of somewhere else or maybe we misheard him and they were supposed to be fed to pigeons but whatever the truth we sold not one pea.

Other failures included toilet tissue made from re-cycled paper that refused to flush away and caused many blocked drains in the area; fishless fishcakes that smelled so bad that the act of cooking them relieved you of any appetite you may have had and Peter's favourite – the 'Pure Organic Negativity Diffuser' that promised to 'Clear your Psychic Environment of Unwanted Negative Energies'. As it consisted of a bottle of odourless liquid that looked suspiciously like water and retailed at £12.99 we didn't sell any.

Peter however, seemed to love it and would often spray it around the shop dramatically saying,

'Oh no! My psychic environment has been contaminated by negative energies, I must disperse it with my Pure Organic Negativity Diffuser immediately.'

Products offered to us by sales reps varied from innovative to weird to downright ridiculous.

Our criteria for including a product in our stock range was difficult to define. We stocked vegetarian foods but also offered tuna in our sandwich menu. We sold wholefoods – unprocessed, natural foods such as rice, lentils, nuts and grains but also stocked products such as TVP (textured vegetable protein) which although was vegetarian was highly processed. Furthermore, it could be argued that some products that were 100% natural were not particularly healthy such as butter, maple syrup and coffee beans.

Lots of products brought to us and described as 'natural' and 'healthy' were anything but. Cereal bars full of added sugar, low fat foods with huge lists of chemical additives and I can't begin to count the number of slimming pills and potions we turned away.

The fact that we ourselves struggled to sum up our mission statement left us open to being offered all sorts of products and also to sometimes being criticised and ridiculed for products we did stock.

One of my better buys was a blend of essential oils that promised to ward off stretch marks. It worked so well that I would enthusiastically extol its virtues to any pregnant women who entered the shop, and would expose my well-rounded stomach to prove how beautifully smooth and unblemished my skin was. This would often prompt the mother-to-be to quickly buy a bottle and rush off home to try it.

'Another lady rushing off to use our stretch-mark oil,' I told Lorraine proudly as she dodged a woman exiting the shop at speed.

'Another poor pregnant woman traumatised by the sight of your belly looking like a space hopper and rushing home for a lie down more like,' she said.

I'd also bought a supply of raspberry leaf tea that I intended to start drinking in the last couple of weeks of my pregnancy. I'd checked with my midwife and she'd said it would be safe to do so. I'd read that raspberry leaf had womb-strengthening properties and could ease labour pains. I was hoping to have as natural a birth as possible.

'Are you sure that's what you really want?' Nadine and Lorraine asked frequently. 'You don't feel pressurised to do that just because we have the shop do you?'

'No I don't,' I told them, not for the first time. 'I just feel that giving birth is a natural function and if you take care of your body it will perform its natural function without any undue stress.'

'Talk about naive!' Nadine muttered. 'Do you not watch East Enders? Have you ever seen a birth scene without the mother screaming hysterically in agony?'

During pregnancy I found that women were very keen to tell me horror stories about birth and pregnancy as soon as they became aware that I was pregnant. There seemed to be some sort of competition as to who could boast the most hours spent in labour and I heard story after story of labour pains that continued for days, stitches in places I preferred not to think about, piles, varicose veins, stretch marks and intimate body places that would 'never be the same again.'

I tried to put these tales out of my head and think positively about the experience ahead of me, but they did get to me sometimes and I had a few sleepless nights dreading what may lie ahead.

I'm sure some women do have bad experiences but I wished they wouldn't terrify first-time mothers-to-be with these sorts of comments. There are so many amazing and positive aspects to carrying a child and giving birth, surely it would be better to focus on these too?

The women at Barbara's yoga class had quite a different outlook on the subject. Olivia, the elderly lady who I'd stupidly vastly misjudged asked me about my pregnancy and told me she was a retired midwife.

'Childbirth is the most natural thing in the world,' she said to me as we chatted at the end of the session. 'It's modern day society that gives women a feeling of fear and apprehension, which encourages them to use all kinds of medical intervention that is often not needed. Years ago, most women gave birth at home surrounded by their families with a minimum of fuss.'

'But surely there were more fatalities and complications then,' I said.

'Well yes,' she admitted. 'I'm not suggesting that medical intervention should be shunned completely. I just think that if women expect and accept that there's going to be bit of hard work and pain they can prepare themselves mentally and hopefully enjoy the whole experience without control being taken away from them.'

'I agree,' Barbara added. 'Giving birth was the most amazing thing I've ever experienced.'

'Me too,' Olivia said. 'Everything is geared up to preparing you for the pain and the struggle needed to bring life into the world, and yes it is hard work and it is painful, but it's nothing compared to the huge feeling of achievement afterwards and of course the immense rush of love when you first hold your child.'

This was much more encouraging and just what I needed to hear.

'So it's not as bad as some women make out then?' I asked.

'I have four sons,' Barbara said. 'Do you think women would have more than one child if it were so bad?'

'Things do go wrong sometimes,' Olivia said. 'And that's when you have to be prepared to take your midwife or doctor's advice. But mostly I found it depended on the attitude of the woman. A woman who is prepared to stay as calm as possible and work with the midwife and accepts she will have some pain and discomfort usually has a much better experience than those who are filled with fear and panic and basically wait for medical staff to take over.'

She took hold of my arm.

'You'll be absolutely fine dear. You have one of the most exciting and wondrous experiences ahead of you. Make your mind up that you are going to enjoy it and you will.'

I was so grateful for her words. I had let the negative comments of others make me lose my faith in nature and in my own body and now I felt optimistic and heartened again.

Barbara's final word on the subject was difficult to get my head around though.

'From a yoga point of view, the Yogis believed that childbirth was the completion of a natural cycle from conception to birth', she said, 'and therefore with the right mental attitude the birth should give as much pleasure and excitement as the orgasm experienced when conception occurred.'

Hmmm.

CHAPTER NINE

The day of the sponsored walk was cold but bright, and thankfully, without snow.

We left my Mam and my mother-in-law Joan in charge of the shop for the day and set off for the coast.

Peter drove into the surprisingly empty carpark at Tynemouth Priory, and pulled into a parking bay.

'Not many walkers here,' Nadine observed.

She shuffled along the backseat of the car looking around at the near-empty carpark.

'The ice-cream man is here, but not many cars.'

Lorraine parked next to us, and I could see Georgina and Nige looking around too. Peter wound down the car window and called to Georgina who was sitting in the passenger seat of Lorraine's car, to open her window.

'Are we too early?' he asked.

'No, it said to meet here at ten-thirty and it's twenty past now,' Georgina called.

'There's a poster over beside the ticket machine,' Lorraine said, pointing. 'Let's go and get the tickets and have a look.'

We got out of the cars, taking care not to have the doors ripped from our hands by the wind.

'Blimey!' I said, as my hair whipped around my face. 'It's wild out here!'

The car park overlooked the two piers that stretched out, solid and safe into the sea, and although the sky was bright ahead, to our left dark clouds behind the Priory camouflaged the stone ruins.

The sea was grey and choppy, and the sight of it made me shiver.

There were a few cars dotted about, one with the engine running. I could see a family inside, wrapped in woollen hats and scarves, and in another an elderly couple poured tea from a thermos.

The ice-cream man slid open the window of his van and looked out hopefully as we walked past towards the ticket machine. We looked at the torn poster attached to the fence and realised why it was so quiet.

'Ah, look at that, would you believe it?' Nadine said. 'We've got the date wrong, it was last week.'

'Oh no!' I said. 'We've been sponsored, we've lost all that money for the charity.'

'Ah well, never mind,' Nige said. 'Let's go home.'

'Or to the pub?' Nadine said. I waited hopefully. It sounded a lot more appealing than walking along the coast in a gale force wind.

'No way!' Georgina said. 'We came to do a walk and we are going to do it.'

'I agree,' Peter said. 'I think we should do it.'

'We can't do a sponsored walk if it's not on,' Nige said.

'This is for Josie, remember,' Lorraine said.

'Exactly,' Peter said. 'We're here and prepared, let's get on with it.'

'But it was last week!'

Nige was not going to give in easily.

A bitter wind from the sea battered us as we stood huddled together. I kept quiet, waiting for a decision. I felt as though we should really go ahead with the walk, but reckoned if the others decided against it I would be quite relieved to get back into the car and go off in search of a warm pub.

The ice-cream man closed his van window and went back to his newspaper.

I looked out to sea. The water hugged by the enfolding piers seemed relatively calm in comparison to the much wilder waves further off.

In the distance a ferry moved slowly away from North Shields and I thought about the people on board setting off for Amsterdam, queueing for food or braving the deck to catch the views, or perhaps just struggling to find their sea legs.

Nige's voice brought me out of my daydream.

'I don't suppose we could just pretend we did it last week…?' he suggested half-heartedly.

'No we couldn't,' Peter and Lorraine chorused.

'Nige, it's for Josie,' Georgina said. 'We can still do it and collect the money for the charity legitimately, even if it is the wrong day.'

Nige sighed dramatically.

'Well I'm not giving up so soon,' Lorraine said. 'People are paying good money for us to do this.'

'It's only five miles,' Peter said. 'Just a stroll really.'

'It would be like letting Josie down if we don't,' Nadine said. Nige gave in.

'Yes, you're right,' he said. 'Come on then, let's get going.'

After returning to the cars with parking tickets to fix on the windscreens, we set off up the hill in the direction of the Priory.

The sun was out, brightening the sky to a vivid blue that was worthy of summer, although the sea was grey and hostile and the wind fought against us as we walked.

'They're brave,' Peter said of two fishermen walking along the far pier, their backs bent into the wind, carrying tall fishing rods that bowed aggressively, threatening to snap with each gust.

'Or perhaps just stupid,' Georgina said. 'They'll end up in the sea if they're not careful.'

'So will that poor dog,' Lorraine said, and we looked to see a woman dragging a ball of billowing fur behind her. 'I hope she's got a firm grip on that lead!'

We slowly climbed the steep hill towards the Priory. I lagged behind, puffing and panting, no longer feeling cold. Peter stopped to wait for me.

'You ok?' he asked.

'Not really, I'm knackered already.'

I unzipped my coat and loosened my scarf. Peter took my arm.

'Come on,' he said. 'This is the worst bit. Once we're up this hill it gets easier.'

At the top of the hill we turned away from Tynemouth village and headed towards the seafront.

The Gibraltar Rock pub stood at the top of the hill looking more inviting than I'd ever seen it.

'Don't suppose there's any chance of a break?' I asked. Nige looked hopeful but the others hurried us on.

We decided to stay on the pavement above Tynemouth Longsands although Peter wanted to walk below on the beach.

'It will be more sheltered down there,' he argued. But for once we went against his advice.

'Wait until we're further along, we'll go down to the beach later,' Georgina suggested.

Apart from the occasional blast of North Sea wind that rocked us across the pavement, the walk was pleasant. The black clouds had moved off and the sun shone, although the sea constantly heaved with frothing waves that battered the shore.

We passed Tynemouth Park, a place that I'd spent many childhood days messing about by the boating pond. In summer, it filled with children on trikes and families eating ice-cream as they strolled around the pond past beds crammed with colour, but today it was deserted. The ice-cream kiosk had been boarded up for the winter and the flower beds were bare but for flapping litter caught on the spikes of the sleeping rose plants.

As we followed the curve of the bay into Cullercoats, the most delicious smell drifted by.

'Chippy's open!' Nige shouted excitedly, and we all cheered and hurried across the road to buy bags of hot salty chips.

'There's nothing like a bag of fresh chips eaten outdoors at the seaside,' Lorraine said, as we ate, huddled together on wooden seats overlooking the bay.

'You all right, flower?' Nadine asked me. 'You are carrying that big lump about with you.'

'I'm fine,' I said. 'It was just that hill at the start that was hard going.'

'Well you won't be carrying him around for much longer,' Lorraine said.

'Her,' I said.

'How do you know?' Nadine asked. 'Did the doctor tell you it's a girl?'

'No. I just have a feeling it's a girl. I don't know why.'

'How long to go now?'

'About four weeks.'

'Just in time for spring,' Lorraine said.

'How lovely, a spring baby,' Nadine said. 'I'm so envious.'

'I'm not,' Georgina said. 'Poor bugger. Have you any idea what you have to go through to get that baby out of you?'

Peter stood up and tossed his chip paper into the bin.

'Come on, let's get moving,' he said.

I knew he was trying to distract Georgina from telling me one of her gruesome childbirth tales but she kept going as we walked along.

'Men don't know the half of it,' she said looking at Peter menacingly. 'It's so easy to be a father. You just had to do the easy bit. Now she has to do the hard part.'

'Yes well nothing I can do about that I'm afraid,' Peter said. 'I'd take the pain if I could.'

'Oh yeah, sure you would.'

'Yes he would. I know he would if he could,' I said loyally.

'Blimey, he's got you brainwashed, hasn't he?'

'No he hasn't, actually,' I said, my anger mounting. How dare she have a go at Peter! Just because she was a hardened man-hater didn't mean she could take a swipe at my husband.

'I'm looking forward to giving birth actually, it will be an amazing and empowering experience,' I said, trying to remember what the women at Elaine's yoga class had said.

'Pah, you won't be saying that when you're screaming in agony.'

'Stop trying to frighten her,' Lorraine said. 'It must be daunting enough without people like you being so negative about it.'

'Let's change the subject,' said Nige, who was always uncomfortable talking about female issues. 'Look at those beautiful clouds.'

'I'm not being negative. I'm just being realistic. She needs to be prepared instead of going into it thinking it's a doddle.'

'Actually, Barbara told me that birth is the completion of a cycle and that giving birth can be as pleasurable as the orgasm when the conception occurred,' I said.

Georgina, for once, was speechless. Nige looked at me pitifully.

'Darlin', even I know that's not true.'

'What! Well I don't know what her definition of an orgasm is, but it's not the same as mine!' Georgina said. 'Eeh! I've heard some shite before but that beats it all!'

Peter took my hand.

'Like Nige said, I think we should change the subject,' he said.

'I was in absolute agony when I had my daughter,' Georgina said. 'There was definitely nothing orgasmic about it.'

'Different women have different experiences,' Lorraine said. 'You obviously had a bad one. It doesn't mean that Chris will too.'

'Exactly,' I said. I remembered the words of Olivia, the retired midwife I'd spoken to at yoga class. 'Women who are filled with fear and panic have a much worse time than those who stay calm and positive. You obviously went into it expecting the worse.'

'Huh!' Georgina scoffed. 'I think you've finally gone off with the fairies.'

'Come on, you two let's agree to disagree and talk about something else,' Nige said. 'It's spoiling the day.' He was right. The happy mood had changed, the energy between us was now tense.

'Yeah,' I said, nudging Georgina with my arm. 'Let's drop it.'

'Ok but don't say I didn't warn you,' Georgina said, always the one to have the last word. 'I didn't enjoy being pregnant at all. I hated the whole thing from start to finish. I'll never forget it. I was screaming 'For God's sake will you get that bloody thing out of me!'

'And that was just the conception,' Peter said wickedly.

We all laughed, relieving the strained atmosphere that had descended and we quickened our pace.

As we rounded the bend, St Mary's lighthouse came into view as the last leg of the walk lay before us.

'Look, you can just see the Rendezvous Café, that white square,' Peter said pointing, and we stopped to look.

'Last section, Cullercoats to Whitley Bay,' Lorraine said, 'Just like in the Dire Straits song,' and we ran down the stone steps from the path to the beach.

It was harder work walking on the sand, but lovely to be so close to the sea. We went down to the tideline and walked alongside the trail of black seaweed scattered with pieces of sea-smoothed wood and discarded plastic.

'Hey, look at this!' Peter said. He bent down and attempted to lift a section of tree trunk, bleached and worn smooth by the sea. Several twisted branches curved from the centre and Nige took hold of one of them and helped Peter to pull it free from tangles of seaweed and old rope.

'That will look great in the garden,' Peter said.

'It is rather beautiful,' Georgina agreed.

'Yeah, but how the heck are you going to get it home?' I asked.

'I'll carry it,' Peter said.

Nadine did not look very impressed.

'You're going to put that horrible old bit of tree in your garden?' she said. 'What's wrong with plant pots like normal people?'

'It'll look great that,' Peter said. 'A few plants climbing over it.'

'Why not leave it there and we'll get it on the way back?' Lorraine suggested.

'What if it's gone when we come back?' Peter said.

'I don't really think anyone else would want it,' Nadine said. So Nige and Peter dragged it a little further up the beach away from the sea and we walked until we came to the steps leading up to the Rendezvous.

'I've never been in here before,' Nige said as we walked across the square-paved promenade to the sandy steps of the café. We were all amazed.

'What! You've never been to the Rendezvous!'

'Everybody's been to the Rendezvous!'

'It's been here for years!'

It had indeed been there for years, the same family had run it since the fifties and little had changed in that time.

'We used to come here all the time when we were small, didn't we Lorraine?' I said, and Lorraine nodded.

'Me too,' Peter said. 'We were here all the time in the summer.'

'My Gran used to bring me,' Nadine said.

'It's fabulous,' Georgina said. 'A true blast from the past.'

We opened the heavy sprung doors and walked across the parquet floor to the counter.

With its little circular Formica-topped tables and spindly-legged chairs, the place was so outdated it had come full circle and was now a genuine vintage cafe. I think that's why so many people loved it - and indeed still do. In such a changing world, this was a place that had defied the passage of time and could instantly transport your mind back to childhood days at the seaside.

'I'm going to have a Knickerbocker Glory,' Peter said. 'They were my favourite when I was a kid.'

'Isn't it too cold for ice-cream?' I asked.

'It's never too cold for ice-cream,' he said. 'Anyway, I'm going to have a hot coffee with it.'

'Mmm, good idea. I'll have a Strawberry Sundae and a hot chocolate,' I said.

We looked at the row of brightly coloured pictures showing the ice-cream desserts available. They were the same pictures that I'd chosen from when I'd been brought here as a child for a treat. Each time we'd visit I'd choose a different one, starting with the Banana Split and working my way along to the Peach Melba, then back to the beginning again.

We took our trays over to a couple of tables near one of the huge arched windows overlooking the sea. I was so glad to sit down. Usually I was quite an enthusiastic walker, but carrying along the extra weight of my bump really did make a difference.

We tucked in to our ice-creams, jokingly discussing which combination of hot drink and cold dessert was the best.

Soon I'll be coming here with my own child, I thought happily as I sipped my hot chocolate. I couldn't wait to be a mother.

As the others chatted, their voices merged into the general contented murmur of customers and I sat back and drank in the atmosphere, watching a mother rocking a pram with one hand as she held a coffee cup in the other. Her other child sat next to her, swinging his feet in their yellow wellington boots as he eagerly scooped ice-cream into his mouth, chocolate sauce covering most of his face.

'What's up with you, sitting there smiling to yourself?' Georgina said.

'Just contemplating life,' I told her.

'Well contemplate this,' she said as the others gathered the empty cups onto a tray.

'We now have to walk back to Tynemouth, but this time with the wind in our face, carrying your husband's bloody great tree stump.'

CHAPTER TEN

The following morning, Sunday February the fourteenth, I awoke to breakfast in bed, red roses and a Valentine card and I have to be honest, it did make me feel very special, deluded female that I am.

'Don't suppose there's any hope of a romantic meal at a lovely restaurant tonight?' I asked optimistically.

'No chance,' Peter said. 'You know I hate going out on Valentine's day, paying extortionate prices for mediocre food, listening to cheesy music and feeling embarrassed sitting amongst loads of other couples trying to out-flirt each other.'

Great, I thought. Sounds like he's been listening to Georgina.

'Anyway,' he continued. 'I'd really like to get the skirting boards finished in the baby's room tonight, thought we could do that together.'

'Lovely. How romantic.'

But I suppose he was right. And I did have a lovely card telling me how much he loved me, and a gorgeous bunch of roses.

I ate my breakfast then snuggled under the duvet. The walk yesterday had really tired me. My legs were aching and my body felt stiff and heavy. Peter was concerned that I'd overdone it.

'Why don't you have another couple of hours?' he suggested. 'I'll go and make a start on the painting and I'll bring you up a cup of tea later.'

'Mmm,' I said, already half asleep.

Later, I joined him in what was to be the baby's bedroom and inspected his handiwork.

'Very good,' I said. 'But you've missed a bit there.'

He handed me a paintbrush.

'Get on with it then.'

We worked our way around the room and when we'd finished the first coat, Peter suggested he go for a take-away before giving it a second coat.

'That paint is quick-drying so we should be able to get the top coat on this afternoon. What do you fancy? Chinese, Indian, pizza…?'

'Well this is romantic,' I grumbled.

I was sitting in the little nursing chair I'd bought from The Narly Neh, and Peter was sitting on the floor as we ate pizza and drank tea.

'Of course it is,' he said. 'What could be more romantic than the two of us preparing our home for the arrival of our first child?'

I looked at him suspiciously but he seemed to be sincere.

'Must have a different understanding of the word 'romantic' then,' I said.

I picked up my paintbrush and dipped it in the paint tin, ready to start work again. I knelt on the floor with my legs tucked beneath me, my bump resting on my thighs as I began painting.

'Romance to me means lovely restaurants, and gorgeous food and music and candles,' I complained as I slapped white paint onto the wood. 'I must be the only woman I know who will be painting on Valentine's Day.'

Georgina's comments had riled me and I grumbled on and on.

'Here am I, in old leggings and a man's sweatshirt doing DIY while everyone is dressed up to kill, being wined and dined.'

'Well we've dined on take-away and you're doing plenty of whining, ha ha,' he joked.

'Oh shut up,' I said, leaning forward to reach the piece of skirting board in the corner. I felt something brush the back of my leggings

'What are you doing?' I asked, turning my head.

'I've painted a smile on your bum,' Peter said laughing, as he added two splodges that I presumed to be eyes.

I got up to go and look in the mirror in our bedroom. Twisting to see my reflection I saw he had, indeed, painted a smiling face on my bottom and unable to be grumpy any longer I succumbed to laughter whilst trying to paint his face with the paintbrush at the same time.

'Well?' Georgina said to me the next morning. 'Did you have a romantic Valentine's evening? Don't tell me... let me guess. You had an intimate little dinner for two and spent the evening gazing into each other's eyes?'

'Something like that,' I said deciding not to share the fact that my Valentine's day had ended with me having to scrub my bottom with turpentine because the smile Peter had painted had soaked through my leggings and onto my skin. Instead, I told her about my lovely card and roses.

'Huh! He only gave you flowers and wrote a load of slop on a card because he knows you expect it,' Georgina said.

'Oh stop being such an old cynic,' Nadine told her. 'He did it because he loves her.'

'I'm not saying he doesn't love her,' Georgina argued. 'I'm just saying he felt compelled to give her flowers and a card because it's what society dictates.'

'I don't agree,' Lorraine told her.

'Thank you Lorraine,' I said, then slapped her when she continued.

'It's because he knows she'd have gone into a mega-huff if he hadn't.'

'I thought better of Peter, mind,' Georgina said. 'Didn't think he was the type to get caught up in all that feeble-minded claptrap…'

'Now just hang on…' I said, as my hackles began to rise.

Peter is my husband and no-one is allowed to criticise him. Except, of course, myself. But I was interrupted by Nige bursting into the shop saying breathlessly,

'Oh I thought you must be in here. I've been knocking at your door for ages. Look! I reckon someone's got an admirer!'

He handed a beautifully wrapped parcel to Georgina. She took the package that was wrapped in red and tied with a gold ribbon saying,

'This is for me?'

'Oh come on Georgina,' Nadine encouraged her. 'Open it!'

Georgina excitedly tore off the paper to reveal a wooden heart, beautifully carved from a piece of driftwood.

'It's from Marc,' she said referring to an artist she'd had an on/off relationship with for the past year or so. Every now and again he would disappear from her life and she would shrug it off claiming they were both free spirits and had an honest, adult relationship. Then news would reach her that he'd been seen with another woman and she would revert to her All-Men-Are-Bastards ranting.

'Oh look what he's made for me,' she said. 'He's carved my name on it too.' She looked around at us, beaming.

'Lucky girl,' Nige said and Lorraine touched the carved letters, exclaiming at how well it had been made.

'It's beautiful,' Nadine said.

It was beautiful, but she had committed the unforgivable crime of insulting Peter.

'Ha!' I said. 'Feeble-minded claptrap! How sad that you've found out he's just the same as other men. Caught up in the mindless compulsion of society!'

'Now, now,' she said. 'Jealousy is not an attractive feature. You really need to let it go. I know you didn't get a hand-made, individual present like mine but not everyone is an individual free spirit. Trying to be catty really doesn't suit you. You are much too nice. See you later!' and off she swept, carrying her carved heart.

I should have remembered that no-one ever gets the better of Georgina.

After the madness of the lunchtime rush, afternoons tended to be quiet, which gave us a chance to get on with the day-to-day tasks that kept the shop running smoothly. After a late lunch we would use the time between serving customers to put together stock orders, tackle paperwork and keep on top of cleaning and replenishing the shelves.

I busied myself filling up the homeopathic remedy shelf with little bottles of white pills, polishing the glass before carefully arranging them.

I loved the abbreviated names of the remedies, all lined up in alphabetical order - words that reminded me of old chemist bottles I'd seen at in the old Apothecary shop at Beamish museum. Apis Mel, Arsen Alb, Belladonna, Calc Carb, Hepar Sulph, Kali Phos, Nat Mur, Rhus Tox.

I was happily straightening the bottles, making sure the labels were perfectly aligned when a bellowing voice brought me out of my daydreaming.

'Mrs Kenworthy?'

I turned to see an authoritative looking, ruddy-faced man with a handlebar moustache, holding a small black case.

'Yes?'

'Weights and Measures. Here to check you over.'

He placed the briefcase on the counter and began to open it.

'You want to weigh and measure me?'

'Not you personally, har har, just some of your stock.'

He showed me an official card, but to be honest it could have been his metro pass, as all I saw was a blurred mugshot as it whizzed past my nose.

'Now then, MeDear. Where are your scales? I just need to check them first, then I'll take a look at some of your merchandise.'

I pointed to the digital scales on the ledge at the back of the display fridge but he had already moved behind the counter towards them.

'Ah yes,' he boomed. 'Excellent, excellent.'

He took some weights from his bag and began to check them on our scales.

I was bit overawed by the sheer presence of the man. He was one of those larger-than-life characters who effortlessly command ownership of their environment and his booming voice made mine feel like a squeak in comparison. Lorraine had just gone to the Post Office and I kept looking at the door, willing her to return.

'Right MeDear, all shipshape. I just need to check a few odds and sods if you'll pardon the expression.'

He strode around the shop collecting bags of dried fruit and flour, then examined the labels carefully, before weighing them.

'Pack these yourself, what?' he asked as he peered at my hand-written label on a bag of prunes.

'Yes,' I piped. 'We buy twenty-five kilo sacks, then repack in five hundred gram bags.'

'Yes, yes. Excellent, excellent. I see you have the sell-by date on there, and the weight and country of origin, all good stuff. That's what you need. And your weights are spot on too. Excellent.'

He handed me the packages.

'Pop those back on the shelf, MeDear, there's a good girl.'

Good girl? I had endured being called MeDear, but really! Who did he think he was speaking to, a child?

'Now look here,' I cheeped, but before I could voice my objection, Peter arrived, striding in and stopping abruptly when he caught sight of the Weights and Measures man.

'Hello Henry!'

'Peter, my good man! Haven't seen you for years, what a hoot!'

He was really beginning to irritate me now. First I was a good girl and now it was a hoot to see my husband.

'You two know each other?' I asked.

'Well either that or we're bloody good actors, har har,' Henry said.

'We were at school together,' Peter said. 'This is Christine, my wife.'

'Ah, excellent, excellent. Got yourself a nice little filly there, old chap.'

Nice little filly? I looked at Peter waiting for him to object to the comparison of the love of his life to a horse, but he just laughed, the big galoot. I gave him a withering look, and he looked back at me with that confused look men give you when they know they have annoyed you but have no idea why.

'Excuse me, I have customers to attend to,' I said and flounced off, leaving them to reminisce about the jolly good old days.

Lorraine returned from the Post Office and asked me who Peter was speaking with.

'Just some old twonk he knew at school,' I said.

'Twonk?'

'It's the most polite word I can think of at the moment.'

'Doesn't seem the type to have gone to school with Peter. Didn't he go to Longbenton?'

'Oh yar, absolute hoot, Longbenton, what?'

'I take it you don't like him?'

'He called me a good girl and referred to me as a nice little filly.'

'Ouch.'

'So you were at school with Hooray Henry then?' I asked Peter later. He laughed.

'He's all right, Henry. Just a bit pompous.'

'Just a bit pompous? So it's ok for him to call me a horse?'

'He called you a horse?'

'He referred to me as a 'nice little filly'.

'Oh that. He didn't mean anything by it. It was his way of saying you are an attractive woman. You can't take offence at Henry.'

'Can't I?'

'No, it's just his way.'

'Well let's hope he doesn't take offence when I refer to him as a pretentious old walrus. That's if I ever have the misfortune of meeting him again.'

'Well that would just be downright rude wouldn't it? I hope you won't say anything of the kind when you see him on Saturday.'

'Saturday? If he's coming back on Saturday I might have to go into the office and polish my paperclips.'

'He's not coming here. We're going out to meet him. He invited us to join his wife and him for dinner.'

'And you said 'Oh dear, what a shame, can't make it'.'

'No, I said 'Thank you we'd love to'. It's at the Red Dragon in Chinatown on Saturday and there are two other couples from his sport club going.'

'What kind of sport club?'

'I don't know, he didn't say. Probably cricket. I seem to remember him being on the school team.'

'So I'm going out to dinner to eat my least favourite kind of food with Hooray Henry who thinks I'm a horse, to talk about boring cricket with his cronies. Great. I can't wait.'

And I am sorry to say I indulged myself in the biggest huff ever for the rest of the day.

CHAPTER ELEVEN

Dried herbs and spices were amongst our bestselling products.

Because we bought them in huge sacks and weighed them into 25g and 50g packs ourselves we were able to sell them cheaply and still make a good mark-up. We added new varieties regularly and our range grew to over a hundred different herbs and spices.

Peter built a high shelf around the shop walls to house our gorgeous vintage sweet jars that we'd bought from an auction. Filled with little packages of herbs and spices and labelled with my hand made signs they looked really effective, until a visiting Health and Safety Inspector requested we change them.

'You'll need to fit a safety rail,' he told us after measuring the height of the shelf and examining the heavy glass jars with their ornately moulded lids and ground-glass necks. He held one up in front of me.

'And these will have to go,' he said.

'But why?' I asked. I loved those jars.

'Imagine this jar fell onto a customer's head.' He demonstrated dramatically. 'One very unhappy customer. And the next thing you know is you're being sued for injuring a member of the public with a jar of...' he peered at the label '...fennel seeds. No you'll have to replace them with plastic jars.'

I was tempted to retort 'Oh so it's ok for a plastic jar of fennel seeds to fall on a customer's head then?' but I refrained. One thing we'd learned was that Health and Safety Officers and Environmental Health Inspectors were very powerful people. It paid to be complying and amenable when dealing with their often petty rules and regulations.

'It's ridiculous,' Lorraine said later. 'Why would a jar full of herbs suddenly jump off a shelf and hit someone on the head?'

'Well I agree with him,' Nige said and we all looked at him, surprised. '*Fennelly* enough I've often wondered what would happen if someone was attacked by a jar of herbs.'

We all groaned except Peter who seemed to be under the illusion that something humorous had been said.

'Nige your jokes are rubbish,' Lorraine told him.

'It was *mint* to be funny,' Peter said and we groaned again.

'Your jokes are rubbish too,' Lorraine said as he guffawed and Nige tittered.

'I like to *cumin* and cheer people up,' Nige said.

'It hasn't worked this *thyme,* Nige,' Peter told him. Honestly, they were as bad as each other.

'Well I'd better go and *curry* on delivering mail,' Nige giggled as he left Peter laughing like a half-wit.

We changed the jars for nondescript plastic ones and it had to be said that they were more practical being easier to handle and to clean.

A delivery of herbs and spices was always received with pleasure as during the unpacking, the shop would be filled with a myriad of fragrances.

Today the delivery arrived just after a delivery from Saffron Chilled and Frozen Foods, so we had no choice but to leave it until the perishable food had been sorted and priced and stashed in the fridges and freezers.

'Just in time,' Lorraine said, as we closed the freezer lid on the last of the frozen vegetable pies. 'We'll have to do the herbs and spices after the lunchtime rush.'

Each day, at a few minutes past twelve, a queue would materialise, weaving its way across the shop. Lorraine, Nadine and I would hurry to our posts, one of us at the till taking orders and money and the other two at the kitchen bench, assembling sandwiches in a mad flurry. This continued until around two o'clock when calmness would be suddenly restored, leaving only a few shoppers and browsers.

We often joked that a trip bus brought them in and whisked them off again, like a group of Japanese tourists descending on a place of interest for a few minutes of frenzied photography then rushing on to the next place. 'The Nutmeg Express is in' became a euphemism for having a shop full of customers.

As we bustled about, making sandwiches and taking orders I noticed an atmosphere amongst the waiting customers. They seemed to be quietly complaining to each other about something and were keen to leave quickly.

'What's going on?' I asked Nadine, as a customer snatched up her sandwich and left wafting her hand in front of her face.

'No idea,' she said, and just then Peter arrived.

'Ugh!' he said. 'It bliddy stinks in here.'

'What of?' I asked, dismayed. Not the greeting you want when you are preparing food for people to buy.

'Like something crawled behind the counter and died. You better check to see if there's a dead rat behind there.'

'Keep your voice down,' I muttered, moving into the shop to let him squeeze through the gap in the counter. As I did, the most rancid, stomach-churning smell rose to slap me right in the face.

'What on earth…?' I gagged as I put my hand over my nose.

By now, the customers had thinned out, many choosing to leave before buying, and the rest eyeing each other suspiciously to ascertain which one of them was the source of the smell.

Lorraine and Nadine continued with their sandwich making, apparently unaware, until I saw Nadine's nose suddenly wrinkle and she held up the dishes of sandwich fillings, giving each one a sniff like a mother sniffing at her baby's bum to see if a change of nappy was needed. I saw her nudge Lorraine and as Lorraine's face puckered I hurried back to the kitchen.

'It's something out in the front of the shop,' I whispered. 'You carry on here. I'll go and find out what it is. Just act normal.'

They arranged their faces into what they must have believed to be pleasant expressions and I left them to carry on, both looking as though they'd had bad face lifts.

'Holy Moley, it smells like the scent of a thousand bums in here,' I heard, and I turned to see Nige holding his nose as he made his way to the counter.

'What *is* that?' he asked as he handed me a pile of mail.

'Stop being so disgusting and be quiet,' I told him.

He unpinched his nose for a second.

'Me being disgusting? Poowee!' he said and immediately pinched his nose again.

'Help me find out what it is,' I said.

There followed a ridiculous scene in which Peter, Nige and I prowled the shop, sniffing at everything in sight. Peter and I tried to be discreet but Nige carried out the task in his own inimitable way, mincing about and dramatically holding his nose in various places, sniffing exaggeratedly.

'Oh my word, it's over here,' he said, gagging and pointing to our delivery of herbs and spices. 'What you got in there? A consignment of sewage?'

Luckily the shop was now devoid of customers so I quickly bolted the door and called Lorraine over.

'We've found it,' I said and we both leaned towards the box to smell it then reeled back.

'Aw yes, it is' Lorraine said. 'What the hell is that?'

'Well I'm not opening it,' I said 'Smells like something's dead in there.'

'Oh no! What if a mouse has crawled in and died?' Nadine said.

'That's worse than a dead mouse,' Peter said. 'More like a dead skunk.'

'Well that's me out,' I said. 'I can't risk being near anything like that, it could harm the baby.'

'Let's get it over with,' Peter said and ripped off the parcel tape, pulling back the flaps to release a new wave of pungency.

'Flippin heck!'

'Blimey!'

'What a stench!'

'That's wicked!'

We all moved back from the box except for Peter, who started lifting out packs of spices. He sniffed each one carefully before throwing them onto the floor.

Sniff, sniff.

'No.'

Sniff, sniff.

'No.'

Sniff… 'Bloody hell, that's it.'

He held up a large cellophane bag full of a whitish powder. The bag had split and the contents sprinkled to the floor as Peter held it.

'Aw, it's on my hands,' he said smelling them and gagging.

'What is it?' I asked. 'Is it drugs?'

'Hardly,' he said. 'I can't see anyone wanting to shove that up their nose.'

A loud knock at the door interrupted us and I looked to see Georgina peering in.

'Come in,' I said, opening the door for her to enter. 'We're trying to identify a bad smell.'

Georgina's face puckered.

'Smells like asafoetida,' she said.

'Asserferwhatta?'

'It is, look. Asafoetida.'

She took up the packet and turned it to show us the label.

'What is it though?' Nadine asked.

'Powdered rat's arse by the smell of it,' Nige said moving towards the door. 'As much as I'd love to stay all day and inhale bad smells with you all I really must be off. Letters to deliver and all that.'

'See you later, Nige,' I said and bolted the door behind him.

Peter went to get the dustpan and brush and started to clean up the spilled powder.

'How could you possibly eat that?' Lorraine asked.

'It's really nice in curries and stuff,' Georgina told us.

'But it absolutely honks,' I said.

'Yeah, another name for it is Devil's Dung. It loses the bad smell when you cook it. It's really popular in India and the Middle East. And it's been used in the east for years as a treatment for stomach problems. It was even used as a contraceptive in some places.'

'Well that doesn't surprise me. A sprinkling of that down your knickers would put anyone off sex,' Peter said.

'Well we can't stock it,' I said. 'It's already stunk out the shop.'

'So why did you order it?' Nadine asked.

'We didn't know what it was. We just ordered lots of new herbs and spices and it was on the list in the brochure.'

'I think you'll do well with it, not many places stock it,' Georgina said.

'Wonder why…' Lorraine said drolly. 'Well this lot is going straight in the bin.'

We opened the back window and the front door to allow a breeze to flow through the shop and even sprayed the Negative Energy Diffuser around but the smell lingered for a while.

We have often been accused of exaggerating the extent of the stink that came into the shop that day when relating the story, but what I later learned was that we had been supplied with the pure form of asafoetida whereas most commercial preparations are a mixture of wheat flour and asafoetida.

Years later I noticed that it was beginning to make a more regular appearance on spice shelves at supermarkets, and when my curiosity forced me to examine a jar, I discovered that although it was doubly wrapped and encased in a glass jar there was still a subtle aroma emanating from it.

I can also reveal that in all our years at Nutmeg, we were never once asked if we stocked asafoetida, nor have I ever used it in my cooking.

CHAPTER TWELVE

A delicious fragrance of ginger, garlic and sweet chilli hit me as I got out of the taxi, making my stomach rumble in anticipation.

'That smells gorgeous,' I said to Peter and I took his arm as we walked into Stowell Street.

'Thought you didn't like Chinese food.'

'I didn't say I didn't like it, I just said it's not my favourite.'

We walked along the narrow pavement past red and green neon signs with Chinese lettering. Ornately painted animals, dragons and fish suspended from the shop fronts swayed in the breeze.

'It's Hooray Henry I don't like.'

'I'm sorry, I know you didn't really want to come tonight,' Peter said. 'But I wish you'd just give him a chance. Please?'

I looked into his eyes, like dark pools, and as always they melted away the last of my resentment and I felt a wave of love bubbling up inside of me.

'Yeah, ok. I'm sorry for being such a misery,' I said, squeezing his arm. 'Let's just enjoy the evening. It'll be fun to meet new people and the food does smell lovely.'

We passed a restaurant with gold lanterns at the entrance, filled with diners eating and chatting over candlelit tables, and a little shop displaying Chinese medicines in its window.

'So how well do you know Henry?' I asked.

'Not that well really. We were in the same year but different classes. He had a bit of a rough time at school, you can imagine how the other lads reacted to his grandiose ways, but I always thought that beneath it, he was a decent lad.'

We crossed the street to The Red Dragon and pulled open the door, releasing a wave of warm spiced air and jovial voices. The interior was opulently decorated with thick red carpets, gold walls and carved tables and chairs. A huge carved dragon adorned the wall above the bar, and red and gold glass lanterns cast a flattering light over the clusters of customers enjoying drinks as they waited to be seated.

I heard Henry's voice at once, resonating across the room from the bar. He was half way through telling an anecdote, but as the jangling strings of gold and red bells on the back of the door announced our entrance, he turned and waved.

'Peter!' he yelled. 'Over here old chap.'

'Why does he keep calling you an old chap?' I muttered as we made our way towards the group of people standing at the bar, a collection of half-empty wine bottles in front of them. 'I didn't think Longbenton would be a place for old chaps.'

'Well it's not really,' Peter said. 'But that's what I mean. It's just his way.'

Henry seemed genuinely pleased to see us.

'Peter. Christine. Excellent, excellent,' he boomed, and he shook Peter's hand and leant to kiss my cheek. 'Let me introduce you to the gang. This is my wife, Luce.'

A long-faced woman with a heavy jaw-line and rather prominent nose turned and barked 'Lucinda' at him, before taking me in from head to toe with an expression of someone who is suffering from a nearby bad smell.

Now that's a horse, I thought as she turned her back, dismissing me without acknowledging my hello.

I smiled and nodded as we were introduced to the other two couples, William and Annalisa, and James and Harriet.

William looked like an overgrown schoolboy, eager to please and hanging on to the every word of the other two men. His wife Annalisa was slim with silky blond hair and a beautifully-cut turquoise dress. Expensive but tasteful jewellery glittered at her throat and wrists. She smiled, revealing two rows of white, perfectly even teeth. She was very stunning and I felt frumpy in comparison.

I'd wandered around the shops in Newcastle looking for something to wear that wouldn't make me look like a walking tent, which was the general style of maternity clothes at that time. I'd finally found a short skirt with a panel of stretchy material at the front to accommodate my bump, and an oversized cream silk blouse. Worn with opaque black tights, sparkly pumps and dangly earrings, I'd thought I looked quite nice, although I still felt enormous. But now, standing next to the petite and gorgeous Annalisa, I felt like a prize pumpkin dressed up as a person.

'So pleased to meet you,' she said, bestowing another of her flawless smiles upon us. Her perfectly made-up blue eyes were glassy, and she swayed on her stilettos, clutching her glass with long manicured fingers. It was evidently not her first drink of the evening.

James was as loud, if not louder than Henry, and seemed to feel the need to end each statement with a braying haw-haw-haw, as though everything he said was excruciatingly funny.

His wife Harriet, tall and angular with crimson lipstick and short jet-black hair, did not appear to find her husband amusing in the least. She stood with one arm flung out to the side, her fingers holding a cigarette that burned with a long curl of smoke. Occasionally, ash would fall from it to the floor, but I never saw her hold it to her lips. Her fringe was cut high, revealing black pencilled eyebrows that made her look startled and she assumed an air of aloofness that bordered on the ridiculous. She assessed me with a bored tilt of her head and said 'Quite.'

Quite what? I wanted to ask, but was on my best behaviour so didn't.

Henry ordered drinks and when I asked for a bitter lemon, Harriet turned her surprised expression and her burning cigarette in my direction.

'How terribly boring,' she said.

'I think I'll have a bitter lemon too,' Annalisa said, smiling and leaning unsteadily towards me, and I smiled back at her, trying not to inhale Harriet's smoke.

'I'm as nished as a pewt already,' she whispered in my ear. 'I had a couple before I came out.'

I wondered if she meant glasses or bottles. She winked at me conspiringly and I warmed to her.

'Dutch courage,' she said.

I wondered why she felt she needed courage to join her friends for dinner.

Our drinks arrived, and we listened politely as Henry told a rather disjointed story about being mistaken for a film star whilst on holiday in the south of France. The others, except Harriet who was probably afraid of her face cracking, laughed heartily at random points during the story.

I had completely lost the thread of the tale and looked at Peter who seemed to be having difficulty in identifying the comical parts, so whenever the others laughed, we joined in, laughing animatedly like a couple of idiots. The part I did find funny was that each time Henry referred to his wife as 'Luce', she would compulsively yell 'Lucinda' like a participant on one of those television hypnotist shows. When he eventually finished relating his yarn, she gave him a look of contempt and said, 'Really, Henry!'

We were taken into the dining area where we were directed to a large circular table. The waiter brought the opened bottles of wine from the bar on a tray and arranged them carefully on our table.

Peter moved to a seat and pulled out the chair on his left for me, but before I could sit, Henry claimed it. I moved around the table intending to sit on Peter's right, but by the time I got there, Annalisa had taken the chair, so there was no alternative but to sit between her and Harriet. Lucinda sat next to Henry with William and James filling the chairs to the right of Harriet.

Menus were passed around and I opened mine, scanning it to find dishes marked suitable for a vegetarian diet.

William and James were laughing together. I couldn't hear what they were saying but I smiled in their direction which seemed to make them laugh harder.

Henry was speaking to Peter so I turned to Harriet and in an attempt to start a conversation said,

'I haven't been here before, it's a lovely restaurant.'

Harriet stared at me from beneath her arched eyebrows as though she couldn't believe I'd said something so inane.

'Quite,' she said then went back to studying her menu.

'Ooh, what are you going to have?' Annalisa asked. 'I'm so hungry but I'm on a diet.'

'I'm not sure,' I said. 'They have a few vegetarian choices.'

'For vegetarians you mean?'

'Yes. Well, for anyone,' I said.

The smoke from Harriet's cigarette was beginning to make me feel queasy so I was pleased when it finally burned down and she stubbed it out. Unfortunately she immediately lit another.

'Right chaps,' Henry roared. 'How about the good old 'Set Menu for Eight Persons?' There was a chorus of agreement and I glanced at the list of dishes offered.

Sticky Ribs, Fried Crab Claws, King Prawns and Salt and Pepper Squid. For the main course there was Roast Pork in Xi Sauce, Char Su Pork, Szechuan Beef, Satay Chicken, Duck with Ginger and Chilli…

I looked at Peter despairingly.

'Um, actually Henry, we'll order separately if you don't mind, we're vegetarian,' he said.

An eerie hush fell across the table and everyone turned to look at us with dismay or shock or both. Harriet's eyebrows had now disappeared beneath her fringe and as I looked around the circle of horrified faces, I almost expected to hear the theme tune from The Twilight Zone.

When I first gave up eating meat, my decision came with quite a few difficulties, the most wearisome being having to constantly explain the reasons for my decision. If I felt that changing my diet was of no interest or importance to anyone else, then I was wrong. My family was fine with it, as were most of my friends. But some of my friends and acquaintances took it almost as a personal insult. The mildest reaction would be a quiet mumble of acknowledgement, given with a shake of the head and a look of disappointment, showing how much I'd let them down. Then there were those who felt the need to justify their own eating habits by telling me that they

'...really don't eat much meat these days, just chicken and fish and the odd roast dinner and occasional ham sandwich, oh and of course bacon, but I could give up eating meat tomorrow if it weren't for the fact that my husband/wife/partner/child loves meat and wouldn't be able to survive without it...'

I honestly wasn't interested in how much meat anyone else was eating or not eating, but would listen politely, changing the subject as soon as I could.

The worst were the ranters who bombarded me aggressively with a long list of objections

'...humans are meant to eat animals and it's all part of the food chain and it is God's plan for animals to be eaten and that's why we have incisors, and cows would become extinct and butchers would become bankrupt and anyway there is a vitamin that only exists in sausages so anyone on a vegetarian diet doesn't get it and they will die eventually and what about if scientists find out that plants have feelings what are you going to do then, eat stones?'

Initially I would defend myself by answering with counter-objections and explanations, but as these were rarely heard I soon tired of the same old arguments being put before me and eventually just refused to talk about the subject.

Often when I ate out with a group and was served my meal, someone would remark, 'What the hell is that? Are you going to eat it?'

And although I really wanted to say 'Eat it? Of course not! I ordered it for the simple purpose of throwing it at you', I'd patiently explain that I was eating a meal based on ingredients such as pulses or tofu or soya while they'd grimace and make disparaging remarks and I'd resist the urge to shout, 'Well excuse me, but actually you are the one eating a dead pig's backside, how is that not more disgusting?'

Others would ask, 'What on earth do you eat?' and at first I'd begin to explain that I ate vegetables, fruit, grains, pulses, nuts, seeds, tofu, soya… but I soon learned that this answer did not satisfy so I'd just say 'just lettuce' which got a much better reaction.

Today most eating places offer at least three or four meat-free dishes, and, if possible, will adapt a dish containing meat when requested.

However, when I first became vegetarian, things were very different. Eating with a group was often a disaster. When friends had decided where to eat, they'd often tell me that the menu included a vegetarian choice. A vegetarian choice meaning one dish suitable for vegetarians.

One dish is not a choice. It is one dish. Which quite often turned out to be an omelette or a mushroom stroganoff, the latter of which I vowed never to eat again after once being served a handful of shrivelled mushrooms thrown into an insipid grey sauce.

At Christmas I'd be served an unseasonal offering such as pasta, when really it was just the turkey I didn't want but apparently had to also forgo all of the usual trimmings.

I'd often be made to feel as though I'd just asked for something obscene as a waiter would huff and puff, unable to hide his displeasure as he was forced to go off in search of the chef to enquire if he had anything suitable for me.

Some places were quite blatantly 'vegetarian-unfriendly' such as the inn serving Sunday lunches in Warkworth which displayed a message beneath its 'Specials of the Day' board which read 'Well behaved dogs and vegetarians welcome.'

But worst of all, was being made to feel like an outcast, purely based on my choice of food.

To my great annoyance, I heard myself apologising for the fact that we did not eat meat and felt my face flush with embarrassment as even Henry seemed lost for words.

Eventually, Lucinda spoke.

'Can't you just eat it this once?'

'No,' Peter said.

'But it won't harm you. It's not like we're asking you to eat something unpalatable.'

'I'm sorry,' I apologised again.

'How inconsiderate,' she said. 'We'll have to order separate dishes.'

'Damned awkward,' said Harriet. 'Surely you can eat chicken? Or duck?

'It's not really a problem, surely,' Peter said.

'Not at all, old chap, not at all.' Henry said. Lucinda turned to him, her annoyance showing.

'Really, Henry!'

'We'll order ours and you can order a set meal for six or whatever,' Peter said. I wished I was sitting next to him so I could hold his hand. I widened my eyes trying not to let the tears welling up in them escape.

Annalisa, looked at me kindly and patted my arm.

'Don't worry about it. We're very open-minded. After all, we're all alike under the skin.'

I didn't really understand what she meant, but I knew she was trying to be kind and I was grateful to her. She took a drink then looked at me thoughtfully.

'What even is a vegetarian anyway?' she slurred.

'Just someone who doesn't eat meat,' I mumbled.

'Actually, the word vegetarian is of tribal origin,' James said. 'It means 'he who can't hunt', haw-haw-haw.'

William laughed, choking on his drink.

'And those who were unable to hunt were forced to subsist on slower prey, such as lettuce and carrots, haw-haw-haw.'

Again William laughed along as though James had said something hilariously funny. Actually, it was quite funny but I chose not to laugh.

'I say, you're not vegan are you?' Henry asked and my answer to his question was drowned by James saying

'My good man, of course she's not vegan. She would have told you within seconds of meeting you, haw-haw-haw. And if you are a ruddy vegan my dear, you can bloody well bugger orf back to Planet Vega, what? Haw-haw.'

William was laughing like a half-wit, until Annalisa reprimanded him, instructing him to be quiet and to go and fetch her another bottle of wine.

'Just ignore them,' she said to me. 'The boys get very silly when they're together.'

I looked at Peter and he gave a forced smile.
'What would you like to eat?' he asked. 'Shall we order a couple of things to share?' We decided on some dishes while the others discussed the menu and made their choices.

The waiter arrived bringing more wine and taking our order. Annalisa put her arm around me and said to the waiter,

'My friend is a vegetable-arian. Have you a vegetable-arian option?'

The waiter began pointing out dishes on the menu and I listened politely although Peter and I had already chosen.

'I'll tell you what option I'd give vegetarians,' James said loudly. 'Eat meat or piss orf, haw-haw.'

'Quite,' Harriet said lighting another cigarette. I coughed as the smoke from it drifted across my face.

'Is my cigarette smoke bothering you? she asked.

'Well now you ask, yes it is actually,' I said apologetically.

'How rude!' she said, and turned to observe James and William in their haw-hawing.

'I think they are being very unreasonable,' Annalisa said to me. 'I mean, I love vegetables. I'm also a vegetable-arian actually. I just eat meat too.'

'My ancestors didn't fight their way to the top of the food chain for me to be a bloody vegetarian,' James said.

'No such thing as a bloody vegetarian,' Peter said. 'That's the whole point.'

Henry, who was looking uncomfortable at the way the conversation was progressing, said,

'Each to their own, ay chaps? Each to their own.'

Two waiters approached carrying silver trays of food that they unloaded onto the rotating platform at the centre of the table.

I was really hungry now and looked to find our vegetable spring rolls and crispy seaweed that we'd ordered for our starter. I spotted the spring rolls but as I moved my hand to spear one with my fork, they moved out of my reach as the platform revolved as the others reached for their food.

'Mmm, spring rolls,' Annalisa said as she helped herself.

Peter managed to swipe one as they spun past him but by the time they had travelled a full three hundred and sixty degrees, the dish was empty.

'I say,' William said. 'How many vegetarians does it take to change a light bulb?'

Oh great. Here we go again, I thought as I managed to scoop a forkful of crispy seaweed onto my plate. But before William could reveal his punchline, James jumped in and beat him to it.

'Two!' he said. 'One to change the bulb and one to read the ingredients.'

William deflated like a leaky balloon as James basked in the laughter of the others.

'And how many meat-eaters does it take to change a lightbulb?' Peter asked. 'None, because they prefer to stay in the dark.'

William began haw-hawing then stopped abruptly when he realised he was the butt of the joke, although Henry and Annalisa laughed.

'Now then chaps, if you give it you have to take it,' Henry said. Lucinda gave him a look of scorn.

'Really Henry!' she said, and Harriet nodded in agreement and said 'Quite.'

I had eaten my few strands of crispy seaweed and looked hungrily at the quickly emptying dishes circling back and forth like sushi on a malfunctioning high speed conveyor belt.

Peter's plate held some boiled rice, and he nodded towards the bowl he'd taken it from, before sending it in my direction. It didn't look particularly appetising but I was ravenous and it was better than nothing.

As the rice came towards me I lunged at it but it changed direction and I grabbed the wooden table centre with one hand and attempted to take rice with the other. As I struggled to keep my grip, I looked up and made eye-contact with Lucinda, who was sitting directly opposite. She too was holding the platform, pulling it away from me with a look of steely determination. For a couple of seconds we grappled with it, until I felt it slip from my fingers and I grabbed at the rice bowl before I lost it. As I seized it, it shot upwards and I looked in dismay as the only meat-free food left on the table flew into the air and rained down onto Harriet.

'So sorry,' I said, and I took a napkin and tried to wipe off some of the white rice grains sitting like oversized nits in her black hair.

'Leave it!' she hissed, then stood and stormed off in the direction of the Ladies.

'Sorry,' I said to the others as I flapped a napkin about amongst the spilt rice. The waiter hurried over and began to clear away the remains of the food and empty dishes.

Annalisa sniggered into her glass.

'That's the funniest thing I've seen in ages,' she spluttered.

I was beginning to really like Annalisa.

CHAPTER THIRTEEN

Harriet returned as the main course was being served. I spotted our tofu in chilli sauce and kept my eye on it, determined to actually eat what I'd ordered this time.

James took a huge portion of every food that passed by him, and I watched in frustration as he piled our tofu onto his plate. I took advantage of the fact that the egg foo yung was placed in front of me, and quickly shovelled as much as I could onto my plate before the food started on its rounds. I suddenly realised that I was being watched by the rest of the group and looked up in shame at being caught diving into the dish like a truffle-hunting pig. Henry came to my rescue, diverting attention from me as he picked up a wine bottle.

'Wine, anyone?' he asked, and proceeded to fill the wine glasses. I covered my glass with my hand.

'Not for me thanks,' I said.

Harriet looked at me caustically. The rice incident had done nothing to lessen her dislike of me.

'So. No alcohol either. Is this because of some religious reason?' she asked.

'Religious reason?' James bellowed. 'Don't tell me they've even vegetarianised the ruddy bible now. I suppose Jesus fed the five thousand with 5 courgettes and two sticks of celery, haw-haw.'

'Really Henry!' Lucinda said. It seemed that he was held responsible for any behaviour or comment of which she did not approve. Poor Henry. I was beginning to see Peter's point of view. Under his cloak of pomposity he was actually a really likeable man. Compared to his friends, anyway.

'There are several religions that advocate a meat-free diet,' Peter said.

'Oh my God, don't tell me you're a member of some weird bloody cult,' James said.

'I'm avoiding alcohol because I'm pregnant.' I said.

Harriet glanced down at my stomach. 'Really? I thought you were rather fat,' she said.

'So you get a bit of meat sometimes then, ey my girl? Haw-haw,' James snorted, which I thought was very crude and unnecessary.

William laughed, and Lucinda snapped,

'Henry, really!' even though he had neither made the remark nor laughed. Annalisa noticing my embarrassment, changed the subject.

'Enjoying the food, everyone?' she asked. We all agreed that we were and James said,

'Bloody marvellous this sweet chilli chicken.'

'Actually, that's tofu,' Peter said. James was flustered at his error.

'Well what's the point of that? If it tastes like meat, why not just ruddy well eat meat?'

I guessed that an explanation of the exploitation of animals in the food industry would fall on deaf ears so I decided not to offer one.

'They say you are what you eat, my girl,' he went on. 'You need to think about that the next time you're tucking in to your nut loaf, haw-haw.'

He lifted his fork to his mouth.

'Enjoying your king-sized prawn there James?' Peter asked and everyone laughed.

'Touche, Peter old chap,' Henry said, raising his glass.

'Well I love animals,' Annalisa said. 'But I must say, I do love eating them too.' She pondered a moment then said,

'Surely if we weren't supposed to eat them they wouldn't be made of meat?' She took a long drink from her wineglass. 'Although I do think it's very condemnable of you to give up eating them.'

I think she meant to say commendable, although I'm not sure.

'I love animals too,' William said. 'Boiled, grilled, fried…' He looked at James to see if he was laughing.

'Save a cow, eat a vegetarian?'

There was something a little pathetic about his desperation to gain attention from James and Henry.

'What about the vegetarian who went to the doctors with a carrot up his nose and the doctor told him he wasn't eating properly?'

My word, he was hilarious.

I scanned the circular platform to see if I could spot any tofu.

So far I'd eaten a forkful of crispy seaweed, a small serving of egg foo yung and a few bits of vegetable I'd managed to fish out from the passing dishes. I spotted the last piece of tofu, glistening with sweet chilli sauce heading my way, and I could not believe my luck as I stabbed it with my fork and put it in my mouth.

It was just one little morsel of deliciousness, a small piece of perfectly cooked tofu smothered in a mouth-watering sweet and spicy sauce, but it was the highlight of my night. I tried to savour it for as long as possible.

'I say my dear,' James called across the table. 'I suppose if you were to go back to eating meat you'd lose your *veginity,* what? Haw-haw.'

Right. That was it, I'd had enough. I stood up, placed my napkin on my empty plate, and picked up my handbag.

'Excuse me, I'm just off to the Ladies.' As I walked off in the direction of the washrooms, I heard Annalisa say,

'Actually, I'll come with you,' and as she stood and followed me I heard Peter's voice but couldn't distinguish what he was saying. I hoped he was having a go at James and William on my behalf.

In the washroom Annalisa asked me if I was all right.

'I'm so sorry they have been rude to you,' she said.

She leaned forwards squinting at the mirror, trying to focus as she applied more face-powder to her perfect complexion.

'I do feel a little out of place,' I admitted.

'Me too,' she said, and I looked at her, surprised.

'But these are your friends,' I said.

'Not really. William met James and Henry at the golf club. He managed to get a membership because he wanted to meet what he calls 'the right people'. So we join them for dinner and parties, and we go on holiday with them.'

'And do you enjoy it?'

'Not much, but James wants us to move on up.'

'Move on up to where?' I asked.

She stopped applying eyeliner, and looked at me through the mirror.

'I don't know,' she said, as though she'd never given it much thought until now. 'He's always going on about bettering ourselves.'

'To be like Henry and Lucinda? And James and Harriet?'

She gave a wry laugh.

'It sounds really silly when you say it like that. But I never feel good enough. We're always trying to keep up with them.'

'Is that why you had a few drinks before you came?' I asked.

'And a few more while I've been here,' she smiled weakly.

I looked at her reflection in the mirror, young, gorgeous, drunk and sad.

'Annalisa,' I said, taking hold of her arms. 'I'm sorry to be blunt but they're a bunch of knobs.' I think I shocked her a little because she laughed suddenly and said,

'That's a bit harsh! Henry's very sweet and the others are just…'

'Knobs,' I finished. Again she laughed.

'And what about my William?' she asked. 'Is he a knob too?'

'Knob in training,' I said, and we giggled together.

'I do love him, you know,' she said, laughing.

'Well don't let him turn into a replica of James and Henry then.'

'You're right you know. James is a knob. But Henry's a darling really.'

'Ok, Henry is a darling as you call him, but he's only the blinking local Weights and Measures man,' I said. 'And James is so far up his own bum it's a wonder he can walk straight. Harriet has the personality of a clothes prop and as for Lucinda! What can I say?'

I knew I was being catty and I usually avoided these sort of conversations, but to be honest I felt justified after the evening I'd had. And the fact that Annalisa was laughing at everything I said encouraged me to keep going.

'I mean, Lucinda and Harriet could play a pantomime horse, and that's without a costume,' I said, at which Annalisa sniggered.

'Which one's the horse's face and which is the rear-end?' she giggled.

'Take your pick.'

We held onto each other and laughed hysterically.

'You really don't need to try to be like anyone, especially not those two,' I said. 'Look at you, you're gorgeous.'

We both turned and looked in the mirror.

'I'm not really,' she said. 'It's all false. Hair, teeth, boobs…the lot. All done to keep up with Harriet.'

'Harriet?'

'Yes, she's had loads of cosmetic surgery.'

'Really?'

'Yes. I reckon if she has any more facelifts she'll have a beard.'

Again we fell against each other, helpless with laughter.

'Even my name is false' Annalisa said, 'I'm really called Ann but James thinks Annalisa sounds posher.'

We were at that stage of hilarity where everything becomes comical and this seemed like the funniest thing I'd ever heard. I wrapped my arms around my stomach.

'Ooh it hurts!' I said, laughing.

'Don't laugh yourself into labour,' Annalisa said, hardly able to speak. 'Unless you want your baby to be delivered in the Ladies of a Chinese restaurant!'

A woman came out of a cubicle and looked at us with disapproval.

'Excuse me,' she said. 'If you've quite finished do you think you could move out of the way so I can get to the washbasin?'

It was more of a demand than a request.

Annalisa threw her arm out to the side, holding her eyeliner pencil between two fingers. Lifting her chin, she stretched her face, raising her eyebrows.

'Quite!' she said, and linked my arm as we marched off together.

'I'm so glad you came,' Annalisa said. 'You've really brightened up the evening for me.'

'And I'm glad you came,' I said. 'Otherwise it would have just been me and the pantomime horse.'

We giggled our way back to the dining area.

We passed a table of people who were being served their food and the delicious aroma reminded me of how hungry I was still.

At least I can have a big fat pudding without worrying about how many calories are in it, I thought as I approached our table. I noticed the table had been cleared and there was no sign of dessert or coffee. Peter said something to Annalisa and they switched places.

'Ok?' he asked as he sat down next to me and I nodded.

'The bill has been paid and the taxi's ordered,' he said. 'James thought it would be easier for us to share so he's arranged a minibus. It will drop the others off first.'

'Aw! I was looking forward to a big pudding,' I said, disappointed. Peter looked surprised.

'I thought you'd had enough of James,' he said. 'I thought you'd be glad to get home.'

'No, I'm having a good time,' I said. 'I would have loved a look at the desserts menu. Never mind.'

We put on our coats and reconvened in the bar area.

'Don't suppose there's time for a brandy?' Annalisa asked hopefully, but the taxi had arrived.

We travelled to Jesmond first to drop off James, Harriet, Henry and Lucinda.

As expected, Harriet and Lucinda were ungenerous in their farewell, ignoring Peter and I, and giving a curt goodbye to James and Annalisa. James, to his credit, shook our hands and told us that it had been a pleasure to meet us and that we were 'decent chaps' considering we were vegetarians.

'Just keep in mind,' he said. 'My food shits on your food, haw-haw-haw.'

Henry too told us how thrilled he'd been to see us and he kissed my cheek and wished me the best of luck with the 'sprog.'

'Goodbye, you old darling,' I said, to make Annalisa laugh, which she did, but Peter looked at me with bewilderment as though he wasn't quite sure if he'd heard correctly.

Our next stop was High Heaton, and as William began to repeat James's parting words, Annalisa said sharply,

'That's enough of that, William. There's going to be no more copying James. You and I are going to have a long conversation when we get home.'

She left us with hugs and demanded we stay in touch.

'They asked us to join them for a game of golf,' Peter said, as the taxi pulled off.

'That'll be fun,' I said.

'I declined.'

'Oh man!' I said. 'Why did you do that?'

'Because I thought you'd hate it,' he said and he mimicked my voice. *'Great! So I'm going out to play a sport that I hate with Hooray Henry and his cronies...'*

'Henry's ok,' I said. 'And it would have been nice to see them all again.'

Peter gave me a look of disbelief.

'Are you serious?' he said. 'Honestly, there's no understanding women.'

We reached home and were presented with the taxi fare.

'Well that was an expensive ride home,' I said to Peter as he unlocked our front door.

'And an expensive dinner,' he said.

We stepped inside and I took off my coat and kicked off my shoes.

'It couldn't have been that much. We hardly had any food. I didn't drink any wine and you only had a few beers.'

'They split it evenly and it would have looked churlish if I'd refused to pay and began adding up how much food we'd had, wouldn't it?' he laughed.

'Ha ha, yes it would have looked really bad if we'd started fussing on about the bill as well as the menu!'

Peter laughed and put his arms around me. I looked up at him.

'Tell you what I'd really love you to do right now,' I said, and he looked at me hopefully.

'Mmm?'

'Run down to the chippy and get me a cheese and onion pie with chips and mushy peas.'

CHAPTER FOURTEEN

'Have you seen Janice lately?' Lorraine asked, as she shredded lettuce. I was next to her at the kitchen bench mixing mayonnaise into the cheese savoury. Nadine was spooning the hummus she'd just made into a glass dish.

'Not for a few days, why?' I said.

'She came in last week for some shopping and forgot her purse. She said she'd drop the money in and as I haven't seen her, I thought perhaps she'd given it to one of you.'

'Uh, oh, alarm bells ringing,' Nadine said. 'She did the same to me.'

'And me,' I said. 'She owes us thirty-eight quid.'

'And twenty-seven,' Lorraine said.

'And forty-five,' Nadine said. 'I thought it would be fine because she always spends so much money here.'

'Me too,' Lorraine said. 'Do you think that was just to lull us into a false sense of security?'

'What, you mean she deliberately gave the impression she's loaded, then she rips us off?'

'Possibly.'

'Ah, let's give her the benefit of the doubt. She'll probably be in soon to pay it off.'

That afternoon we cleared up the sandwich-making debris more quickly than usual as we were expecting a visit from Jean Harding, the reflexologist therapist.

'Have you two washed your feet?' Lorraine asked. 'We don't want the poor girl passing out when you whip off your socks for your foot massage.'

'Hadn't thought of that,' Nadine said jumping up and rushing up to the washroom.

When she returned, I went up and used our hand soap to wash my feet in the tiny hand basin - a difficult task made more so by my baby bump, but I managed.

At two o'clock prompt Jean Harding arrived. She was an attractive, gentle spoken woman and I immediately felt at ease with her. There was something quite compelling about her and I felt drawn to her. She had a delicate, almost ethereal aura about her and her eyes held depths of compassion.

She looked around the shop enthusing about our stock range, and after we'd shown her our newly painted therapy room she briefly explained the principles of Reflexology to us.

'Basically, the therapist applies pressure to reflex points, usually on the feet or hands but also sometimes the ears, which stimulates energy flow to different zones of the body,' she told us.

'By alternating pressure on these points I can detect areas of imbalance within the body and begin to stimulate energy flow and healing to needed areas.'

I really wanted to believe in what she was saying but struggled with the credibility of some of the concepts she was explaining to us.

'I use the chakras a lot in my work,' she said.

Nadine was fascinated.

'Oh yes,' she said. 'The chakras, I've heard of those.'

'Me too,' I said, thinking vaguely of some sort of African musical instrument. 'I love that whole world music thing, you know, Paul Simon and all that.'

Lorraine, Nadine and Jean looked at me blankly.

'Paul Simon…Gracelands… you know?' I burst into song '…don't I know you from the cinematographer's party? I said who am I to blow against the wind…'

There was a moment of silence then Lorraine tutted and Jean, looking at me kindly, said,

'The chakras are the seven main energy centres of the body. There are of course many more but these are the main ones that we work with.'

'Yes!' said Nadine. 'That's what I thought! Spinning vortexes of energy that respond to different emotions and colours.'

Apparently she had read a book on the subject the previous evening in preparation, and appeared very knowledgeable. The swot.

'That's right,' said Jean. 'Most natural therapies embrace the chakras of course.'

'Of course,' I mumbled. 'Yes, I know that.'

'Why don't I give you each a treatment and you can see how you feel?' Jean offered, and Nadine and I struggled to push each other out of the way to get into the therapy room first. I won.

Jean's reflexology treatment was wonderful. I rarely had the chance to take time out and relax properly, so lying in our new little therapy room with gentle music and the scent of geranium and vanilla candles drifting over me as my feet were massaged was heaven.

Jean told me that she could detect areas of tension within my body that she would work on through my feet, and presumably did a bit of appropriate toe-twiddling to tackle it.

'That was wonderful!' I told Nadine and Lorraine as Nadine hurried in for her turn but Lorraine was not impressed.

'Huh, as if someone fiddling about with your feet wasn't bad enough, that drippy music is enough to stress me out!'

'I liked the music,' I said. 'I think I'll buy a couple of CDs to keep in there for therapists to use.'

'Me too,' said Lorraine. 'Something like 'Bat out of Hell' by Meatloaf would be good.'

Afterwards we drank herbal tea and chatted to Jean about the types of ailments that reflexology treatments could help, and we devised a system for booking appointments with customers. She hugged us all before leaving saying that she hoped to be back soon.

'What a lovely woman,' Lorraine said.

'You've changed your tune,' I said to her. 'I thought you didn't think much of reflexology.'

'It's not that I don't think much of it, it's just not for me. I hate having my feet massaged, it's too tickly. And I find that sort of new age music irritating rather than relaxing. But I do think she's a lovely woman.'

'Why don't you have a treatment with the Indian Head Massage therapist, she's due in soon?'

'No thanks, I'll leave the sampling to you and Nadine, I'll stay on shop duty.'

Martha Rydale swept in like a whirl of energy, talking rapidly.

'Sorry I'm a little early,' she said as we introduced ourselves. 'I can wait if it's inconvenient? I came on the Metro you see, and it got me here a little earlier than I'd planned. But not to worry, I can wait if you like, it's no problem.'

'Not at all,' I answered. 'Perfect timing. Our last therapist left not long since.'

I led her into the therapy room, trying to get ahead of Nadine.

'I think it's my turn to go first actually,' she said, pushing me out of the way.

Martha pulled forward one of our chairs and motioned to Nadine to sit.

'That's it my darling, just sit yourself there and relax. Nice and comfortable.'

Although Martha was very different to Jean, she shared the same flair of instilling a feeling of confidence and I warmed to her immediately.

'Now then, I'll just take this coat off and get myself sorted,' she said as she placed her bag and outdoor things on the therapy couch. She then stood behind Nadine and breathed deeply as she rubbed her hands together.

'Now I take some nice deep breaths to start and I ask you to do the same.'

I inhaled deeply.

'Not you my darling, your turn next.'

Nadine closed her eyes taking in a deep breath.

'Now I rub my hands together to stimulate the energy flow and off we go.'

Martha put her hands onto Nadine's head and began massaging her scalp.

'Is that ok for you there, my darling?' she asked and Nadine mumbled her assurances, obviously thoroughly enjoying the experience.

'Indian Head Massage also involves massage of the neck and shoulders as well as the head, taking in pressure points that can help release any blocked negative energy,' Martha told us. She began kneading Nadine's shoulders.

'As you know, a build-up of negative energy in one of the chakras can lead to disease and injury.'

She moved her hands up the back of Nadine's neck and began to massage the sides of her head.

'Many ailments such as headaches, insomnia, depression and anxiety can be helped by this method.'

I listened attentively, asking questions and trying again to digest all this information about these amazing spinning whirlpools of energy that were the chakras.

It seemed incredible that I'd had no idea of their existence, let alone their function, until this very morning, and yet they were apparently paramount to my well-being and indeed my whole existence! I was intrigued by what to me was a whole new concept of the human body and wanted to know more.

'This is fascinating, isn't it?' I said looking at Nadine, but it seemed that she had drifted off into some sort of trance and had melted into the chair, a look of pure bliss on her face.

When it was my turn I realised why. It was heavenly. I tried to sit up and stay alert but it was impossible. I gave into it and felt my whole body relax as what seemed like years of tensions were released by the movement of Martha's hands across my scalp. I'll have to get Peter to learn how to do this, I thought before drifting off into a semi-sleep.

I tried to explain the technique to Peter and he had a go, but to be honest, my head felt like a piece of dough being kneaded because he was watching the match at the same time and wasn't really concentrating. And every time Newcastle came close to scoring I received a slap on the head so at the finish I just thanked him and said it was lovely and went to put the kettle on.

'I have a surprise for you,' he told me when I returned with a pot of tea and a packet of chocolate biscuits. 'Tickets to see 'Rebecca' at the People's Theatre.'

'Great, when's it on?'

I loved 'Rebecca'. It was one of my favourite books and although I had both read it and seen it performed many times, I never tired of it.

'Friday evening. I thought we could go for something to eat first if you like, just to make up for the Chinese with Henry and co.'

'Aw, you didn't have to do that. I told you. I enjoyed it. But I'm glad you did. I hope they've got a handsome Max de Winter.'

'Shall I book us a table at Georgio's then?'

'Yes, that would be lovely.'

By the end of the week we had five therapists signed up for our Therapy Room. As well as Jean and Martha, we had a Reiki practitioner, a Crystal Healing therapist and a young girl called Sandra who practised something called Body Energy Release Therapy.

Our appointment diary was filling up nicely. I had tried most of the therapies and while Lorraine was still a little sceptical about what she called the 'airyfairyness' of it all, I had to admit that the therapies, especially the Reiki, had left me feeling refreshed and energised.

The only therapy I hadn't yet tried was the Body Energy Release Therapy, which Sandra seemed unable to explain to Lorraine and I. She gave us a vague explanation about it being a type of 'tension relieving relaxation therapy' and that it involved 'many hands-on techniques'. I was not convinced, but ignored my gut feeling, letting my impatience to get the therapy clinic up and running override my doubts.

We charged the therapists by the hour for the use of the room, and as they often recommended our products to their clients, we also made a lot of extra sales on the days that the room was fully booked.

We also had a Feng Shui Practitioner who, although did not need to use our room as she visited clients in their homes or places of work, suggested we take appointments for her. At £200 for a consultation I didn't think we'd get many takers but I agreed. At that time Feng Shui was still a relatively new concept in Britain.

'Have you heard of Fung Shooey?' I asked the others.

'I've heard of Hong Kong Fooey,' Peter said and started singing the theme tune to the old cartoon. As usual, we ignored him.

'I read an article about it,' Lorraine said. 'Didn't make much sense to me. Going on about using a compass to change all your furniture around.'

'What for?' I asked.

Lorraine shrugged, but once again, Nadine, our fountain of knowledge seemed to have the answer.

'Well you see, each area of your home relates to a different area of your life, such as love, finances, work and such,' she explained. 'Richard and Judy were talking about it on 'This Morning.' It's all about how chi flows through your environment. Chi is energy and you can make it flow differently by the way you position things in your house and the colours and things you use. So you use appropriate colours and arrange the furniture in each area to be the most auspicious.'

'What a load of tripe,' Peter said.

'I've got a bagua mirror in my hall to deflect chi and slow it as it enters my house,' Georgina said.

'My love corner is in the downstairs toilet,' Nadine said. 'Not really the best place. So I've hung a Chinese flute on the ceiling and put a picture of George Clooney in there.'

Georgina nodded as if this made some sort of sense.

'And what's that going to do, like?' I asked.

'Well it should stimulate the chi in my love corner and better my chances for finding my soul mate.'

'A flute and George Clooney in your netty? I don't understand how that's going to get you a partner.'

'Me neither,' said Peter. 'It's all Chinese to me, he he.'

'It's an ancient art,' Georgina told us. 'Each area of a building is related to an area in your life. What you place in each area is very important to improve that part of your life.'

'So what does this therapist do that's worth two hundred quid then?' Peter asked.

'Well obviously she must map the client's home or workplace, and advise them if they need to move anything to improve their flow of chi.'

'I could do that,' Peter said and he sauntered around the shop, peering at an imaginary map in his hand.

'You need to move your coffee table a bit there missus if you want to get a bloke. That's two hundred quid, ta.'

'Anyway, I don't need any help with my love life,' Georgina said smugly.

'Oh, so it's all back on with Marc is it?' Lorraine asked.

'It was never off. We're adults. Free spirits. We don't need to live in each other's pockets…'

'Yeah right,' I said. I'd heard all this before.

'He's back up here in Newcastle. Staying with a friend. We're going to meet up tomorrow.'

'Thought he'd be staying at your place,' Lorraine said.

'Oh honestly. What are you like?' Georgina said. 'We just like to give each other a bit of space. It's fine for him to stay with a friend. We don't own each other.'

'Morning, people,' Nige said as he skipped in with our mail. 'Hey, I see that artist you used to hang about with is back in town,' he said to Georgina. 'Gus was telling me that he...'

Georgina sighed.

'Yes I know he is, what about it?' she said irritably.

'He's staying with a friend,' Lorraine said. 'She's seeing him tomorrow.'

'They're just giving each other a bit of space,' I said.

'Well he's not giving *her* much space is he?' he said, indicating to the window, where on the other side of the road, Marc was walking with his arm wrapped around an attractive copper haired woman who was snuggling into him.

We watched Georgina's face turn purple as Marc gallantly opened the door of the Saffron cafe and the woman smiled coyly at him as they entered.

'Who the f..?' Georgina started. 'What does he think he's doing, the bastard? Who the hell is she?'

'That's what I was saying,' Nige said. 'Gus was telling me he saw him at the auditions for a play he's involved with at The Tyne Theatre. Apparently he's staying with Diana Lacey who has the lead role, and she brought him along to audition for a part in the chorus.'

'Oh dear,' Lorraine said as Georgina called Marc some names I'd heard before and some I hadn't. 'Looks like she's a pretty close friend.'

'Gus said he thinks he'll get the part so he could be around for a while,' Nige said. 'He said he has a lovely falsetto voice.'

'He'll need a lovely falsetto teeth when I've bloody finished with him the two-timing, cheating, lying git,' Georgina ranted and she stormed off, banging the shop door behind her.

We arrived at the theatre early, so bought drinks at the bar and looked at the leaflets advertising coming shows before going into the auditorium.

Our seats were ideal, centre of the front row and although there were a few people already in their seats, those to either side of us were still empty. We chatted, enjoying our drinks as we looked about to see if we could spot anyone we knew. Peter nudged me.

'Look, there's Norman Wisdom,' he said.

It was a silly game we played. If we saw someone who bore a vague resemblance to a famous person, we'd say, 'Oh look, there's Bruce Forsyth/Bette Davis/Donny Osmond and the other person would have to try to identify who we were referring to.

Peter was rubbish at it. The people he picked out rarely resembled the person he thought they did, so I was quite surprised to spot Norman Wisdom's doppelganger being greeted near the stage. As he came closer I could not believe the similarity.

'Good lord, he's the spit!'

'It's Norman Wisdom.'

'I know, ha ha. Very good.'

'Chris, it's Norman Wisdom.'

'Ha, ha. Yes, well done.'

The man was shown to the front row and smiled at me as he approached. And then I realised.

'My God, it is! It's Norman Wisdom!' I couldn't believe it.

He was with two other men and a woman, and I held my breath as they contemplated seats, the woman sitting next to me, and he sitting to the right of her.

'Norman Wisdom,' I mouthed at Peter and he nodded.

'Yes, I know.'

I peered sideways, trying to get a good look at the man whose films had been such a big part of my childhood. Lorraine and I had loved them when we were children, laughing hysterically at his silly antics. There was a particular scene in one of his films with Hattie Jaques as a singing tutor giving Norman a lesson that had us falling about every time we saw it, and we would act it out until we drove our Mam and Dad mad.

The lights went down and there was a hush as the curtains opened.

'Last night I dreamed I went to Manderlay again...'

Although I practically knew the words by heart, I spent most of the first act squinting at my childhood hero until I noticed he'd dozed off and I turned my attention back to the play.

Sitting one seat away from Norman Wisdom at a theatre overthrew my top name-dropping brag of having once been at a party with Ian Dury, and I became quite adept at manipulating conversations to a point where I could link any subject to The Time I Sat One Seat Away From Norman Wisdom In A Theatre.

CHAPTER FIFTEEN

Monday morning was very busy and rather stressful and Lorraine seemed to get the brunt of it. As Nadine and I prepared food, she dealt with two difficult phone calls.

The first was a woman who had bought a bottle of Aesculus to treat her varicose veins and said it hadn't given her any relief even though she'd twice bathed her legs with it.

Lorraine patiently explained that the remedy needed to be taken orally and the woman became abusive, saying that she had not been told that when she'd bought it. Lorraine had then told her that she found this difficult to believe as it was our policy to explain the use of remedies to customers adding that even if we hadn't, the instructions were clearly set out on the accompanying leaflet. The argument went on and on, Lorraine becoming redder in the face and eventually having to back down and agree to a refund.

Just as she put down the phone - none too gently - it immediately began to ring again.

This time it was a very determined woman intent on staying on the phone until she'd sold Lorraine an insurance policy. The woman would not accept a polite refusal, causing Lorraine to eventually hang up on her.

It just didn't seem to be Lorraine's day.

Val arrived with the sole intention of telling someone about her ingrown toenail and as Nadine and I were busy with other customers she targeted Lorraine.

Once she'd managed to get rid of Val, Lorraine was then caught by the space-invading biscuit salesman and turkey-trotted around the shop a couple of times before he left with his order.

'What is it with me today?' she complained. She stood on the little flight of stairs that led to the sink area as Nadine and I made sandwiches for customers.

'I've had people whinging on the phone, I've had to look at Val's deformed toenail and I've had to deal with that creepy sales rep.'

'Looks like your luck is changing,' Nadine said as a builder from the nearby site came in. He'd been coming in for a few weeks now, since work had started on the new houses close by and Lorraine had taken a fancy to him. She always made sure that she made his sandwich, choosing the biggest bread roll she could find and giving him extra tuna mayonnaise.

As he approached the counter she flicked back her hair and smiled at him.

'Hi,' she said, leaning alluringly against the bannister. Suddenly, she lost her balance and slipped off the step, giving a high pitched yelp as her feet flew out from beneath her. Her body seemed to stiffen in mid-air before falling to the stairs with a crash and she slid to the bottom like a plank of wood. She tried to regain her dignity by standing and reaching for the stair post, but unfortunately she missed it and lost her balance, crumpling to a heap on the floor.

Nadine and I scuttled, giggling, into the office, leaving Lorraine to make his up-graded tuna sandwich with a red face and a stiff gait.

Once he'd gone we came out sniggering and obviously Lorraine wasn't very happy with us.

'I could have broken my neck,' she yelled. 'And you two just buggered off and left me to make a sandwich.'

We apologised and showed concern about her bruises, but I caught Nadine's eye, causing her to snort and we were off again.

The phone rang and I went to answer it leaving Nadine to take the rap for our childish behaviour.

It was a Kinesiology therapist ringing to ask if she could rent the therapy room.

Of all the therapies I'd researched, Kinesiology was the one I found most difficult to understand.

I told the therapist, whose name was Coral that she could certainly rent the room and asked if she'd like to come and see it. I thought it would be the perfect chance to ask questions and gain some clarity.

'Why don't I come in and give you a free treatment?' she offered. 'I'm free this afternoon I could come in at about three-thirty?'

'That would be lovely,' I said. 'See you then.'

Nadine was very excited.

'What is kinesiology?' she asked.

'I'm not entirely sure. Something to do with muscle testing and balancing energies. I'm hoping that Coral will enlighten us.'

'Do you mind if I stay to see her? I want to find out all about it.' Nadine finished her shift at two but often stayed later to help out or just to sit and chat.

'Of course you can.'

'I want to have a treatment so that I will be able to explain to our customers how it could help them.'

'She's offered a free sample session. I was going to have it because I know nothing about kinesiology but I could ask if you could have one another time?'

'Yeah, that would be great,' Nadine said happily.

Nadine was a very conscientious about her job with us. She always whizzed through her chores, never complaining like Lorraine and I often did, running circles around us as she untiringly chopped salad, mixed fillings and served customers. She read up on all the health products we stocked and tried all the foodstuffs so that she was confident in advising customers and answering their questions.

She was good at selling too. She had a way of effortlessly persuading customers that what she was offering was exactly what they needed to buy. She even used to tell people that the products they were buying were on special offer, buy one get one the same price and it was surprising how many people fell for it.

'Actually, I think it's my turn to have a free session. After the day I've had I could do with a bit of pampering,' Lorraine said.

I was disappointed but I knew it was fair. Nadine and I had enjoyed free treatments from all but one of the therapists.

'Ok,' I said. 'You'd better go and check that the therapy room is tidy because she'll be here soon.'

Coral was in her early sixties and arrived dressed like a nursery-rhyme character. She wore a spotted dress with puffed sleeves and a ruffled skirt, pale blue Mary-Jane shoes and had a ribbon tied in a large bow on top of her blond corkscrew curls. She carried a shopping basket and walked with a skip in her step.

After the introductions, we showed her the therapy room and told her that Lorraine would like to have the sample treatment. She asked for a glass of water and after she'd downed it in one, asked for another.

'Now then,' she said. She balanced her glass of water on one of our shelves, next to some jars of tomato chutney. Looking about, she spotted our chair near the counter, carried it to the front of the shop and set it down in the middle of the floor.

'Come and sit yourself down, Lorraine,' she said.

'I thought you wanted to use the therapy room,' Lorraine said.

'No, no. I thought I'd do it here and then your customers can see what I'm doing. Hopefully it will create interest and Christine can tell them all about it and maybe even take some bookings for me.'

She beamed widely, gesturing for Lorraine to sit in the chair.

'I'd prefer to go in the therapy room, really, I'll find it much easier to relax and…'

'Come along, sit down. You'll be fine here, I'll have you relaxed in no time.'

Lorraine sat down hesitantly and I tried not to laugh. Lorraine hated being the centre of attention and I knew she'd now be wishing she had left the free treatment to me.

Coral took a large white handkerchief from her basket and shook it.

'I'll just place this on your head, it will help you to absorb the energies and will keep my hands clean,' Coral said.

I could tell by Lorraine's body language that she wasn't happy.

'I washed my hair this morning, actually. I'm sure your hands will be fine.'

'I was speaking in an energy-related way,' Coral said. 'It's to keep the energies separate.'

She draped the handkerchief over Lorraine's head and I choked back a giggle. I looked at Nadine and saw that she too was struggling not to laugh. She pulled a face at me and I pulled one back but unfortunately Coral turned and saw me so I quickly incorporated it into a performance of an extremely loud sneeze. Nadine snorted and coughed and Lorraine lifted the edge of the handkerchief to peer at us.

'Dear, dear. Sounds like you two have the sniffles,' Coral said.

Lorraine narrowed her eyes and looked at us cynically.

Coral rearranged the handkerchief, making it look even more comical by pulling it over Lorraine's eyes so that the edge just skimmed her nostrils.

'So what exactly are you going to do?' I asked, trying not to look at the white cloth, gently billowing and falling as Lorraine breathed.

Coral clasped her hands, gave a Mary Poppins-esque click of her heels and launched into a well-rehearsed speech.

'Kinesiology is the study of movement, and Applied Kinesiology is a non-evasive therapy which uses muscle testing to determine imbalances in the body. An imbalance in any part of the body affects the function of the body as a whole, so what better way is there to help the body regain its balance than to ask it directly for information?'

She paused, looking at us with raised eyebrows, waiting for an answer. I couldn't think of one so I nodded wisely and said 'What indeed?'

Coral looked at Nadine, waiting for an answer from her.

'I don't know, what better way is there to help the body regain its balance than to ask it directly?' she repeated, as though she'd been asked a joke from a cracker.

Coral smiled triumphantly.

'None!'

She told us that she was going to communicate directly with Lorraine's energy system by applying pressure to her arm muscle and monitoring the responses. This would reveal strengths and weaknesses in different areas of the body. She went on to tell us that she would question the muscle and it would respond by tightening or weakening, signifying yes or no in answer to the query.

To be honest it didn't make any sense at all to me, but I bobbed my head in what I thought to be an intelligent way, aware of Lorraine waiting beneath the handkerchief.

As Coral moved Lorraine's arm into a position that she said would give her access to a contracted muscle, a woman arrived, asking for rye bread, so I went off to the counter to wrap a loaf and take payment.

'What's going on there like?' the woman asked, nodding towards where Lorraine sat near the preserves and pickles, handkerchief on head. Coral appeared to be having a conversation

114

with Lorraine's hand. She would ask a question then press Lorraine's muscle causing her hand to wave, then she would react as though she'd been given an answer, thanking the hand for the information it had given.

'How about the heart chakra? Is the heart chakra balanced? Yes? Yes. Thank you. And the base chakra? Yes? No? No. That's a no then? Please confirm that. Ah, no. Ok. Right, that's a definite no. Thank you.'

Nadine stood nearby, her face showing an expression of bewilderment.

'What're they doing?' the woman asked.

I was about to relate what Coral had explained to us, but thought better of it.

'Haven't got a clue.'

The woman took her loaf and made to leave but Coral stopped her, asking her to stay and watch.

Each time a customer arrived, Coral would ask them to stay to watch her demonstration and would repeat her prepared talk.

'Kinesiology is the study of movement, and Applied Kinesiology is a non-evasive therapy which uses muscle testing...'

In between performances of her oration she would ask Lorraine's hand a few questions and then work at balancing her energies by wafting around Lorraine's head as though batting off a persistent fly.

It was one of the most bizarre, hysterically funny things I'd ever seen, made more so by imagining Lorraine's thoughts as she sat silently beneath her head cover, unable to see what was happening around her.

I had a fleeting thought that perhaps it would look less weird if Lorraine wore a Sooty puppet on her hand.

Occasionally, Lorraine would begin to answer a question or give a muffled 'Pardon?' and Coral would respond by saying,

'I'm talking to the hand.'

I avoided looking at Nadine. We were gigglers at the best of times, if we were to make eye contact we would be uncontrollable.

Eventually, Coral finished her hand-questioning and fly-swatting and explained to her audience – Nadine, myself and four women - that Lorraine's energies were now fully balanced.

'Once the body's energies are stable, I can then find out what changes or healing it needs. This could be anything from a change in diet or lifestyle, to a particular type of therapy.'

Coral took a step back, clicked her heels and bowed slightly, and after a short pause one of the women hesitantly began to clap her hands and the rest of us followed suit, giving Coral a half-hearted round of applause.

'Now then,' Coral continued. 'While I have you ladies here together, I'm going to show you a very simple exercise you can practise at home to help avoid breast cancer.'

There was a murmur of interest. Here at last was something we could understand. Something useful that surely would be of interest to all women.

Once Coral was sure she had our undivided attention, she began to instruct us.

'There are energy points on the body that if pressed gently, can help to stimulate the lymph glands and clear toxins from the body, thus lessening the chances of cancer in the breasts.'

There was silence as we all listened intently, waiting to find out this secret that could potentially save our lives.

'To locate the precise position, I would first like you all to place a forefinger directly on each nipple.'

I hesitated, waiting for the others to move first as we looked at each other sheepishly, the air thick with our mortification. Slowly, hands came up and fingers were pointed and I joined in with an approximation although to be honest it was difficult to be accurate when fully clothed.

One of the women who had been slowly backing away from us suddenly made a run for it, scurrying out of the door as we watched, envious of her great escape.

I noticed that the woman who'd bought the rye bread was standing with the finger of her left hand pointing at least four inches higher than the right and I looked away in embarrassment.

'Now then, the spot you need to work on is located three centimetres below the nipple,' Coral told us. 'Give it a good massage.'

We dutifully lowered our fingers and began to massage, and that was the moment that Peter arrived to see us standing in a row rotating our forefingers into our bosoms, each of us exhibiting a face as red as a baboon's rear end, except for Lorraine whose embarrassment was contained beneath the white cotton handkerchief.

CHAPTER SIXTEEN

'What on earth did I just walk in on?' Peter asked when Coral had gone up to the washroom. He'd taken one look at us and scuttled into the office where he'd stayed until Coral had finished her demonstration.

'I'll explain later,' I said.

Lorraine had carried her chair back to the counter and was making an appointment for one of the women who'd watched the kinesiology session and wanted a consultation with Coral.

Nadine picked up the brush to sweep the floor and I took it from her.

'Your shift finished ages ago!' I said.

She grabbed the brush back.

'You know I don't mind,' she said, as she expertly whipped the brush around the floor.

'Do you still want to have a session with Coral?' I asked. 'Or has that put you off?'

'Oh no, it hasn't put me off at all, I'm even more intrigued now,' she said. 'Although I'd prefer not to have it in the centre of the shop. I'll have a word with her when she comes down.'

Coral seemed pleased that Nadine wanted a treatment but said she was unable to stay as she had an appointment.

'Why don't you pop around to my house this evening? I'm just up the road. I have my conservatory set up as a therapy area, I could do it there if you like?'

'Thanks, that would be great,' Nadine said happily.

The next morning Lorraine rang the local paper, The Evening Echo to place an ad about our therapy room.

'Were you really clear on the wording?' I asked her. 'You know how good they are at getting it wrong.'

'Surely they can't get this wrong,' she said. 'It's just a small advert about the therapies available with our address and telephone number.'

'Yeah, I'm sure it'll be fine this time,' I said. 'And we do need to spread the word about the therapies we can offer.'

We'd also had leaflets printed which my Mam and Dad offered to deliver to local houses and also to local community organisations and doctor's surgeries.

Lorraine and I couldn't wait to find out how Nadine's kinesiology session had gone so as soon as she arrived at ten we bombarded her with questions which she fended off as she went into the office to take off her coat and put down her bag.

'Yes, it was interesting. No, I didn't have a hanky on my head. Yes, it was weird and no, it didn't involve bosom-prodding. Now let me get my apron on and my hands washed and I'll tell you properly.'

We settled ourselves down with cups of blackcurrant tea to listen to her tale.

'I got to Coral's house at about half past six. It's absolutely beautiful, one of the old Georgian houses on the way to the hospital. Honestly it's *gorgeous*! Great big hall with a polished wooden floor and a huge staircase with this carved bannister and the most beautiful carpet...'

'Yes, yes,' Lorraine said. 'Never mind the carpet. What was the therapy like? What did she do to you?'

'I'm coming to that,' Nadine continued. 'She took me through to the conservatory, and it's a proper conservatory mind, not one of those little modern things that they stick on the end of buildings these days. This was the real thing, old stone floor with a big rug, loads of flowers and a big cage with these cute little zebra finches in.'

'And the treatment?'

Nadine ignored this.

'It had these gorgeous bamboo chairs with covers embroidered with birds and huge pots with massive plants, great big ferns and palms, and it overlooked this amazing garden with a big hedge at the bottom so it was really private and I thought wow this is fantastic, not like my little garden with next door's cats keep coming in to poop in me flower beds and auld Mrs Herron nebbing in me windows all the time...'

'Nadine, can you please get to the point, the Nutmeg Express will be coming in soon.'

'Well anyway, she had this therapy couch set up by the wall beside the windows and I thought, that's nice, I'll be able to look out of the window at the garden. But then she says to me, 'If you just slip all your clothes off,' and I said 'Eh?' because I didn't think I'd have to do that and she says 'Oh well you can leave your panties on if you're shy.

So I said, 'Well what about the windows?' and she says 'Oh don't worry, no-one can see past the hedge.' So I took me things off and God help us, I'd forgotten I was wearing a thong. Of all the days to be wearing a thong, and I thought, eeh I wish I'd put me granny knickers on the day.'

She paused for breath and we urged her to go on.

'So there I was with all me wobbly bits out in their glory and me backside practically bare, so I said 'Coral I'm so sorry, I would have worn bigger knickers if I'd known, me backside's hanging out,' and she says 'Don't worry about that, everyone has a bottom,' and I thought aye but not the size of mine.

So I lay on the couch and she did that thing with me hand, asking it questions and stuff then she said she couldn't get the energies to balance so she asked me to stand up and she explained that my aura was a little ruffled…'

'Your what?' I asked.

'My aura. It was ruffled so she said she could smooth it by going over it with a hairdryer.'

'Get lost,' Lorraine said.

'Honest, she did. I had to stand there lifting me arms and legs up and down while she blasted me with hot air…'

'Ha ha ha! In your thong?' Lorraine said as we laughed at the scenario Nadine was describing.

'Yes, in me thong and nowt else.'

'And what's that supposed to do?'

'Coral said it smooths your aura. She explained something about positive and negative ions but to be honest I didn't really take it in because I was just standing there, mortified. And then if that wasn't bad enough, a flash of yellow caught my eye from the bottom of the garden, and when I turned to look, wasn't it the number forty bus, just pulled up behind the hedge? And everyone on the top deck turned to look at me standing on one leg while Coral blow-dried me aura.'

Lorraine and I were falling about now, our faces streaming with tears.

'Maybe they didn't see you,' I laughed, trying to reassure her.

'Oh they saw me,' Nadine said. 'I could tell because they were pointing and laughing.'

Lorraine and I sniggered.

'Well they shouldn't have done that,' I said. 'That wasn't very polite of them.'

'No, it wasn't,' Lorraine said. She was still wiping tears from her eyes. 'I mean, there was no need for that, I wonder why they did.'

'Maybe because a fat girl standing on one leg in a thong while she has her bum blow-dried in a conservatory is not a sight you see every day?'

Nadine laughed with us, enjoying our laughter as she told the story.

'So did it work? Did it smooth your aura?'

'Apparently so. At least, my hand said it had. Then she said she could get to work finding out what my body needed to ensure its maximum state of health. So she questioned my hand for a while and it told her I need to eat less sugary food and more green vegetables and stop all the yo-yo dieting and just stick to eating good unprocessed food.'

'We've been telling you that for ages,' Lorraine said.

'Yeah, but this came directly from my hand,' Nadine said. 'Anyway, it also said that I needed some crystal healing so Coral asked it which crystals she needed to use then told me to lie on my front so she could place them in the right spots. One of them was a bit awkward because it was right at the base of my spine and it kept slipping down and she kept having to fish it out so at the finish she got a bit of sticky tape and stuck it down. She said I needed to relax for twenty minutes so she put some music on and left me lying there.'

'So was it relaxing?' I asked.

'Well it would have been if I hadn't been so aware of my bare bum. I just lay there trying to work out what time it was and worrying whether another bus was due.'

'I got off quite lightly with my hanky treatment then,' Lorraine said. 'Although I have to say, I did feel better after it and I slept really well.'

'Me too,' Nadine said. 'That's the thing. It sounds totally crazy but I actually did feel great afterwards.'

'I know you said you wanted a treatment so you could tell customers about it, but I think maybe you need to be selective in the parts you tell them,' I said.

'I agree,' Lorraine said. 'Telling them they are going to have someone talk to their hand, blast them with a hairdryer and then shove a crystal up their bum might not be the best way to encourage people to book an appointment.'

'I'll just tell them to wear big knickers.'

CHAPTER SEVENTEEN

As my pregnancy approached the ninth month, I found myself needing more sleep and after the lunchtime rush would sometimes have a nap on the therapy couch if the room was free.

'Sorry Chris, there's an appointment in fifteen minutes,' Lorraine said, giving me a nudge to wake me. I stretched and yawned.

'Two more minutes,' I said.

Sandra had booked the room for a Body Energy Release Therapy session, whatever it was. I still wasn't sure.

She arrived with her client and as she spoke to Lorraine I positioned myself behind the front row of shelves and squinted between the bags of flour to get a good look at the man. He appeared to be in his mid-fifties, an ordinary inoffensive looking man with thinning grey hair and a neatly trimmed moustache. He was dressed in dark blue jeans and a fawn sweater, similar in fact to any other middle-aged man you might see.

Sandra led him into the therapy room and the door closed behind them. I came out from my spying place.

'What exactly does Sandra do?' I asked Lorraine.

'Body Energy Release Therapy.'

'Yeah, I know that, but what is it?'

'No idea,' Lorraine said. 'I thought you knew.'

'No, she kept making excuses when I asked for a demonstration.'

'Well she's had quite a few customers. Whatever it is, it's popular.'

'Only with middle-aged men,' I said.

Lorraine looked at me.

'So what are you saying?' she asked.

'Nothing. Just seems a bit dodgy to me. I mean she only ever treats older men. There's a lot of gasping and grunting while she's in there and then they both come out hot and flushed.'

Lorraine looked horrified.

'Gasping and grunting? What do you think is going on in there?'

'I don't know, I just have a bad feeling about it.'

I couldn't really explain, I just felt uncomfortable with it and didn't have a logical explanation.

'Go and have a listen,' I urged her. 'Put your ear to the door and see if you can hear anything.'

Lorraine moved quietly to the therapy room door and put her ear against it. She listened for a while and then said in a whisper,

'I can just hear a muffled conversation.'

'You need a glass,' I whispered back. 'It amplifies the sound.'

I gave her a glass and showed her how to hold it with the open end to the wall and hold her ear against the base.

'Where did you learn this?' she whispered. 'And why?'

'I've seen it on the telly.'

She listened for a while.

'I can't hear anything.'

I picked up another glass from the kitchen shelf and joined her. We listened in silence then looked at each other wide-eyed and open-mouthed at the sound of a long deep-pitched groan.

'What the…?'

'Sh! Keep listening.'

We strained to hear through our glass tumblers as a muffled female voice could be heard.

'What did she say?' Lorraine hissed.

'Can't make it out,' I said and then the sound of a high pitched giggle penetrated the door. Lorraine and I turned our eyes to each other.

'Look through the keyhole,' I said, looking down at the door. 'Oh, there isn't one.' The giggling resumed accompanied by a deep moan.

'Right,' I said. 'That's it. Let's go in. I'll follow you.'

'We can't just go in! It's a private therapy session.'

'We have a right to know what's going on in our shop.'

'What if we find them in a compromising position or in a state of undress? It could be embarrassing for them.'

'Well tough. She shouldn't be using our therapy room to get into compromising positions in a state of undress should she?'

The man spoke now and I strained my ears trying to decipher his words.

'Do you think we should bring someone else in to be a witness, or get a camera to record the evidence?' I asked.

'Who do you think you are, Miss Marple?'

Before our conversation could develop into a squabble, there was a scuffling movement behind the door.

'Quick they're coming out!'

We scuttled behind the counter as the door opened and Sandra emerged followed by her client, his face flushed and wet with perspiration like a steamed beetroot. He murmured his thanks to Sandra and slunk away.

'I'll just clean up before I go,' Sandra said and the therapy room door slammed.

'Why did she say 'clean up' and not 'tidy up'?' Lorraine asked me.

I chose to ignore this and said,

'When she comes out, ask her what she was doing in there.'

'I can't just ask straight out like that,' she said.

'Course you can,' I said. 'It's easy.'

'Well you ask her then.'

'But it would sound better coming from you.'

'And why is that exactly?'

The door opened Sandra emerged, and Lorraine and I threw insincere smiles in her direction.

'Everything ok?' I asked.

'Great,' she said. 'I'll be back tomorrow, got another session at three-thirty.'

'To do ...er what exactly?' I asked.

'Just the usual,' she said.

Lorraine and I smiled and nodded then Lorraine nudged me.

'So they like it do they? I mean, it's useful is it? Your...er...clients? It helps them? This...therapy that you do?' I stuttered.

'They do and yes it does,' Sandra said with a smile. 'See you tomorrow.'

She hitched her bag over her shoulder and walked jauntily towards the door, her ponytail swinging in time with her strides.

'Oh great, now we've put her on her guard,' I said as she left the shop.

'On her guard?' Lorraine said. 'I think we're getting a bit carried away. I'm sure what she's doing is all above suspicion. We just need to find out what she's actually doing.'

'Well, you ask her tomorrow,' I said.

'I can't just ask straight out like that,' Lorraine said.

'Course you can.'

'Hang on, I'm getting deja vu here. We've had this conversation before.'

The shop door opened and Lorraine's face dropped as she looked past me.

'Uh, oh I'm off' she said and scooted into the office.

I looked around and realised the reason for her sudden departure was the arrival of Val. She hobbled in breathing heavily.

'Have you anything for an upset stomach?' she asked as she rested her forearms on the counter, slumping dramatically. I knew she wouldn't buy anything that I suggested, but I also knew she wouldn't leave without having a good whinge so I said,

'Well it depends on the cause, but anything with natural healthy bacteria such as live yogurt can help re-balance your system. Or you can buy supplements such as acidophilus in tablet form.'

'Ooh I can't afford tablets,' she said. 'And I couldn't eat yogurt. To be honest I can't face eating anything right now. I just hope I don't lose loads of weight and fade away.'

This seemed highly unlikely but I made sympathetic noises as I knew it would please her and she continued.

'I bought a family pack of custard tarts from SuperSavers because they were reduced. I ate a couple and they didn't taste right, so I ate a couple more, just to check and they made me feel really queasy. By the time I'd had another one I was feeling really off colour. I had terrible stomach pains by the time I'd finished the pack.'

I found it impossible to feel any sympathy for such wanton greed so I forced a smile and let her go on.

'I was ill all night. I don't sleep well anyway, I have terrible insomnia and I just lay there thinking that I could wake up dead in my bed tomorrow and no-one would know. But I soldiered on. I'm not one for self-pity. I've always had to look after myself being all alone in the world. It's an awful thing when you know no-one cares if you live or die and you only have yourself to rely on. But I'm used to it. It's made me what I am. Strong in spirit and independent in character.'

Blimey, I thought. She's excelling herself here.

'Of course I went back to SuperSavers and I was given a refund but the assistant was very impolite. She said, 'I would imagine if eating something makes you feel ill, finishing off a whole family pack will only make you feel worse.''

'How rude,' I said.

'Very. I think she was trying to insinuate that I'd been greedy.'

'Oh, is that what she was getting at? How strange.'

'I nearly told her that I wouldn't be shopping there any more due to her attitude but I didn't because it would be cutting off my nose to spite my face. They sell stuff very cheap when it goes past its sell-by date.'

Sometimes I found it really difficult to think of a polite reply to Val's comments so I just smiled and nodded and shook my head at what I hoped were relevant points in her conversation.

'Actually,' she said, looking at the fridge. 'Do you have anything in here that's out of date? I need something for my tea.'

When she'd gone Lorraine came out of the office with plenty to say about how greedy and self-pitying Val was.

'I mean, who would eat a whole family pack of custard tarts anyway even if they didn't taste off?' she said.

'Oh shurrup man,' I told her. 'I've just had to listen to it all from Val, I don't need to go through it all again from you.'

'Ooh, tetchy!'

'Well I didn't see you rushing out to give her the benefit of your opinion,' I said. 'All alone in the world...waking up dead in her bed...gawd.'

'I'll make you a nice cup of tea,' Lorraine said. 'I think you need one.'

I served a few customers then when they'd left I wandered about the shop with my cup of tea, tidying the displays and straightening odd packages.

I loved the way the shelves looked, especially just after a big delivery from Karma, when they would be fully stocked again. I spent hours arranging and re-arranging everything to look as appealing as possible – or 'fannying aboot' as Lorraine called it.

I was especially proud of my dried pulses. I had arranged them in a spectrum of colour from black beans through brown lentils, maroon kidney beans, khaki-green lentils, bright orange lentils, yellow split peas, creamy butter beans and various other beans in shades of beige, fawn and taupe.

I loved the neat rows of packages and jars, the bags of jewel coloured dried fruits and the bread shelves behind the counter filled with unbleached white, wholemeal, granary, seeded and rye breads in all sorts of shapes and sizes.

The display fridges were always filled with dishes of olives, capers, hummus, coleslaw, vegetable pates, salads and huge cheeses, and every type of vegetarian pie, pastry and quiche you could think of. The glass shelves at the top held hand-made cakes, scones and flapjacks and tempted many a customer as they waited for their sandwiches.

There were so many eye-catching areas of the shop; wooden bookshelves full of cookery books, rows of pickles and preserves, glass bottles filled with bath oils and skin lotions, boxes of beautifully fragranced hand-made soaps, bottles of fruit and vegetable juices, rainbow coloured candles hanging on a rack. I loved it all.

I don't think the others understood how I could get so much pleasure from just looking at our displays, tweaking a packet here and there and constantly repositioning the eggs in their straw lined basket every time a customer dared to spoil my carefully positioned arrangement by buying some.

I put down my tea mug in order to straighten bottles of homeopathic pills and as I moved along the shelves tidying vitamins and herbal remedies, I came to the essential oils and noticed that there were many gaps in the display.

'Have you sold a lot of essential oils today?' I asked Lorraine.

'No, just a couple of bottles of lavender, oh and a bergamot oil, but that's all.'

'There are loads of gaps here,' I said. 'I know for a fact there were more than this last night because I tidied them before I left.'

Lorraine came over to have a look.

'You don't think we've had a shoplifter do you?' she said. 'They are quite small bottles. Easy to slip into a pocket.'

'Looks like it,' I said. 'And it's the more expensive ones that are missing.'

'I'll go and get the stock book and check the numbers.'

As someone who always returns to a shop if I'm accidentally undercharged even a few pence because I feel so guilty, it came as a great surprise to me to discover that customers stole from us.

I mean, I'm not naïve enough to think that shop lifting is a rare occurrence. I just didn't think anyone would do it to us. We were selling bags of oats and lentils for goodness sake, not designer watches and high priced jewellery. We were a small family-run business, not a huge faceless chain-store. And we were *nice*.

But people did steal from us - in various ways.

We had the basic common-or-garden thieves who slipped something into their pocket when no-one was looking.

Then we had pond-life who took charity boxes full of change from the counter.

We had our share of change-fiddlers; customers who would purchase something with a low price, then bring out a twenty pound note and ask for change as they shuffled notes and piles of coins around like some sort of Tommy Cooper trick trying to bamboozle the person behind the counter.

Luckily for us, these tricksters would hit different shopping areas at different times, and when they targeted our street, started near the Metro Station where they'd arrived. By the time they worked their way up the bank to our shop, we would have been warned by the local business owners' grape-vine and so were primed for them.

Nadine and I once managed to keep a particularly incompetent pair of fraudsters in the front of the shop while Lorraine telephoned the police, by pretending to have accidentally jammed the till drawer shut. They waited patiently as we apologised, and even offered to help us to break into it and were taken completely by surprise when two police officers arrived to arrest them.

Some customers had the audacity to try all kinds of ways to cheat us, like the man who bought six jars of honey then returned to tell us he'd dropped them on his way home so could he have a replacement free of charge?

Or the woman who regularly bought our bread then returned to tell us that it had a strange texture and could she please have a refund -although she never had evidence of the offending loaf as it had always been eaten, presumably under great sufferance.

There were customers who would come to browse at our bookstand, reading a few pages a day until they'd finished the book of their choice, often asking for a seat so that they could have their free read in comfort. One woman asked for a piece of paper and a pencil so she could copy some recipes from one of the cookery books for sale. When Lorraine told her that we weren't a bloody library, she asked if she could borrow the book until the next day to give her a chance to photocopy it.

We even had a customer who tried to return a product that I'd just watched him steal.

It happened that Co-enzyme Q10 was a very popular food supplement at the time.

Co-enzyme Q10 (or Co-Q-10) is a naturally occurring substance that is essential for basic cell function in the body. There had been a lot of claims in the press that levels of Co-Q-10 deplete with age and that taking a supplement could help with many health issues.

We stocked packs of 30 tablets at £6.99 that were selling really well. The sales rep suggested we also stock packs of 150 tablets that sold at £29.99 saying that they would sell well when customers realised that they would save money by purchasing the larger pack.

We decided to take just three packs with the agreement that we would telephone the rep as soon as they sold and he would post replacements to us. We displayed the large packs on the shelf near the smaller ones along with a sign explaining the benefits of Co-Q-10 and the prices of the different packs.

I was replenishing our display fridge with bowls of olives when I noticed a customer looking at the shelves. His behaviour caught my attention as he seemed to be systematically scanning the shelves looking at the price tickets on goods. I watched from the corner of my eye as he worked his way along the supplement shelves and as he selected a 150-tablet pack of Co-Q-10, I thought happily,

I've just put those out ten minutes ago and I'm going to sell one already!

He put the pack on the counter in front of me.

'Can I return this please?'

'Return it to where?' I asked, puzzled.

Did he mean back to the shelf? Had he changed his mind about buying it?

He coughed.

'I mean can I return it and have my money back?' I looked at him, amazed at his temerity.

'My wife bought it here and she picked up the wrong box.'

'No she didn't.'

'Eh?'

'Your wife didn't buy it here.'

'Yes she did.'

'No she didn't.'

There was a pause as we looked at each other, both deliberating the best way to play this.

'Sorry love,' he said. 'I must have the wrong shop.' His hand reached out and as I realised he was going to take the box I reached out and snatched it up.

'Well you're right about that,' I said angrily. 'You've got the wrong shop.'

'Couldn't you just give me a refund anyway then you can sell it again?' he suggested.

'I haven't even sold it once yet, have I?' I snapped. 'I've just seen you take it off that shelf and walk over here and ask me for a refund.'

He looked at me. I could see he was frantically thinking of an explanation and I waited in anticipation.

Let's see you talk your way out of this one mate, I thought. A couple of seconds passed and then he spoke.

'I didn't.'

'Yes you did.'

'No I didn't.'

'YES YOU DID.'

'I didn't.'

I wondered how long we could keep this going. I decided to take a different tack.

'It will have been caught on tape by the security camera,' I lied. Let's have a look at it shall we?'

His eyes quickly scanned the area above my head in search of a camera.

'I'll just nip out and get my wife from the car and she'll be able to explain,' he said. I hurried around the counter to follow him but as soon as he left the shop he took to his heels and shot off down the bank and around the corner, never to be seen again.

CHAPTER EIGHTEEN

It was Wednesday and we were having our usual morning gathering. Lorraine placed a tray of hot drinks on the counter and Nige, Nadine and Georgina each took one.

'Tea's up,' Lorraine called to me.

'I'm just cleaning this glass,' I said as I polished my way along the front of the large display fridge.

'Nest building that's what that is,' Nadine said, and they all turned to watch.

'Don't be silly,' I said. 'I just noticed it needed a clean.' I took a sip of tea then started on the upright fridge.

'What?' I asked, looking towards where they all sat looking at me with smug expressions.

'Won't be long now,' Nadine said, 'It's a sure sign. Baby's on its way.'

'Let's enjoy it while we can,' Lorraine said. 'Not often I see my sister cleaning without complaining.'

'I'll give you a hand,' Nadine said picking up a cloth and coming to join me.

'I'm just doing a bit of routine cleaning,' I said. 'Stop making such a fuss.'

I didn't want to admit that there probably was something in what they were saying. I'd spent the last few evenings systematically cleaning out my kitchen cupboards, which wasn't particularly unusual. What was unusual was the fact that I'd thoroughly enjoyed doing it.

Nige had brought our day's mail with him, including a large package.

'Wonder what this is?' Lorraine said as she pulled it open. 'Oh it's the music CDs we ordered for the therapy room.'

She pulled out a pile of CD boxes and read the titles aloud.

'Voices of the Angels, Relax and Refresh with Melodies of Nature, - that sounds good. Tranquillity Dreams, Music to Heal the Chakras, and Inuit Throat Singing.'

'What was the last one?' Nadine asked. 'Inuit Goats Singing?'

'*Throat* singing.'

'Throat singing? What's that like?

'Haven't a clue,' Lorraine said. 'I'll go and put it on now.'
She went into the therapy room to switch on the CD player. Peter
had fixed up speakers in the shop as well as in the therapy room so
that we could choose to play music in either or both places.

As I continued polishing my way around the shop, a very
angry looking woman burst through the door and marched up to the
counter. She slammed down her handbag then hitched up the sleeves
of her jacket as though preparing herself for confrontation.

'Can I help you?' Nadine asked politely as Lorraine returned
to the shop front, reading the back of the CD box.

'Oh yes, I've heard that you are very good at helping people
in here, very good indeed.'

I stopped my cleaning and turned to look. A prolonged low
grunting sound suddenly emerged from the speakers.

'Well, we do like to think so,' Lorraine said, a little fazed by
the woman's animosity.

'Yes well this area can do without help from those such as
you, thank you very much.' The woman's face was crimson with
anger and she looked close to tears.

'What exactly is the problem?' Lorraine asked.

I peered through the shelves and vaguely recognised the
woman as a customer who came each Saturday to buy our bread. She
was in her forties and always dressed expensively but plainly, her
hair well cut, but not in a particularly flattering style and her face
make-up free. She was not an especially friendly woman. Although
never unpleasant she was very abrupt in her manner and clipped in
her speech. She'd shopped with us practically each week since we'd
opened yet she'd never conversed with any of us except to ask for
her bread order.

I was aware that the volume of the Inuit Throat singing had
increased as another grunter had joined the first at a lower pitch.

As I watched, Nige and Georgina shuffled on their seats to
get a better view of the conversation. Nadine left Lorraine to deal
with the woman and walked over to join me in peeping through the
shelves.

'What exactly is the problem?' Lorraine repeated and I saw
Nige and Georgina lean forwards, curious to hear the woman's
answer.

'I demand to know the whereabouts of that strumpet,' she yelled.

I looked at Nadine, wondering if I'd misheard and she was trying to locate a missing musical instrument.

I heard Lorraine say, 'I beg your pardon?' as Nadine whispered to me,

'What's a strumpet? Are they like crumpets? We don't sell crumpets, do we?'

'It's an old term for a tart,' I whispered back.

'Oh, well we sell those. There were some apple ones come in with the delivery this morning.'

Nige and Georgina were watching the proceedings in silent fascination.

The woman's voice became shriller and louder as her anger increased. She leaned across the counter and shrieked

'I suppose you're all in the same business are you? Don't think for one moment that you can fool me with your pretence of a healthfood shop. I know what's going on here.'

Realisation that the woman was not referring to apple tarts caused a look of outrage to descend over Nadine's face and she marched around the shelves from where we'd been crouching and confronted the woman just as a chorus of gargling throat singers swelled to a crescendo.

'Now just a minute, are you calling me a trumpet?' she said. 'Because if you are I'll sue you for slander. I'll go to my solicitor and...'

The woman held up her hand so that her palm was in front of Nadine's face.

'Excuse me,' she said. 'I am talking to the organ grinder, not the monkey.' She turned back to Lorraine as Nadine spluttered her indignation.

'I can assure you, I shall be going to the police and I can guarantee that I will see to it personally that you will be closed down.'

She hesitated and turned her head in the direction of the speakers.

'What *is* that disgusting noise?'

The singers were now grunting alternately like two warthogs mating. She regained her composure and continued her tirade.

'And I shall be contacting the local press.'

'Now look here,' Lorraine said. 'I've no idea what you are talking about. You need to either calm down and explain yourself properly, or leave.'

'Calm down? I'll give you calm down you trollop!'

I felt that perhaps I should be supporting Lorraine instead of hiding behind a shelf so I moved forward and spoke to the woman.

'Don't speak to my sister like that! How dare you!'

'Oh I dare,' the woman said, and as she turned to look at me, her eyes moved to my bump. Her eyes narrowed.

'Aha!' she said, pointing at my stomach. 'Ho ho!'

It was not often that Lorraine and I were speechless when dealing with difficult customers. We looked at each other, each waiting for the other to say something.

Nige sniggered, unable to control himself any longer and the woman turned to face him.

'And I don't know what you seem to be finding so amusing,' she said to him. 'I suppose you come in here to find loose women?'

This remark seemed to tickle Nige even further.

'Well hardly, flower,' he said to her, wiping tears of laughter from his eyes. Georgina snorted loudly, unable to hide her laughter and as the woman turned to confront her she said,

'Just singing along to the music,' then gave a succession of deep grunts. Nige laughed harder.

'Eeh, that's really good!' he told Georgina. 'You sound just like those goats or whatever they are!'

The woman snatched up her handbag then marched towards the door. She wrenched it open then turned and shouted:

'Right, I'm going to fetch my husband from the car so that he can identify which of you it was.'

'What on earth was all that about?' Georgina said as the woman slammed the door behind her, leaving the bell jangling furiously. 'Unless I'm mistaken she seems to be under the impression you're running a brothel here.'

'Eeh, this is better than Coronation Street,' Nige said. He was obviously thoroughly enjoying himself.

'I knew that bloody Sandra was up to no good,' I said. 'This must be something to do with her.'

'Give me that phone,' Lorraine said. 'I'm going to find out what she's been up to.' She started punching numbers into the phone and I moved to the counter to greet a customer who'd just come in. It was Fee.

'Hello there,' she said. 'I've just come to ask if you would be willing to donate a raffle prize for the school summer fayre?' I looked at her, trying to focus on what she was saying.

'It's ok if you're unable to,' she said, her facing turning red. 'I know you must get lots of people asking...'

Lorraine put the phone back in its holder, none too gently.

'Answer-machine!' she said. 'I'll go in the office and keep trying.'

I turned back to Fee.

'No...yes... I mean, it's no problem. Sorry Fee, I'm a bit distracted, just had a bit of a strange encounter with a customer. I'll put a little hamper together for you, would that do?'

'Oh that would be wonderful,' Fee gushed. 'I'm so excited, the fayre is always so popular. We have a tombola and face painting...bottle stall...cake stall... and my favourite, the pet show, the children love it. And so do I.'

'Sounds good, let us know the date and we'll try and come along.'

'I'm going to exhibit my canary,' Fee said clasping her hands in front of her chest.

'Now there's a novelty,' Nige said and collapsed into a giggling heap.

I gave him a warning look, glancing at Georgina for support, but she was just as bad, sniggering and nudging Nige.

'Last year my hamster, Mr Tuggy – well actually, he died – he won first prize.'

'Must have been a crap pet show if a dead hamster won it,' Georgina said and she and Nige held onto each other as they roared with laughter.

'No, no...silly me,' Fee laughed, embarrassed. 'I mean he wasn't dead when he won it...he died after. Well not straight after...' her face fell.

'I knew what you meant,' I told her. 'That's very sad. I'm sure you loved him.'

'Oh I did,' Fee said. 'I still have his little trophy. So this year I'm hoping Captain Tweety will win.'

The throat singers reached their chorus again and Fee's eyes widened.

'Actually, if you don't mind me asking, is that whale music or something you're playing?'

'It's Inuit goats singing,' Georgina told her.

'Really? How…unusual.'

'It's very relaxing don't you think?'

'Oh yes…yes,' Fee said as Georgina once again launched into her low tuneless throat singing, this time accompanied by Nige. Fee seemed stuck for words.

'Lovely,' she said eventually.

The shop was now quite busy with customers and Nadine who'd been speaking to two women turned to me and said,

'This lady is asking about free treatments. She says it said in the Evening Echo that we were giving free therapy sessions.'

I sighed. Surely that blasted newspaper hadn't messed up our ad again.

'It did, didn't it Betty?' said one of the women.

'It did, Mary, you're right,' the other said and she shuffled her bust with her forearms. Nige giggled.

'Eeh, you two are like them two off the telly,' he laughed.

I knew straight away what he was getting at and anxious that he might mention something that would make the two women realise they were being compared to Les Dawson and Roy Barraclough, I said to him,

'Don't you think you should go and do some work?'

'Not likely,' he said, and he and Georgina looked at each other hitching up imaginary bosoms and sniggering.

'It definitely said they were free, didn't it Betty,' said Mary.

'As true as I'm standing here,' Betty said. 'It said complementary treatments available.'

'Oh I see what you mean,' I said, realising the misunderstanding. 'It doesn't mean free therapies, it means complementary therapies.'

'Yes. Well that means free,' Betty said.

'You're right again, Betty,' said Mary. Nige tittered and I kicked him in the shin at which he let out a yelp.

'No, no,' I said. 'It means alternative therapies.'

'Well why does it say complementary?'

'That's a good question, Betty.'

'Because they are therapies that complement any medical treatments you may be having,' I explained.

'Well that doesn't make much sense to me, does it to you Mary?'

'No it doesn't. I mean when we get complementary tea at the bingo it means it's free, doesn't it Betty?'

'It does.'

'Me and Betty have come all the way from Seghill for this you know. I thought I could get me corns done. Didn't I Betty?

'You did Mary. You said, I might see if I can get me corns done.'

'Ooh the plot thickens,' Nige said and I looked to see the angry woman returning with a very sheepish looking man.

'Right Harold,' she said, pushing him forward. 'I want to know which one it was.'

'Excuse me there's a queue here,' Betty said.

'You tell her Betty, pushing in like that,' said Mary.

'Why don't I make you two ladies a nice cup of tea before you leave?' Nadine said as Harold's wife pushed him around the shop, her voice shrill as she berated him with a tirade of accusations.

'Come and sit here and enjoy the show while you have a cuppa,' Nige said pulling another two stools from behind the counter.

'Well I'm not paying for it, mind,' said Betty.

'So it's a complementary cup of tea is it?' Mary asked. 'Because I don't want any of that alternative tea with herbs and stuff in it.'

'Just a nice cup of PG Tips,' Nadine told them and Nige beckoned to them to take a seat.

'Mind you'll have to turn that noise off, it's doing me head in, whatever it is,' Betty said.

'Goats,' Nige told her.

'Goats did he say Betty?'

'Aye that's what he said.'

'Never in this world. Goats eh? Fancy. Well I can't say I'm partial. Gives me the heebyjeebies.'

'Eeh, it's horrible that. I'd rather listen to nails down a blackboard.'

'That's on next,' Georgina said.

Poor Harold was now being pushed in front of each of us in turn in his wife's quest to identify which of us had allegedly compromised him.

'I'm so sorry,' Harold mumbled. 'My wife has got the wrong end of the stick.'

'It's who got the right end of the stick we're all waiting to find out,' tittered Nige.

'I'm sure I recognise your face,' Fee said to Harold and as his wife stepped forward he stammered his denial.

'No, no, you must be mistaken.' He held up his hands. 'I've never met her before in my life.'

I was aware that Georgina, Nige, Betty and Mary were sitting listening so I tried to be calm and defuse the situation.

'I'm sure we can sort this all out,' I said. 'My sister is in the office now trying to get in touch with the therapist who treated you.'

'Treated him to what though?' asked Nige rolling his eyes and the woman turned on him.

'Would you please be quiet and mind your own business,' she shouted at him.

'Actually Nige I agree with her,' I said. 'Shut your face, you're not helping.'

My head was pounding and my stress levels were rising rapidly. I was sure my blood pressure had gone up.

The pulsating grunting of the Inuit singers was plucking at my nerves and the urge to lose control and scream like a frustrated toddler was growing at an alarming rate. The shop was quite full now and I tried to serve customers as I fended off the woman's angry comments trying to calm her down.

Lorraine appeared from the office.

'Can you please turn that bloody music off,' I said as the droning singing rumbled from the speakers like gargling camels. Lorraine ignored my request.

'I can't get in touch with Sandra,' she said. 'I think her mobile is switched off. She may be on her way in, she is supposed to have an appointment at half past three.'

'Well I'm staying here until she arrives. I'm not leaving until I hear what's been going on. I want to hear it from the horse's mouth,' the woman said.

'I'll get you a stool,' Nadine said. What was Nadine playing at providing chairs? I thought. The place was starting to look like a bloody doctor's waiting room.

I closed my eyes and rubbed my temples where a piercing headache was beginning to form.

'Any chance of being served here darlin'?' I heard and I opened my eyes to see a regular customer of ours standing at the counter.

'Have you come for sex?' Harold's wife shouted at him.

'Well I came for a tuna sandwich love, but if you're offering...'

'Usual is it?' I asked, trying to behave as though everything was normal. 'Tuna mayo on white with salad?'

'Champion, darlin',' he said and I picked up a bread roll and went to make his sandwich.

Harold's wife was now wound up to fever pitch.

'Oh I see, you get better treatment in here if you're a man then?' she said.

'No,' I said calmly. 'We treat everyone alike.' I looked around for support but unfortunately it was Georgina who gave it.

'Oh aye that's true,' she said. 'They treat everyone the same in here. Like shite.' She clutched at Nige and they laughed hysterically.

'Ooh it hurts,' Nige said, clutching his stomach.

'I'll bloody hurt you in a minute,' I hissed at him.

'I'm glad we came now Betty,' Mary said. 'It's good in here isn't it?'

'It is Mary, it is. I'm enjoying it. Lovely cup of tea an' all. Better than what you get at the bingo.'

I gave the customer his tuna sandwich and as he paid he said, 'Any idea who the silver Nissan belongs to?'

'That's ours,' Harold's wife said. 'Why?'

'You're blocking me in, could you nip out and move it love?'

'No I couldn't. I'm waiting for someone and I'm not moving until she arrives.'

'I'll move it,' Harold said.

'No you won't,' his wife said. 'You're going nowhere.'

'Well it looks like I'm not either,' the man said, and he sat on an upturned box and began to unwrap his sandwich.

I looked at Nadine who was ringing in a sale at the till and I shrugged helplessly.

'I'll go and get you a seat,' she said, misreading my look.

'And a cuppa would be great love,' he said.

Customers now had to squeeze around the collection of stools and chairs to get to the counter. Fee was getting on famously with Betty and Mary and had invited them to the summer fayre, although she kept puzzling over where she'd seen Harold which did not do anything to help calm his wife.

The noise level in the shop was at a high, a babble of raised voices competed with the unearthly droning sound of the throat singers. My head was pounding and I was having difficulty concentrating.

Nige and Georgina seemed to be finding everything hilarious and were having a great time. Harold had given up protesting his innocence and his wife seemed to be unable to contain her rage and took swipes at customers as they entered.

'And I suppose you've come for sex too,' she said to an inoffensive looking delivery man as he walked in with a box.

'I am the egg man,' he said.

'I am the walrus, goo, goo g'joob,' chorused Nige and Georgina. I took the box of eggs from the man and paid him.

'Sorry,' I said to him as he snatched his money and scuttled off.

'Excuse me,' Fee said to Harold. 'I've been trying to think how I know you. I'm sure you're the father of one of my children.'

CHAPTER NINETEEN

When I was in my early teens I went through a stage when I would occasionally faint, usually in some crowded place, causing me acute embarrassment when I came round, usually with my clothes disarrayed and with the concerned faces of a circle of strangers peering down at me.

Now I wondered if it was possible to pass out on demand and found myself almost willing a faint to envelop me so that I could just sink into glorious oblivion. I even considered faking it but realised I would just have to get back up and carry on after lying on the floor looking ridiculous for a few minutes. I took a deep breath and tried to compose myself.

Thankfully, the CD had come to its natural end, I just hoped Lorraine hadn't put it on repeat.

Harold's wife pushed him into a chair that Nadine had carried through from the back shop. She looked like she was about to have some sort of fit. Fee was sitting next to her whittering her explanation about being a school teacher and mistaking Harold for a parent.

Oh no! I thought as I saw Val enter the shop. That's all we need.

'My, it's busy in here today,' she said. 'I've come to ask you about a bit of an embarrassing health problem,' she said.

'We're a bit crowded in here at the minute, Val' I said, nodding my head at the row of chairs and their occupants. 'Perhaps you might want to come and talk to us at a more quiet time?'

But Val was delighted at seeing an audience ready and waiting and took to the stage.

'I've got terrible heartburn and indigestion,' she said, looking towards her spectators. 'I don't know what's causing it.'

'Is it an ulcer?' asked Betty.

'I don't know,' Val said. 'But I feel terribly queasy in the mornings.'

'Gallstones!' said Mary. 'That's what it sounds like to me.'

'I've got the most awful pains in my lower back and I'm so tired.'

'Could be your kidneys love,' the workman chipped in.

What was this? Some kind of bizarre game show? Guess the ailment?

I saw Janice enter the shop and move behind the shelves. I hoped she had come to pay off some of the money she owed us.

Val was now explaining about her dizzy turns while she acted one out.

'Change of life?' Georgina asked.

'I hardly think so,' Val said, affronted. 'I'm only thirty.'

What! Surely not. I was due to turn thirty in a few weeks. Val and I can not be the same age, I thought. Lorraine saw my shocked face and must have guessed my thoughts.

'She's lying,' she murmured. 'Has to be at least forty-five.'

'Anaemia!' Betty shouted. 'Am I right?'

'I think you could be right Betty,' Mary said. 'That sounds like anaemia. I was like that after me fourth. Doctor gave me iron pills. They did the trick but they didn't half bung me up.'

'Syrup of figs, Mary.' Betty said. 'Works a treat.'

'Have you had a pregnancy test?' Georgina asked suddenly. 'Could be that, you know.'

Val launched into her best dramatic performance to date. She staggered backwards as if she'd been pushed.

'Oh my heart!' she said, clutching her chest. 'How dare you! I am an unmarried woman. How dare you suggest that I have had immoral relations!'

'Well you must be the only one in here who hasn't,' Harold's wife interjected.

Val was well on her way to an Oscar. She threw her hands across her face.

'I've never been so insulted in my life! I am a chaste woman.'

'There you go,' Georgina said. '*That's* the root of your problem. A good shag would do you the world of good.'

Val let out a wail and backing into a nearby shelf slid down it to the floor into the faint that had escaped me. As we all moved forward to assist her I saw Janice head towards the door.

'Janice!' I called, intending to have a quiet word about the money she owed. Janice turned and as she did two bottles of essential oil slid from her sleeve and smashed to the floor.

For a second I looked in disbelief at the broken glass and paths of scented oil that were slowly weaving across the parquet flooring, but her look of guilt immediately eradicated any doubts I may have had.

'You thieving cow!' I shouted. 'It's you isn't it? The essential oil robber. You've been coming in here all sweetness and shite, and all the time you've been stealing from us. Well you'll wish you hadn't messed with me...'

Janice took to her heels and ran and I did the same, chasing her through the shop as fast as it was possible to do with a nine month baby bump. I was furious. I couldn't ever remember feeling so angry.

'Stop her!' Lorraine yelled, struggling to get through all the chairs, and for a moment I thought she meant Janice until she tried to grab me.

Georgina was close behind Lorraine, followed by Nige, all of them calling to me to stop and to think of the baby. But I couldn't think of anything except that I wanted to kill her. A red mist had descended and as I struggled to keep up with her I shouted to stunned shoppers, who parted hurriedly to let me pass, informing them that Janice was a thief and a liar and many other things besides.

I heard Georgina shouting for me to stop, and I glanced behind to see the builder running after Nige with his half eaten tuna sandwich still in his hand and saw that Betty and Mary had joined the chase. Even Val had managed to rouse herself and was moving at quite an impressive pace for someone who had just suffered from a shock-induced collapse.

'Come back here!' I yelled as we wound our way around pedestrians and lamp posts like a chase scene from Benny Hill only with more clothes on.

Janice disappeared around a corner, and I wrapped my arms around my heavy bump as if to lighten it by carrying it as I swerved to miss an elderly man coming the other way, narrowly missing tripping over his Jack Russell.

My heart felt as though it was clanging against my ribs and I was struggling to breathe now. As I lost pace Georgina grabbed me by my right arm and Lorraine by my left and to my utter contempt I found myself pinned against the wall of the hardware shop. I struggled furiously and voiced my objections loudly, until to my

145

absolute shame, I was forcibly frog-marched down the bank with Betty, Mary, Nige and the workman walking ahead calling out to onlookers to move along and that there was nothing to see.

CHAPTER TWENTY

Three days later, on the first of April, our beautiful daughter made her entrance into the world, bringing more joy into my life than I ever knew possible.

I could not believe that I'd somehow managed to create this tiny, perfect person and deliver her into the world. I could not stop gazing in awe at her beauty; her tiny fingernails, her dark curling lashes, her rosebud mouth.

We named her Rose Sarah.

She was a sweet-tempered baby who although woke regularly through the night, would fall asleep contentedly after being fed. She quickly became known as Rosie, due to her lovely nature and her adorable dark features and pink cheeks.

The shop was temporarily forgotten as I fell into a cycle of feeding, changing and pacifying, snatching moments to eat and sleep when I could.

Peter, as I'd known he would be, was a loving, attentive father. We shared the changing, the laundering, the pacing up and down rocking and soothing.

We had both fallen utterly and completely in love with our new daughter. We constantly discussed her beauty, and relived every milestone, filling albums with photographs, capturing hours of footage on videotape and boring everyone senseless.

I called in at the shop regularly, bringing Rosie with me. I would help, when I was compelled to, with chores such as shelf-filling and sandwich making, although I had little interest in business matters, preferring to sit behind the counter, showing off my beautiful little daughter.

Lorraine would brief me on what had been happening, and I would listen distractedly, waiting for a pause in the conversation so that I could bring the subject back to Rosie.

For me, her radiance outshone everything. Life before her had been so mundane, meandering along without a real focus and I'd had no idea! I was overflowing with new-mother-love and for a while everything else faded into insignificance.

Over the weeks, reality came slowly back into my awareness and life settled into a manageable routine.

When Rosie was four months old, I returned to working at the shop. I reduced my hours so that I could spend as much time with her as possible. I was very fortunate when it came to childcare; I had two willing baby-sitters – my Mam and my mother-in-law Joan.

Some days I brought Rosie into the shop with me for an hour or so. When she was old enough we installed a playpen behind the counter and she was quite happy to play and sing, entertaining the customers for half an hour or so while I joined in the lunchtime rush.

I quickly caught up with the events I'd missed as we gossiped over morning cups of herb tea.

Apparently Sandra's therapy had been perfectly above board, if a little unorthodox.

She practised a treatment that manually drained toxins from the lymph glands. This involved massaging several pressure points around the body including those located in the groin. However, after the altercation with Harold's wife, Sandra had decided that in future she would only treat female clients and had secured the lease of a small treatment room in a large women's health club in Newcastle.

'I'm glad she's gone, really' Lorraine said.

'Me too,' Nadine agreed. 'Authentic or not, poking around in men's groins is bound to lead to trouble.'

'Well it's a lesson learned,' I said. 'In future we will vet any therapists very carefully before agreeing to promote their services.'

'Ah yes,' Lorraine said. 'That reminds me. I have a replacement for Sandra. A new therapist who is going to book the room.'

'Great. What does she do?'

'She's a medium and clairvoyant.'

'A what? You're having a laugh!'

'No, it's all set up. Her name is Mariana and her first session is next Friday.'

'And the connection with natural health therapies is what exactly?'

'I think she'll be really popular,' Lorraine said, ignoring my question, and Nadine agreed with her.

'She's going to give us all a free reading,' she said. 'I can't wait!'

'But it's not really a complementary health therapy is it?' I said. 'Lots of people are a bit funny about stuff like that.'

'A bit funny in what way?' Nadine asked.

'That it's meddling with things we don't fully understand and stuff.'

'Well if they feel like that they don't need to come, do they?' Nadine said.

'As long as it doesn't put any of our regulars off.'

'I don't think it will,' Lorraine said. 'Most people are open-minded about things and like Nadine said, if they don't like the idea of it, they won't book an appointment. Let's wait until we meet her and then we can decide.'

CHAPTER TWENTY-ONE

I was expecting Mariana to arrive draped in scarves and jangling bangles with heavily kohl-lined eyes and an air of mystery.

Disappointingly she arrived draped in easy-care polyester with an over-tight perm, orange lipstick and an air of despondency.

'Good morning love,' she said, as she carefully put her huge shopping bag on the floor. 'Although I don't know what's good about it. I'm the medium, come to give you some free readings.'

'Oh you must be Mariana,' I said. 'Lovely to meet you. Would you like a cup of tea?'

'I'd love one, pet. I'm as dry as an old stick. I've just had the journey from hell on that number thirty-nine. And by the way, me real name is Maureen. I just use Mariana for the punters. Makes it sound a bit more exotic.'

'Oh right. Ok, well I'll just pop the kettle on.'

I set about the tea making process as Maureen complained about the bus driver and her journey to the shop.

I introduced her to Nige and Georgina who arrived, with their usual impeccable timing, just as I was pouring tea. Georgina looked a bit sceptical but Nige was enthralled.

'Please to meet you,' he said sitting down next to her at the counter. 'I hope you're going to tell me that I'm in for a lovely future. You see I've got this partner called Gus, and he's an actor and...'

'Not at the minute please Nige,' I said, knowing he would dominate the conversation if we let him. Georgina obviously thought the same because she nudged him and said rudely,

'Pipe down Nige, keep your life story till you're asked for it.'

Maureen, however, seemed oblivious and carried on with her complaining, although she seemed to have a way of moaning generally without always pinning down what she was unhappy about.'

'Eeh, what a life, eh?' she said. 'Still, we've just got to get on with it, what else can we do?' She took a sip of her tea and then said suddenly,

'I can hear you.' We all looked at her.

'Who? Me?' Nige asked timidly.

'No not you,' Maureen said.

150

Nige clutched at my arm and we all surveyed the space above Maureen's head, waiting for some ghostly apparition to materialise.

'I don't believe in all this stuff anyway,' Georgina said and Maureen gave her a look of contempt.

'Are you comfortable there me little love'?' she asked. Nige looked around warily.

'Are you talking to a spirit?' he whispered. 'Is there one here now?'

'I'm talking to Billy,' Maureen said, as she stood up.

'Billy? Is that your spirit guide?' Nige asked and we all joined him in looking around expectantly.

'Don't be so daft,' Maureen said as she unzipped her bag and lifted out a small pug puppy. 'Billy's me dog. Who's Mummy's good boy then? Have you had a lovely nap?'

Billy snuffled and licked Maureen's face and there was a chorus of 'Aw he's gorgeous.'

We all had a turn at holding Billy while Maureen kept up her rather negative observations.

'No, there's not a lot of good in this world. It's a terrible place indeed. If I didn't have my Billy to love, I don't know what I'd do.'

Billy was a sweet little thing. After we'd all cuddled him, Lorraine said,

'Will he be all right back in your bag Maureen, just we're not supposed to have dogs in here. Health and safety and all that.'

'Yes, he'll be fine, won't you my little love?' Maureen said, kissing Billy's snout as she tucked him back into her shopping bag, where he settled down.

'He seems quite happy in there,' I said.

'Well it's good to see someone happy,' Maureen said. 'It's not something I know a lot about, is happiness.'

'Gawd, we'll have to introduce her to Val,' Lorraine said to me quietly. 'They'll get on like a house on fire.'

Nadine arrived and seemed disappointed when she was told that the plump middle-aged woman slurping a cup of tea and describing the pain of her corns was actually Mariana the medium.

'You don't look like a medium,' she said.

'More like a large, I'd say,' Georgina said.

Maureen turned to look at her.

'Just a joke,' Georgina said.

'Not one I haven't heard before, many times.'

Georgina pulled a face as Maureen turned her back and Nadine said,

'It must be wonderful having such a gift. It's so exciting! I can't wait to have a reading, I'm really looking forward to it. So amazing!'

'Me too,' said Nige.

Georgina laughed scornfully.

'How can you say it's amazing? She hasn't even told you anything yet!'

'Ah, we have a non-believer in our midst.' Maureen shook her head. 'Not the first and won't be the last. Wait till you get a message from the other side, love. Then you'll change your tune.'

'I doubt it,' Georgina mumbled.

'I just meant it must be amazing to be able to contact those who have left us,' Nadine told Georgina.

'They didn't leave us Nadine,' Georgina said caustically, 'they *died*.'

'We never die, our souls live forever in different forms,' Maureen said poignantly, but then added, 'At least I hope it's in different forms because I couldn't stand another bliddy life like this one.'

'It is a marvellous gift, though,' Nige said.

'Eeh love, you wouldn't call it a gift if you could see what I see,' Maureen said. 'More like a curse. I can see things before they happen, you see. Now take my friend Linda. Sixty-two she was and full of life. 'Maureen,' she says to me, 'I've booked a holiday of a lifetime for me and my Dougie. We're going on a cruise next summer, right around the Med. It'll be smashing, you should see the brochure. The ship's got restaurants, bars, cinema…the lot.' I looked at her and I thought, no you won't, you'll be dead by Christmas.'

She stopped to take a mouthful of tea and Nadine asked,

'So did you tell her?'

'Why no,' Maureen answered. 'You can't go around telling people they're going to kick the bucket. So I just said to her, 'Well make sure you've got good insurance, that's all I'm saying on the matter.' And as sure as I'm standing here, she dropped down dead the Sunday afore Christmas.'

'Really?' I asked, feeling a cold shiver move down my spine.

'Yes, I'm telling yer. Right as rain she was, then halfway through dishing up the Sunday dinner her number was called and woomf! Gone. Like her Dougie told me later, she didn't even manage to get the Yorkshires out of the oven. They were burnt to a crisp by the time he realised.'

Maureen paused for dramatic effect and it had the desired intent as a hush settled over us. The silence was broken by Georgina sniggering loudly.

'What a load of tosh.'

Maureen looked at her and said,' I wouldn't mock if I were you, love. You have no idea what I might be seeing as I look at you.'

'Oh don't tell me. I suppose I'm in for the same fate as poor old Linda? Yorkshires in the oven and woomf! Gone. Ha ha ha...'

'Hardly dear. You don't really look the type to make a decent Yorkshire pudding, let alone a Sunday dinner.'

'And you look like someone who's eaten plenty of them,' Georgina retorted.

Maureen's psychic vibes must have been contagious as I had a sudden vision of Georgina being walloped with Maureen's handbag so before it could happen I picked up the bag in which Billy lay sleeping.

'Let me show you our therapy room, Maureen,' I said, and she struggled to her feet.

As I showed her how to adjust the temperature on the heater and told her she was welcome to use the CD player for background music, a gentle snoring reminded me of the sleeping Billy and I placed the bag carefully on the carpet.

Maureen did not show great enthusiasm for the room, but I was not too discouraged. I had already accepted that Maureen was a 'glass half-empty' sort of person and so stood back as she looked around touching things and muttering 'It will have to do,' and 'Beggars can't be choosers,' and 'It never rains but it pours.'

She went to collect some more bags that she'd left by the door.

'Give me ten minutes to get ready then send the first punter in, my love,' she said.

In the shop we argued about who was to go first.

'I'll go first to find out what she's like' Nige offered.

'No, I work here, I should have priority,' Nadine argued.

'I think it should be me,' Lorraine said. 'You two are much too gullible, you'll give her information to work on.'

'In that case, I'll go first,' Georgina said. 'I'll soon see through her psychological trickery.'

I kept quiet. I wasn't sure that I even wanted a turn at all, let alone go first.

'Right, let's draw for it,' Nadine said and she fetched a box of matches. She counted them out and snapped one, discarding one of the halves. After arranging them in her fist she turned to me.

'Choose,' she ordered and I pulled out the snapped match.

'Wow, how lucky are you?' she said

'Aw, I didn't even have a chance,' Nige said with disappointment.

I considered telling a lie and saying that I'd cheated and ask if I could choose another match but then I thought I might as well get it over with.

'Off you go then,' Georgina said. 'Go and hear about tall dark strangers and journeys overseas.'

'Here I go!' I said with a half-hearted smile, and I pushed open the therapy room door.

CHAPTER TWENTY-TWO

The first thing to hit me was the fact that the room was filled with an eerie purple glow and the second was the heady aroma of incense.

The room had been draped with lengths of jewel-coloured fabrics, and joss sticks burned in holders dotted about. A tie-dyed scarf wrapped around our table lamp created the ghostly purple light. The chairs and table were also draped with cloths and the CD was playing what Peter would have called 'plinky plonky' music.

Maureen was seated behind a huge crystal ball. At least I thought it was Maureen. I squinted through the thick spirals of patchouli smoke to see a bronze-faced, black-haired woman, glittering with gold jewellery and sparkling scarves. It was indeed Maureen, heavily made up and wearing a wig of unruly black curls.

'Ha ha, Maureen! Wow, you look so different,' I said.

Maureen lifted a hand to silence me.

'I am Mariana, seer of the unseen, perceiver of what is and of what is yet to be. Be seated and I shall call upon the spirits to impart their wisdom.'

I gulped on a laugh that was bubbling up my throat and stepped over Billy who was sitting on a red velvet cushion with a tiny stretchy turban pulled over his ears. I perched on the edge of my chair and after a bit of hand wafting and head rolling, Maureen looked into the crystal ball and spoke in a voice several octaves lower that the one she'd used to tell us about her corns.

'I see your past. You have experienced many things, good and bad. You have had many thoughts, achieved many things and made many plans. You now leave your past behind as you look towards your future.'

Hmmm. Not impressed so far.

Billy yawned then brought his hind leg forward in order to give his bits a thorough licking, pulling his turban over one eye in the process.

'And now for the present.' More head rolling and hand waving. 'I see a tall, dark man.'

'That'll be Peter, my husband,' I blurted out, then immediately berated myself for giving out information so easily.

'This man adores you, he worships you, he lives for you,' Maureen said dramatically.

Wow, that's better, I thought. She's actually quite good.

'I see a child…a beautiful child.'

'That's Rosie my baby girl,' I said excitedly. Shit, I'd done it again.

'It is a girl child. I see the initial 'R'. She will bring you much happiness.' She raised her hands and looked to the ceiling.

'I now call upon the spirits to show me the future,' she said huskily, which would have been quite atmospheric if Billy had not at that moment farted then jumped from his cushion in fright.

I waited as Maureen contemplated my future. I hoped the giggle that I was desperately trying to hold onto would not escape.

Billy put his front paws on the edge of my chair so I picked him up and straightened his turban as I waited for the spirits to enlighten Maureen. He snuffled and licked my face as I cuddled him - he really was a lovely little dog.

'I see many things ahead. I see laughter and happiness. I see new experiences and I see travel and success.'

'Could you be more specific?' I asked timidly.

Maureen closed her eyes and raised her hands to her temples.

'I see…a china cup. And a red car. I see…a celebration and I see…' here she held her head as she moved it back and forwards then suddenly opened her eyes and said flamboyantly, '…new light through old windows.'

'And what do those things mean?' I asked. Maureen shushed me.

'We do not question the wisdom of the spirits,' she said. 'The significance of these signs will become apparent as your future arrives.'

She again raised her eyes, and her hands towards the ceiling.

'I am Mariana, seer of the unseen, perceiver of what is and of what is yet to be. We thank you, O spirits, for your wisdom.'

I waited, not sure of what was to happen next, then Maureen, still looking at the ceiling, waved her hand at me several times and pointed to the door and I realised I was being dismissed.

I gave Billy a last cuddle and placed him on his cushion before murmuring my thanks and leaving the room.

CHAPTER TWENTY-THREE

'Well?' Lorraine said. 'What was it like?'

'Was it crap?' Georgina asked, hopefully. I hesitated, not sure how to describe what I had just experienced. Somewhere between a hallucinogenic dream and a pantomime with a farting dog thrown in for good measure.

'She's still in awe,' Nadine said. 'I'll get you a cuppa, darlin'.'

'Actually, I think it's best if I let you make your own judgements,' I said.

'Whoa, as bad as that eh?' Georgina said.

'Doesn't she just tell people what they want to hear?' Lorraine asked.

'No, not really. She told me that I had a tall dark man who adored me and that I had a beautiful child whose name began with R.'

'Wow, that's incredible,' Nige said.

'Like that's not what you want to hear?' Lorraine said scornfully.

'That's amazing!' Nadine said as she poured me a cup of tea. 'How did she know that Peter is tall and dark and that Rosie's name begins with an 'R'?'

'Did you give her any clues?' Georgina asked.

'Well I may have inadvertently mentioned something without intending to,' I said. 'She told me she could see a china cup, a red car and a celebration in my future. Oh and something about seeing new light through old windows.'

'Well there's your china cup,' Lorraine said as Nadine placed my tea in front of me.

'So, sometime in your future you're going to see a red car. Wow! I'm blown away. That's incredible,' Georgina said.

'Oh stop being so harsh,' Nige said. 'At least wait until you have a reading yourself until you start criticising.'

'I wonder what you will be celebrating?' Nadine asked thoughtfully.

'Err, her birthday? Peter's birthday? Anniversary? Christmas?' Georgina said. 'Hey, why don't you just let me do it? I'd be great.'

She held up her coffee mug and peered into it.

'I see food. This means you will eat something today. I see a bed…You will go to bed tonight. I see …a bathroom, yes you will definitely use the bathroom in the near future.'

Lorraine and I laughed but Nadine and Nige didn't.

'If you feel like that then you shouldn't go in,' Nadine told her. 'Not if you're just going to mock the poor woman.'

Georgina stayed in character and continued her performance.

'I see a number thirty-nine bus…' she said dramatically, then changed her voice in an imitation of Maureen's.

'Eeh, it's me bus home. I hope that bliddy bus driver doesn't start with his cheek, me corns are giving us hell.'

Lorraine and I laughed. Georgina was a good mimic, she could impersonate voices and mannerisms accurately and she really did sound like Maureen.

'Very funny I don't think,' Nige said. 'If you don't want to see her, I'll go in next.'

'Oh I want to see her! I can't wait, I'm really going to enjoy it.' Georgina said.

'I hope you won't go upsetting her,' I said, thinking of the sight that would greet Georgina.

'Ah, I won't. Stop worrying. I'll just be my usual self.'

'I think that's what she's worrying about,' Nadine said.

'Anyway, who's next?' I asked. Lorraine held up half a matchstick.

'Me,' she said, 'Here I go!' She went off to the therapy room and I sat down to drink my tea.

'Hey, here's another of your predictions coming to fruition,' Georgina said and she pointed to the window where the window cleaner was dipping his squeegee into a bucket of soapy water. 'You'll be seeing new light through old windows any second now,' she said.

And we all laughed as we watched the bemused window cleaner cover our windows in suds.

Nadine pulled the next winning match and she and I busied ourselves preparing salad and sandwich fillings while Lorraine was in with Maureen.

We had a way of working together without needing to discuss who was doing what. Nadine picked up the box of salad that Lorraine had collected from Derek's shop earlier and began rinsing tomatoes while I put chick peas and tahini into the blender ready to make hummus.

Nige was as jumpy as a puppet waiting for his turn.

'I'm going to have to go,' he said. 'I'll have to come back later. Unless you swap with me Nadine and let me go before you?'

'I don't mind waiting till last.' Georgina said. 'I've got plenty of time.'

'No chance,' Nadine said as she expertly sliced tomatoes at record speed, throwing the slices into a plastic container. 'I need to get in and out before the lunchtime rush.'

'It's ages till lunchtime, ah go on, let me go next' Nige wheedled, but Nadine was having none of it.

'No, sorry Nige,' she said. 'If I go in after Lorraine I can finish my jobs when I come out and be all ready for the Nutmeg Express.'

Lorraine came out of the therapy room as Nige flounced off in a huff.

'Flippin' heck,' Lorraine said. 'That was surreal!'

I laughed.

'Don't say too much, you don't want to spoil the surprise for Nadine and Georgina!'

Nadine whipped off her apron and smoothed down her hair.

'Wish me luck,' she said as she rushed off for her turn.

Lorraine went up to the sink to wash her hands as Georgina and I waited to hear the predictions for her future.

'Well, what lies in store for you then?' Georgina asked.

'Did she tell you what you wanted to hear?' I said.

'No she bloody didn't.' Lorraine said. She took an apron from the hook in the kitchen and tied it around her waist. 'Basically I'm never going to be rich, I'm going to have to work hard all my life and I won't find true happiness until I'm in my fifties.'

'No! She never said that!' Georgina said.

'She did.'

'Fifties! That's ancient!' I said with the ignorance of someone who had just turned thirty.

'Actually your forties and fifties are the best time of your life,' Georgina said.

'I didn't mean that *you* were ancient,' I said, trying to back pedal. 'I just meant…well it is pretty old isn't it?'

The look on Georgina's face told me it was probably best to change the subject so I asked Lorraine if Maureen had said anything positive at all.

'Only that I'd always have good family and friends around me,' Lorraine said.

'Well that's very positive,' I said. 'Not everyone has that.'

'And you'll need good people around you by the sound of it if you're going to be miserable and skint till you're my age,' Georgina added.

'Thanks for that, Georgina. Anyway, you're both talking as though it's all true. It's a load of rubbish.'

'Ah, I knew you'd see that in the end,' Georgina said smugly.

'Well, honestly! Who would want to pay to hear stuff like that?' Lorraine said.

'Excuse me, you were the one who brought her in here in the first place,' I argued. 'I told you I had doubts about it. And we're going to be a laughing stock when people come out of there having paid to see that spectacle.'

Lorraine laughed. 'I know! What a performance!'

'What do you mean?' Georgina asked. 'What kind of performance?' Lorraine and I looked at each other and laughed.

'Just wait and see,' I said.

Nadine came out of the therapy room like a puppy let out of a box. If I didn't know better I'd have thought she'd been in there to inhale helium.

'Oh my God,' she squeaked. 'That was amazing! She has real powers - it was like a spirit had possessed her. She had taken on a whole new persona. Her voice, how she looked everything!'

'And what did she say to you?'

'She said I'm going to meet the man of my dreams. My perfect partner. She said it's someone I've already met but I haven't realised. He's Sagittarius and he works with wires.'

'Wires? Like an electrician?' I said.

'Oh yes!' Nadine said. 'An electrician. Of course! I never thought of that. Anyone know any electricians?'

'Could be a trapeze artist,' Georgina said and Nadine's face brightened for a couple of seconds until she realised she was being teased.

'Or maybe it's that bloke in the Co-op with no teeth who works on the deli counter?' Georgina suggested and we looked at her, puzzled. 'He's got a little wire to cut the cheese with.'

'You can ridicule all you like Georgina. I can't wait to hear what the future has in store for you.'

'Neither can I, I'm going in now,' she said and off she went.

CHAPTER TWENTY-FOUR

I was packing a bag of groceries for a customer when I heard the resounding thud of the therapy room door crashing against the wall followed by Georgina's raucous laughter and Maureen shouting loudly.

'I am Mariana, seer of the unseen, perceiver of what is and of what is yet to be... THE SPIRITS WILL NOT BE MOCKED!'

I quickly handed over the customer's purchases as Georgina staggered into the kitchen clutching her stomach and laughing hysterically as the therapy room door slammed violently behind her.

'Ha ha ha. Oh my Lord! I've never seen anything like that in my life! Hee hee, what a hoot! I am Mariana, seer of shite... ha ha ha, ooh it hurts!'

'I thought something like this might happen,' Lorraine said. 'Georgina! Get a grip, we've a shop full of customers.'

'Ha ha ha...oooh hoo! Even the poor dog was in on it...ha ha ha! Sitting there with a bliddy turban on...'

Customers had stopped browsing and come to watch as she flopped over the counter, her eyes streaming with tears.

'Eeh, I nearly wet meself!'

'Get her out of sight quickly,' I said, as Lorraine dragged her by the arm and forced her up the stairs to our tiny washroom.

Nadine and I left Lorraine to deal with her while we served customers pretending, rather unconvincingly, not to have noticed her behaviour.

As soon as there was a lull in the queue, I told Nadine that I was going to check if Maureen was all right and left her to serve a man who was asking about homeopathic remedies for his horse.

I knocked gently on the therapy room door.

'Maureen?'

'Come on in, my love, I'm just about sorted.'

I opened the door to see Maureen, minus her Mariana get-up, folding the lengths of silky fabrics that had adorned the room. Billy, sans-turban, was investigating the carpet in the corner where he seemed to have caught the scent of something interesting. I hoped he wasn't looking for a suitable spot to pee.

'Are you ok?' I asked. 'I'm so sorry about Georgina. She's doesn't mean any harm, she just has a rather infantile sense of humour sometimes.'

Maureen looked up at me, surprised. She still had a little smudge of bronze make-up in the crease of her nose and the black wig lay on the chair with its curls flicked out in a halo like a prize-winning guinea pig.

'Oh don't worry about that my love. I face non-believers and ridiculers all the time. It goes with the territory.' She picked up the folded fabric and the wig and placed them carefully in her bag.

'If I were to take what people say about me to heart, I'd be done for. Now if you don't mind I'll just take Billy out because I'm sure he'll be ready for a tiddle, then I wouldn't mind a nice cup of tea before I go.'

'Of course,' I said. 'I'll go and make a pot.'

Georgina had been sent home in disgrace by Lorraine and Nadine.

'Maureen's all packed up,' I said.

'How is she?' Lorraine asked.

'She's fine. She's going to take Billy out for a minute while I make some tea.'

'That was an absolute disgrace,' Nadine said. 'I can't believe the way Georgina went on. So disrespectful. She was still laughing and carrying on as she went up the street! We could hear her from here.'

'She did go a bit over the top,' Lorraine said. 'But then, it was all rather bizarre. I had to try really hard not to laugh when I saw Maureen...sorry, Mariana...seer of the unseen...ha ha!'

'Me too,' I said. 'Especially when I saw Billy with his little turban on, poor little bugger.'

'Well I don't think there was anything to laugh about,' Nadine said. She was obviously still upset about Georgina's behaviour. 'She was very professional, it's a serious thing talking to spirits.'

'Shh!' Lorraine said as Maureen appeared with Billy, who was whining excitedly and pulling on his lead towards the door.

'Calm down, my little love, I'm going as fast as I can.'

She staggered towards the door as Billy's paws slithered about, his claws clacking on the wooden floor.

'Won't be a tick,' she told us as she was dragged out of the door.

When she returned, she sat and slurped her way through a pot of tea and chatted to us, while we took turns to deal with customers. Nadine was desperate to make sure Maureen had not been hurt by Georgina's antics.

'Don't take any notice of her, she's always like that. Very immature for a woman approaching sixty,' she told Maureen.

'Oh I could tell from the start that one would be trouble,' Maureen said as she sucked at her tea. 'I come up against it all the time, it doesn't bother me. I'll have the last laugh when they pop off and realise it's all true.'

'Well, that's very philosophical of you, Maureen. Very admirable,' Nadine told her.

'Do you think she was surprised at the…' I stumbled on my words '…considerable change in your appearance? It did rather take me aback when I first saw you.'

'Maybe people could find it a bit distracting?' Lorraine suggested.

'Oh no, they love it,' Maureen said. 'And anyway, I need to do it. It gets me in the right frame of mind, you see. It's a sort of ritual. By the time I've finished getting ready, Mariana just sort of takes over and sometimes it's as though I'm possessed for a while, I often don't remember a lot of what I've told people.'

She picked up her cup and drained it.

'You should video it,' Lorraine suggested. 'I think you'd find it quite…enlightening.' Maureen put her cup down suddenly and turned to me.

'Sorry for changing the subject,' she said. 'But there's a tall man here. He's showing me a pithead. Is this your place of work…yes? Ah, he was a miner, his name is Joseph…Joe?'

My whole body shivered. My maternal grandfather was a miner called Joe. And he was a very tall man. I'd spent lots of my childhood with him and he'd died when I was in my early teens.

Lorraine too looked shocked.

'That's our Grandad,' she said.

Nadine's eyes were as large as stotties as she looked at Maureen with awe.

164

'Well he just wants you know that he's happy and well and he says…' she closed her eyes and Lorraine and I waited in anticipation.

'He says…' Maureen concentrated and we waited.

Nadine looked as though she was about to either burst with joy or throw herself at Maureen's feet in an act of worship.

'He says…' she opened her eyes and picked up her cup. 'No, sorry, he's gone. Any chance of a refill?'

Later, after the lunchtime rush, Nadine ran the hot tap to fill our enormous sink so that she could begin the washing up process.

'You've been promising to get me a dishwasher for months,' she grumbled as she began stacking empty dishes and gathering the used utensils.

'But you do such a good job, Nadine,' Lorraine said, filling rolls with leftover cheese savoury and chopped lettuce for our lunch.

'I'll come and dry,' I said.

'I'm back!' Nige said as he burst through the door, making the bell jangle madly. 'Where is she? Mystic Maureen? Am I too late?'

'Only by a couple of hours,' Lorraine told him. 'She left ages ago.'

'Aw no!' Nige said. 'I can't believe I've missed her, I've done my delivery at record speed.'

'Well that's a first,' Lorraine said.

'So, tell me…what was she like?'

We answered in unison.

'Brilliant.'

'Rubbish.'

'Ok.'

'Well which one? Was she brilliant, rubbish or ok?'

'I thought she was really good,' Nadine said.

'And I thought she was rubbish,' Lorraine said. 'It was all drama and acting and the few things she did tell me were pretty depressing.'

'So you must have thought she was ok then?' he asked me.

'Yeah. Like Lorraine I thought a lot of it was pretentious over-acting, she was actually better when she was out of character.'

'What do you mean, out-of-character?' he asked excitedly 'Did she turn into someone else? Was she possessed, like, did she lose sense of everything?'

'If you mean did she lose possession of her senses, then yes,' Lorraine said.

'Really? Was there ectoplasm? Did she go into a trance? Aw, I wish I'd seen that!'

'No she didn't. Lorraine's just joking,' I told him. 'I just meant she seemed to be more accurate when she was just having a cuppa with us than when she was in a one-to-one situation.'

I wanted him to see Maureen aka Mariana without any preconceptions.

'You have to agree, Lorraine, she was pretty accurate about our Grandad.'

'Well yes, she was,' Lorraine admitted. 'But I hope her predictions about my life are wrong. Fifty! Gawd, I could be dead by the time I find happiness.'

CHAPTER TWENTY-FIVE

I loved bringing Rosie to work with me. I was so lucky to be able to do so.

When I was at home with Rosie I often felt bad that I was at home having a lovely time, while the others did my work at the shop. I was able to spend valuable time with my child while still receiving my full salary thanks to Lorraine and Nadine working full time, their workload increased because of my absence.

When I was working at the shop, I missed my baby girl so much I ached, and had to stop myself from constantly telephoning to check on her day.

Having her with me at the shop was the perfect compromise. The customers loved to see her and were often disappointed if she were not there when they called, although I was sometimes subjected to criticism that it was not an appropriate place for a child. I would feel the need to explain that she spent only an odd hour at the shop and that mostly she was at home with myself or her grandparents.

Having my ability as a mother condemned was the most wounding form of criticism I'd ever endured. Having my writing rejected or being ridiculed for my vegetarian lifestyle were mere pinpricks compared to this gash to the soul.

There is so much guilt involved with motherhood.

Balancing work and motherhood is such a difficult thing. Mothers are judged in a way that fathers rarely are; there is an ongoing struggle to prove which is better for both mother and baby, a working mum or a stay-at-home mum, and sadly most of the judgement comes from other mothers.

Bringing up children is the most important job in the world and we should support each other instead of putting each other down.

When Rosie was at the shop, Lorraine and I would take turns to take her for a walk in the pram. The intention was to walk around the park, but we encountered so many familiar people on the way, stopping to chat and see Rosie that it took an age to get down the bank and we usually only got as far as the churchyard.

Sometimes my Mam or Joan would come to take her out for the afternoon, giving me a little longer to get things done in the shop, and then we'd pick her up on our way home.

Today, after the Nutmeg Express had been and gone, Lorraine picked Rosie out of her playpen and cuddled her.

'Are you going to come for a walk with your Auntie Lorraine to see the dead people, my little angel?'

'Lorraine! Don't say that to her, it sounds awful.'

Lorraine sat down with Rosie on her knee, gently easing her arms and legs into her little snuggle-suit.

'Well that's where we go isn't it?' she said to Rosie, kissing her head. 'To the churchyard to see all the dead people. Say bye to Mammy.' She held her up so I could kiss her then tucked her into her pram. 'See you later.'

I found that the shop had gained many new customers during my maternity leave, and although this was great for the business, I was not happy when people assumed I was a new member of staff.

When I went to serve people they would look disappointed and ask where the other ladies were, or they'd ask if I was new.

One woman even told me not to worry and that I'd soon get the hang of it, when I'd made an error on the till.

Lorraine had been gone about five minutes when a small middle-aged woman entered the shop. She was bright-eyed and rosy-cheeked and smiled warmly.

'Now then,' she said, looking around. 'Where's the other lady?'

'Just me here at the moment,' I said. 'Can I help?'

'Oh, that's a shame. I was hoping to see Lorraine. She's an absolute marvel.'

The woman looked at me kindly.

'Well, I supposed you'll have to do. Are you new?'

'No, no,' I said. 'I've been on maternity leave so I haven't been in for a while. What can I get you?'

'I wanted some more of that stuff Lorraine sold me, it's marvellous.'

'And what was it?'

'I can't remember, but it did the trick, she's a marvel, Lorraine.'

'Can you remember the name of it?'

168

'No. Oh, what a shame Lorraine's not here. She would have known straight away.'

'What was it for?'

'Oh it was marvellous! It was for my husband. I came in a while ago just on the chance I might get something to help him and Lorraine sold me this stuff and it worked wonders! I tell you, that girl is an absolute marvel.'

'Indeed she is. Now if you could just tell me a bit more about your husband's condition I may be able to work out what it was she sold you.'

'Well, he had been poorly for *ages*. He hadn't been able to get out of bed for nearly seven years. I gave him some of that stuff Lorraine sold me, and it's the God's honest truth, as I'm standing here, he jumped out of bed and papered the wall.'

'Really?' I said. 'I'm not sure what that could be.'

We sold some good natural remedies and we'd often had customers return and thank us when they'd had good results, but this story took a bit of believing.

'He was up that ladder before I could say Jack Robinson.'

I had no idea what Lorraine could have suggested that would have had such an amazing result.

'And you can't remember the name of the remedy?' I asked.

'No.'

'Can you remember how much it cost? Or what the bottle looked like?'

'No.'

'Was it a vitamin supplement? Or a herbal remedy?'

'I've no idea. I just asked Lorraine, and she recommended this stuff and I'm telling you it worked like magic. She's an absolute marvel.'

'Right,' I said as I looked at the shelves, perplexed as to what this miracle-in-a-bottle could be. 'I really can't think of what it could have been.'

'Don't worry dear, it's not your fault,' the woman said. 'You'll get to know more about all this stuff when you've been here a bit longer.'

'I'm not new, like I said I've been away having a baby.'

'How lovely. Well I'm sure Lorraine will teach you all you need to know. She's a marvel, she is.'

The temperature in the shop had cooled, and I looked up to see drops of rain on the window.

'Well, speak of the devil, here she is, the marvel herself,' I said as Lorraine pushed the pram through the door.

'It's spitting on to rain so I thought we'd better head back, it looks a bit threatening.'

The woman turned and her face lit up when she saw who had just entered.

'Hello there,' she said to Lorraine. 'I'm just telling your new girl here what a marvel you are. That stuff you gave me for my husband worked a treat.'

'I'm not actually a new girl, I've been on maternity leave…'

'Ah that's good,' Lorraine said.

I took the pram from her and seeing that Rosie was fast asleep, pushed it carefully behind the counter.

'I've come for another bottle for him, it's amazing. Remember I told you he'd never left his bed for seven years? Well after I gave him some of that stuff, he jumped out of bed and papered the wall, didn't he?'

The woman looked towards me for confirmation as though I'd been there to witness this miraculous event.

'He did indeed,' I said.

'Wow!' Lorraine said.

'Yes. Wow,' I said.

'So what I'm after is another bottle, please.'

'Certainly.'

Lorraine reached for a bottle of Echinacea Tincture and placed it on the counter.

'That's six ninety-nine please.'

Aha. So it was Echinacea that had caused the miracle. Echinacea was a popular herb for boosting the immune system and we'd had a lot of success with it but I'd been unaware that it had the power to propel a man from his sick bed to the top of a ladder.

'Thank you dear. You're an absolute marvel. I've told everyone about you.'

'You're very welcome, Lorraine said, modestly. She put the bottle of Echinacea into a paper bag and rang the sale into the till.

The woman was still singing Lorraine's praises.

'I told everyone at church, I said to them, if you ever need sorting out, get yourself down to that health shop and see Lorraine, she's a marvel.'

I'd heard enough about the marvel that was my sister so I picked up the brush and started to sweep the kitchen floor – a task that we carried out intermittently throughout the day.

'That's right dear, give it a good sweep,' the woman said. 'Lorraine will keep you busy.'

I gave a forced smile and carried on sweeping as she thanked Lorraine and took her leave.

'Well, what can I say?' Lorraine said. 'Bloomin' marvel, I am!'

'Bloomin' lucky, you mean.'

'Lucky? Excuse me, you heard what she said. That man had not been out of bed for seven years!'

'Aye, that's probably why he got up and papered the wall,' I said. 'Must have been sick of lying there, looking at it.'

Lorraine laughed.

'That'll be why she came back for another bottle,' she said. 'Probably wants the other walls doing!'

'Perhaps we should put a poster in the window. Echinacea – for all your DIY jobs,' I said. We laughed, and hearing a gurgle I peered into the pram. Rosie looked back at me, her eyes huge and dark and her face flushed from sleep.

'Hello, my darling,' I said, picking her up. 'Your Aunty Lorraine, the Bloomin' Marvel, is just going to make me a cup of tea.'

CHAPTER TWENTY-SIX

The shop was quiet so we had a lovely half an hour, playing and laughing with Rosie and singing silly songs to her. There were loads of jobs to do; filing invoices, cleaning shelves, preparing orders…but they were ignored as we sang and clapped, absorbing Rosie's tinkling baby-laugh like basking in warm sunshine.

My Dad, having heard on the grapevine that Rosie was in residence, arrived and offered to take her to Paddy Freeman's Park, where he'd spent hours with Lorraine and I when we were small, pushing us on the swings, and sailing home-made boats on the pond.

He would do this whenever he could; luckily he was self-employed and so could prioritise his working hours for his most important tasks, such as spending time with his little granddaughter.

We watched them go off, waving as they passed the window, and sighing as we now had to return to work.

'What do you prefer? Cooking dinner or getting the accounts up to date?' I asked Lorraine.

On quiet afternoons, one of us would catch up with paperwork while the other cooked dinner for us to take home.

'I'll cook,' Lorraine said. 'I might make a vegetable curry. Then we can do our own rice and nan breads at home. Fancy it?'

'Sounds great,' I said.

'And I'll do a little dish of vegetables to mash up for Rosie too.' She took off her apron and picked up her bag to go and buy some ingredients.

'Won't be long,' she said.

I carried our big ledger through to the front of the shop and settled myself on a stool at the counter with a pile of invoices and a calculator, but every time I made a start on a list of figures, I'd have to stop to serve someone. Although I was happy that people were buying from us, I wished they'd hurry up so I could get a couple of uninterrupted minutes to add up my invoice totals.

I served a run of customers, taking money and packing goods into our recycled paper grocery bags.

There was just one woman browsing now and she seemed unlikely to be about to buy anything. She was dressed in a drab grey raincoat that matched the colour of her skin. In fact it matched her whole countenance.

She wandered about, randomly looking at shelves.

Probably a time-waster, I thought. We often had people come in to keep warm for a few minutes, then as soon as they saw the number 39 bus trundling down the bank they would hurry out to the bus stop.

I sighed loudly as she set off for a second traipse around the shelves. I wish she'd hurry up and leave so I could concentrate on my figures.

Lorraine returned, placing a cauliflower, carrots, peppers and a paper bag of mushrooms on the bench in the kitchen, then picked up the kettle and went up to the sink to fill it. The woman was now standing motionless, gazing at the display of essential oils. I sighed again and walked over to her.

'Can I help you,' I asked.

As she turned toward me my impatience was immediately replaced by concern as I saw her face. Her skin was pallid and she had the look of a person who had not slept peacefully for a long while. Her skin was tight and papery over her cheekbones, but swollen beneath her eyes, showing she had shed many tears.

As I looked at her, I was almost moved to tears myself as a wave of compassion engulfed me. She looked defeated, as though her whole spirit had been crushed. Her eyes held a great pain, I could see that the very act of being was difficult for her.

'Are you all right?' I asked, this time more gently.

'I'm looking for some lavender oil,' she said. 'I was told it's good for helping you to sleep.'

'Yes. It's right here,'

Although lavender oil was great for relaxation and inducing sleep I felt that her problems ran much more deeply and I asked if she'd seen her GP.

'Yes, he's given me some pills to help,' she said. 'It was one of the nurses at the hospital who suggested lavender oil.'

She suddenly lost her balance and I held her arm to steady her.

'Are you sure you are all right?' I asked again. 'Would you like a cup of tea?'

'Actually, I'd love one,' she said. 'How kind.'

Lorraine poured three cups of tea and I carried a stool to the edge of the counter and helped the woman sit down. Her hand shook as she reached for her cup.

'Are you ill?' Lorraine asked.

'No…no, not really.' She breathed deeply then said 'It's my little boy you see. He's on a life support machine at the hospital. There was an accident… he's very…poorly.'

I felt my eyes immediately fill with tears. I'd always been over-sensitive but since becoming a mother my emotions were even more raw to the suffering of others and now I felt an actual physical pain as the woman told us her story.

'He was hit in the head by a cricket ball. It was just one of those freak accidents really. No-one's fault… just a terrible, terrible accident and now he's brain damaged and won't survive and they can't do any more for him.'

I choked on the lump that had moved into my throat and unable to speak, I reached out and touched her arm. Lorraine bit on her lower lip as her eyes brimmed with tears. I could see she was struggling to hold them back, but the woman was dry-eyed. She was beyond tears, defeated and broken by one of life's unjustifiable adversities.

'One of the nurses said maybe I should get out of the hospital for a while and get some fresh air. She suggested I come here because she said the staff are always so lovely and she said I could maybe buy some lavender oil for later tonight to help calm me.'

I gulped at the obstruction in my throat and tried to breathe normally.

'You see, they are going to turn off his machines this evening and the nurse said if I had a walk I'd feel fresher for saying goodbye.'

Lorraine's tears spilled and she leaned forward and hugged the woman. I could not cry. It was as though I had a huge stone blocking my throat and nothing could shift it.

'It's his birthday next week, he would have been three…just three. He wanted a toy tractor. He loved tractors.'

It was difficult to know what to say.

In the end we didn't say much. We just listened, occasionally squeezing the woman's hand and hugging her as she drank her tea and talked about her little son's love of his uncle's farm and especially the tractors.

She held no anger, showed no blame. She was numb, as though her life had been frozen, suspended like that of her little boy.

She did not stay long. She was keen to get back to her son's side.

Lorraine offered to take her back to the hospital in the car, but she refused, thanking us for our tea and our kindness and leaving with a bottle of lavender oil which she tried desperately to pay for, but we would not take her money.

We sent her off with hugs and our love and watched as she set off down the bank towards the hospital, an inconspicuous figure, weaving her way through shoppers and office workers who had no idea that the small woman in grey walked with such a heavy cloud above her.

Lorraine gave vent to her tears in the shop, but mine were a solid painful mass that I could not ease.

It was not until much later that night that I held my precious baby daughter close to my heart and was able to weep long and hard for a little boy whose name I did not know.

CHAPTER TWENTY-SEVEN

Since opening Nutmeg, Lorraine, Nadine and Peter and I had gradually changed many of our living habits, and all claimed to feel better for it.

We ate less processed foods and more wholefoods; drank less caffeine and more water and juices and herbal teas. We learned about preventative health measures, took vitamins and supplements suited to our needs, and used herbal remedies and treatments for any minor ailments.

The shelves became our personal dispensary. If we came into work with a headache we opened a bottle of feverfew tablets. A bit hung-over and we headed for the milk thistle. We had arnica for bruises, melissa for period pains and lavender oil for the burns we regularly incurred as we grappled with hot pans. Any bottles we opened were stored on a shelf in the office along with the first aid box.

We had not set out to change. It was an unintentional process that happened naturally over the months as we learned about and sampled the products we stocked.

I felt lighter and more energised and suffered less from headaches and coughs and colds, and this, along with the fact that I'd given birth without the aid of pain relief, convinced me that this was a path I needed to stay on.

I still occasionally ate chips and chocolate and desserts, but I seemed to lose the taste for fatty and sweetened foods and became naturally drawn to 'healthier' options.

The more I learned about natural therapies the more I wanted to know and I read everything I could find about the subject, ordering books from bookshops and scouring the library.

I particularly enjoyed reading the books of Jan de Vries, a well-respected naturopath who had a clinic in Scotland.

Originally from Holland, he had graduated in pharmacy then gone on to study osteopathy and acupuncture. His books were informative and his advice easy to put into practice, as he advocated using a combination of orthodox and 'alternative' treatments best suited to the patient.

We ordered copies of his books and also his collection of products which included herbal teas and essences specifically blended for a range of ailments and conditions.

When I heard he was to give a talk at the Civic Centre in Newcastle I was eager to go. Lorraine offered to come with me.

'What's he like?' she asked. 'Is he very old?'

'I've no idea,' I said. 'Never seen him. He'll be in his fifties I would think. His books are really good, lots of down-to-earth advice.'

'I think I'll borrow them and read them before we go, if that's ok,' she said.

'Yeah, of course. But you'll have to be quick. The talk is tomorrow night.'

'Tomorrow? I'd better ring now to order tickets then.'

She went into the office to use the telephone and I set about sweeping the floor and tidying the kitchen as I heard her speaking on the phone.

'I've reserved two tickets,' she said putting down the phone. 'We collect them on the night.'

I was about to speak when she shushed me.

'What was that?' she whispered.

'What was what?'

'That noise.'

'What noise?'

There was a scrabbling noise that seemed to come from above our heads. We both looked up.

'That noise,' she said. 'I heard it earlier this morning too.'

We listened to a series of scratching and tapping noises coming from behind the wooden pine panels that covered the ceiling. We concentrated on the sounds, trying to locate the exact spot where they were coming from.

'There's someone in the gym,' Lorraine said.

'There can't be,' I said. 'It's been empty for months now.'

On Guy Fawkes Night the gym on the floor above us had been badly damaged by fire when a lit firework had been pushed through the letterbox. The fire had spread to our shop, destroying our kitchen, blackening everything and rendering our stock unfit for sale. We'd come very close to losing our business and it was only because of the support from our fellow shop owners and customers that we were still here and trading.

The proprietors of the gym – named Ug and Pug by Lorraine and I because of their caveman looks and lack of intelligence – had fled after the fire and the property had been locked up and left empty by Mr Stoker, the landlord. He had left a key with us so that he could send potential tenants to collect it and view the property without any inconvenience to himself. I think he may have been expecting a rush of interest as the property was in a very desirable position for business, but there had been no enquiries and the key had been put under the cash drawer in the till and forgotten.

'Do you think there are rats up there?' Lorraine asked, as more scratching and a louder bump was heard.

'I hope not,' I said. 'We'd have to get someone out to kill them.'

'We'd better go up and take a look.'

'I'm not going up there!' I said. 'There could be a squatter living up there or anything.'

'Don't be so daft. It's probably just mice. If we get up there first we could put some humane traps down rather than wait till Mr Stoker finds out and goes up there with poison.'

'Yeah, I see what you mean,' I said.

We both hated the thought of killing anything, even creatures that others looked on as vermin. 'We'll go up when Nadine gets in.'

Nadine arrived just before ten, and put on an apron ready to make a start on the sandwich fillings.

'We're going to take a look upstairs in the gym,' Lorraine told her. 'We've heard strange noises coming from up there.' Nadine, who'd been drying her hands, put down the towel and looked at us.

'What kind of noises?'

'Tapping and scratching,' I told her.

'Oh my Lord!' she said. 'It's since Maureen's been in here, making contact with spirits. She's left one here and it's haunting us!'

Lorraine laughed. 'You're as daft as she is,' she said, nodding towards me. 'She thinks we've got an old tramp living up there.'

'An old tramp!' Nadine said. 'I never thought of that.'

'And I never thought of a lost soul haunting us,' I said.

'Honestly the two of you are nuts. It's mice, that's all,' Lorraine said.

'Have you ever been up there?' Nadine asked.

'Just once, ages ago,' I said.

I'd been up to introduce myself to the gym owners but had left very quickly when they began making inappropriate remarks and suggestions.

'I haven't,' Lorraine said. 'Actually I'm quite curious about it, I wonder why we've never thought of having a snoop about the place before.'

'What's it like?' Nadine asked.

'I didn't get much of a look around,' I said. 'But from what I saw it's pretty bleak. Dark and smelly and dirty.'

'And that was before the fire, it'll be worse now,' Nadine said. 'I'm glad I'm not going up with you.'

Lorraine opened the till, and lifting the cash drawer, took out the key.

'Come on then,' she said. 'Let's get it over with.'

'Hang on,' I said, and I went to the window shelf to open the loose panel where the electricity meter was. I pulled out the torch we kept in there.

'We won't need that!' Lorraine said.

'Yes we will, the windows are boarded up remember. It'll be pitch black in there.'

Nadine shuddered.

'Do you think you should take some garlic and a bible too?' she suggested.

'For the last time, they are only MICE. Not vampire mice or ghost mice, just ordinary little scrabbly squeaky MICE,' Lorraine said. 'Now stop winding each other up and let's go.'

I picked up my torch and followed her out.

We walked around the side of the shop to the door of the gym. Lorraine unlocked the door and as she pushed it open, a sour smell of dust and burned wood seeped out.

After the fire, minimum repairs had been carried out to the property, enough to make it safe, but anyone taking it on as a business premises would have a lot more work to do.

In the entrance, rough panels of wood had been used to repair the walls and floor, and also the narrow stairs that disappeared into the darkness above.

Lorraine closed the door and started to climb the stairs.

'Don't close it,' I said, and I quickly opened the door, leaving it ajar behind us. 'We might get locked in.'

I switched on my torch and followed her.

The stairs groaned and creaked as if in pain as we stepped on them.

The top of the staircase opened onto a large room and my torch swept across dismantled and discarded weight training apparatus to the abandoned boxing ring at the far end of the room. The boarded up windows added to the look of decay.

'Ugh, it's horrible up here,' Lorraine whispered.

'Why are you whispering?' I whispered back.

'In case anyone hears us.'

'Like who? I thought you said there was no-one here.'

'Well, I just meant the mice.'

'You meant the ghosts didn't you? Or the tramp?'

'Stop it! You're spooking me out.'

The bravery that Lorraine had shown downstairs seemed to be leaving her as we stood in the dark, straining our eyes to pick out things in the torchlight.

An archway led to a room that had obviously been used as a kitchen An old microwave oven stood on a filthy fridge that had its door hanging open, revealing grimy shelves and a rusted beer can lying on its side. Next to it was a stainless steel sink filled with a couple of inches of slimy water and some unwashed dishes.

Behind this room was a shower block; heaps of broken tiles lay in the shower trays and rust marks ran from the old shower heads down the few cracked tiles that were still attached to the walls. The musty smell was so strong I could taste it.

'Ugh, let's get out of here,' I said, and we turned and made our way back into the main room.

Again I moved the torch across the room and the beam from it illuminated an open door at the back of the room behind the boxing ring.

'Through there,' Lorraine said, and we clung together as we picked our way across the creaking floor, through empty boxes and bits of rubbish, climbing over exercise equipment and over the boxing ring to reach the door.

'It's the stairs to the attics,' I said as I shone the torch to reveal a dark narrow stairwell that ascended for a few steps then turned a corner and disappeared into blackness.

I didn't want to go up. My heart was pounding and I had an overwhelming urge to turn and flee, back across the assault course that we'd come across, down the decrepit stairs to the safety of the shop.

The stairs were too narrow for us to climb side-by-side, but as we didn't want to let go of each other, we ascended side-ways, our arms linked together.

The walls of the stairway were bare plaster, which had crumbled in places, dropping chunks onto the stairs which made them even more difficult to negotiate as we stumbled upwards.

The stairs turned again, the last flight taking us to the first attic which was sparsely furnished with an old bed and wardrobe. There was a smell of dampness and dirt, and disturbed dust motes lurked in the light of the torch. The beam of light fell across a pair of filthy pillows lying on a stained mattress and Lorraine and I cried out our disgust in unison.

'Eww! That's minging!' Lorraine said. 'Who the hell has been sleeping on that?'

'It's the tramp, it's the tramp,' I wailed.

Fear had taken a grip and I was near to hysteria. The fact that Lorraine too was beginning to show signs of panic was really freaking me out, she was normally level headed and unaffected by anything melodramatic.

'Oh my God!' she screeched, as the torch lit up a dirty plate and mug set upon an old packing case. 'You're right, it's a squatter, he's living up here!'

I clutched her arm tighter.

'But where is he now?' I said in a half-whisper, half-squeak and I slowly moved the torch around, dreading the moment when it would illuminate our wild man, crouching in a corner, ready to pounce.

Every muscle I had was clenched to its limit as I scanned the space in terror. The room was empty.

'Through there,' Lorraine whispered, pointing to a doorway leading to the second attic room.

Clinging together, we made our way past the bed and through the doorway to the second attic room.

As I lifted the torch, a blood-curdling scream emerged from Lorraine and then we were scrambling our way back through the attics screaming hysterically at the horror we had just seen.

CHAPTER TWENTY-EIGHT

'The police are on their way,' Nadine said.

She handed me a bottle of Rescue Remedy.

'Take a few drops of this for the shock,' she said. I took the bottle from her with a shaking hand and took a swig from it then handed it to Lorraine.

'To think that's been right above us and we didn't know anything about it,' Lorraine said with a shudder.

'Don't think about it,' Nadine said. 'I'll make you both a cup of hot sweet tea, my Granny used to swear by it for things like this.'

'Things like this?' I said. 'You said that as though this is a regular occurrence.'

Lorraine and I prowled about the kitchen, unable to settle or focus on anything. Nadine seemed fairly calm.

'Aren't you shocked?' I asked her.

'Well of course I am but it's not going to help if I get into a state too, is it?' she said. 'And I didn't actually see it.'

'No,' I said. 'I wish I hadn't either.'

'I wish we hadn't gone up there,' Lorraine said.

'That would have been worse, imagine if it had been months before anyone went up there.'

Lorraine winced. 'Don't!' she said.

The Police Officer arrived quickly.

'Have you come on your own? I asked.

'Don't worry,' he said. 'I'll just ask a few questions first to assess the situation then I can decided if I need to call for back up, although I did get the basic facts that you reported over the phone.'

He took out his notebook as we led him into the kitchen to talk. The shop was filling with customers and his presence was causing quite a stir.

'What's the problem, Officer?' a man asked.

'Mind your neb,' I said, which was a bit rude but I was very distressed.

'Nothing for you to worry about, sir,' the Officer said, at which the man suddenly developed a great interest in some organic tampons that were displayed near the till, picking them up and pretending to read the box as he strained his ears to hear our conversation.

'Get away,' I hissed at him, as if I were chasing a cat getting ready to poop in my garden. He ignored me and continued loitering.

'Will you be all right looking after things for a while?' I asked Nadine.

'Course I will,' she said, and moved behind the counter.

'Don't I need to speak to you?' the Officer asked and Nadine gave him her best smile.

'You can speak to me any time you like, Officer,' she said and I gave her a look of disapproval.

How could she think of flirting at a time like this? I felt really jittery and close to tears and I could see Lorraine was really shaken too.

The Officer smiled back at Nadine.

'I'm sure I'll have time to come and have a word with you before I go,' he said. And the name's Brian. He gave her a wink. Nadine winked back.

'I'll look forward to that, Brian.'

Lorraine gave a sniff of indignation.

'Excuse me,' she said. 'This is not a speed-dating service. We have a serious matter to attend to.'

'Now then,' Brian said. 'First things first. Any chance of a cuppa?'

I couldn't believe his audacity.

'A cuppa?' I said. 'A cuppa? There's a dead body hanging upstairs! Don't you think you should be up there instead of asking for a cuppa and chatting up our assistant?'

The man at the counter dropped his tampons.

'A dead body! There's a body upstairs!' he yelled, running about in a Corporal Jones type flap. I expected him to start shouting 'don't panic!' but he didn't. After provoking a commotion amongst the customers waiting to be served by Nadine, he took off into the street.

The customers were like a brood of worried chickens fearing the imminent arrival of a fox.

'A dead body! A dead body!' they shrieked as they fluttered about squawking and clucking.

'Now that's just what I was trying to avoid,' Brian said as the news was carried out of the door and into the neighbourhood, as people rushed to be the first to tell what they'd heard.

'Right then,' Brian said. 'Forget the tea. I'd better take a look. You have a key you say?'

'It's open. We didn't stop to lock the door behind us,' Lorraine said.

'And you say the body is hanging in the second attic at the top of the building?'

Lorraine and I nodded, and Brian picked up the torch Lorraine held out for him and went to investigate.

'Come on let's go after him,' Nadine said.

'No chance,' I said. 'I'm not going up there again.'

'I just meant outside,' she said. 'Come on! It's the most exciting thing that's happened around here since that man streaked around the Co-op. Don't let's miss it.'

Lorraine and I reluctantly agreed to go outside with her and by the time we'd locked the shop and walked the short distance to the gym door, there was a crowd waiting and the word on the street was that there were at least three bodies up there.

'There's been a murder,' a woman told us. 'Apparently three people have been shot.'

'I heard there were five,' another woman said. 'And all strangled.'

We were told that the Police Officer had entered the building alone, and my respect for Brian grew. There was no way I would have set foot in the place, and he had gone in unaccompanied.

Stories circulated as we waited, each more incredulous than the last. The number of alleged victims rose in proportion to the size of the crowd and theories about drug money and gang crimes were bandied about.

We didn't have to wait long for Brian to reappear.

'All right, excitement over,' he said as he appeared at the gym door. 'If you three ladies would accompany me into the building, I just need you to confirm what you saw.'

'I don't want to go in,' I said in a hushed voice to Lorraine.

'We'll have to,' she said.

'I don't need to though, this is nothing to do with me,' Nadine said. I grabbed her arm.

'If we have to go up there, then you're coming too,' I said.

The ascent up the stairs to the gym didn't seem so frightening with the reassuring figure of Brian leading the way. His down-to-earth manner and cheery countenance helped to disperse any feelings of fear we may have had. Having a masculine presence gave us a feeling of protection, although I made a mental note not to mention anything of the sort to Georgina.

We crossed the gym and climbed the narrow steps to the attics. As we approached the entrance to the second attic, my stomach fluttered with dread at having to look at the horror again.

'Now then, is this what you saw?' Brian asked, and Nadine, Lorraine and I clutched each other as the torch illuminated an ancient misshapen punchbag hanging in the corner. The leather cover was cracked and split, revealing what looked like old horsehair stuffing and with a bit of imagination, its shape did resemble that of a human form.

'There's your corpse, girls,' Brian said, looking at us and my immediate feeling of relief was overtaken by one of embarrassment and I almost wished there had been a dead body as I thought of the excited crowd waiting outside.

The onlookers reluctantly dispersed after Brian told them to move along and that no bodies, dead or alive, had been discovered in the gym. Lorraine and I shuffled into the shop red-faced as they grumbled their disappointment at being cheated out of a murder story.

Brian took the key to lock up the gym and returned carrying a cardboard box that he placed on the floor.

'Serious business, wasting police time,' he said as he opened his notebook and began to write in it.

'It really did look like a body,' I said. 'It was hanging there in the dark and when the torch lit it up…well, we just ran for it.'

'So you didn't have a proper look then, before deciding to call me out and waste my time?'

'Well no I suppose we didn't,' I said. 'We were nearly breaking our necks to get out.'

Brian laughed. 'I'm just teasing you,' he said. 'Wait till the lads hear about this!'

'How about a cup of tea and a cake to make up for it? Lorraine offered.

'Sounds great,' Brian said. 'And how about you coming out for dinner tomorrow night?' he asked Nadine.

'I'll check my diary,' she said, trying to play it cool but giving herself away with the huge grin that spread across her face.

'Oh I nearly forgot,' he said, and he carefully lifted the cardboard box. 'This is the little fella that's been making all the noise up there.'

He gently lifted the lid to reveal, huddled in the corner, a starling with a broken wing.

'Oh, the poor thing,' Lorraine said. 'What are you going to do with him?'

'I have a friend who works for the RSPB, he'll know how to put him right. I'm going to take him along there on my way home.'

And Lorraine, Nadine and I beamed at him as he suddenly went up in our estimation.

'Have another cake,' I said.

CHAPTER TWENTY-NINE

Of course Peter found the whole thing hilarious.

He arrived at lunchtime and after having a cup of tea and a sandwich, took the key to go upstairs and have a look for himself.

'Good imaginations you two have,' he said when he returned.

'It looked like a body in the torchlight,' Lorraine said.

'It looks like what it is – a punch bag,' Peter insisted. 'All that stuffing hanging out of it. Who did you think had been murdered? Worzel Gummidge?'

'You went in there knowing what to expect, we came across it while we were looking for a suspected intruder,' I said.

'You *even* had me taken in for a while,' Nadine said, as though she was the least gullible person in the world. 'But I knew it couldn't be true. Not really.'

Georgina and Nige were disappointed to have missed the fun.

'What a hoot,' Georgina said. 'I wish I'd been here. What a couple of jessies you two are.'

I was beginning to get a bit fed up with all the jeering.

'Look here, you weren't there so I don't think you're qualified to comment. It's easy to sit here and laugh but if you'd gone up there in the dark you'd be telling a different story.'

'I don't think so. A bag of straw wouldn't have scared me. Huh!'

'Really.'

'Yeah, really. It's because you two are so flappable and panicky all the time.'

Lorraine, who had been ignoring the conversation turned to Georgina.

'Who are you calling flappable and panicky?' she said. 'Me?'

'Yeah. Well more so, her,' she said pointing at me.

'Me?' I said.

'Yeah. You're the biggest chicken going.'

'Oh really? So how come I gave birth without any pain relief after you'd told me I'd be screaming in agony like you were?'

'That's a completely different thing,' Georgina said. 'That's about pain threshold.'

'Ah, get stuffed, Georgina. You just change facts to suit yourself.'

'Well I think most people would agree that screaming with the pain of childbirth is more comprehendible than screaming at an old punch bag, actually.'

I could sense that both Nige and Peter were becoming more uncomfortable as the tension between us grew.

'Tell me about the Police Officer,' Nige said. 'Was he nice?'

'Nadine thinks so, she has a date with him,' I said.

'Ooh have you? I like a man in uniform,' Nige said.

'He doesn't work with wires though,' Nadine said sadly. 'So he can't be 'the one'.'

Nige looked puzzled and I explained to him that she'd been told by Maureen that the man she was destined to be with worked with wires.

'Wires? What, like he makes coat hangers in a factory or something?'

'We're not going to live this one down, are we?' Lorraine said as the topic of conversation changed to Maureen's predictions and Peter left to return to work.

'No,' I said. 'They'll go on about this forever.'

I turned my attention to a smartly-dressed middle-aged man who was browsing at our herbal remedies shelves.

'Do you need any help there?' I asked.

He turned and smiled, his eyes twinkling from behind his spectacles.

'I am admiring your selection of herbal tinctures and natural remedies,' he said.

He had a soft, soothing voice and spoke with an accent that I did not recognise.

'You have a very impressive range of products.'

He was one of those people who have a presence that draws you to them.

I thought perhaps he was Scandinavian and had arrived by ferry at North Shields. We often had visitors passing through on their way to Newcastle before travelling further north into Northumberland and then up to Scotland.

He seemed to be genuinely interested in our shop, asking questions and talking about different products and I happily chatted to him, telling him of my favourite range of products from Jan de Vries.

Lorraine joined the conversation and showed him our range of books, pointing out those written by Jan de Vries and enthusing about what a knowledgeable and enlightened author he was.

'What a lovely man,' I said when he'd left.

'Very,' Lorraine said. 'Isn't it strange how some people seem to make you feel better just by being in their presence? As though they are radiating some sort of positive energy.'

'And some are quite the opposite,' I said as I saw Val huffing and puffing up the bank towards the shop.

Lorraine and I jostled with each other, trying to get from behind the counter to the office, but she escaped first and I was left to serve Val.

'Hello Val, how are you?' I stupidly asked.

As Val began to relate her tales of woe, I pulled out a seat from beneath the counter and sat down. I flicked through the latest Health Trade Retailer magazine, nodding and agreeing periodically as she spoke. I knew it was very rude of me but honestly, once Val started I could have stripped naked and danced on the counter and she would have carried on, unaware.

I continued nodding and agreeing, to make her think I was paying attention as I flicked through the magazine. I noticed an article about the coming Health Trade Fair in Brighton, the one Jim had mentioned to us ages ago.

Bugger, I thought. I'd forgotten all about it. We were supposed to ring the hotel to book one of their special deals. They'd be all booked up by now.

'…and I've got a blister on my toe,' Val finished with a flourish.

'Oh,' I said.

I was long past being able to summon up any false sympathy for Val and sometimes thought that the less response she got the more quickly she became bored with her own complaints and left.

'Actually,' she said. 'That's why I've come in. To see if you have a plaster to put on my toe.'

'Sorry Val, we don't sell them.'

'I know you don't sell them, but surely you have one in your first aid box, I'll just have one of those.'

She sat herself down with a thud on the chair we kept near the counter for frail and elderly customers and I grudgingly went into the office to get her a plaster.

Lorraine was hiding in there and had heard the conversation.

'What a cheek!' she said. 'Tell her to get lost.'

'Tell her yourself,' I said and I handed Lorraine the plaster. I put my head around the office door.

'Just slip your sock off, Val,' I said. 'Lorraine's coming to put it on for you.'

CHAPTER THIRTY

'That was a dirty trick you played on me,' Lorraine said later as we rode the Metro into Newcastle.

'I thought it was funny, especially when she asked you to cut her toenails while you were down there because she couldn't reach them!'

'Ugh, don't remind me,' Lorraine said.

'And then when you told her cutting toenails in a food shop was prohibited by Health and Safety regulations, she believed you,' I laughed.

'Well I'm sure it is prohibited. Can you imagine finding one of Val's toenails in your egg mayo?'

The Metro slowed to a halt and after being told to mind the doors please, we stepped out of the carriage and joined the crowd of people pushing their way onto the long escalator that took us up to the Haymarket.

The town was busy, full of workers making their way home, revellers arriving early to start on a famous Newcastle night out, and late night shoppers.

We turned onto Northumberland Street, passing up the offer of end-of-day blooms from the flower seller and leaving the scent of Bimbi's fish and chips behind us.

We crossed the road, taking a short cut through the church grounds and made our way to the Civic Centre.

We walked around to the entrance opposite the university and followed the signs to the hall.

Inside, rows of chairs faced a low raised platform where I assumed Jan de Vries would stand to give his talk. Many people were already seated, and many others mingled at the back of the hall where a range of books and products were offered for sale.

I found a couple of books I didn't have in my collection, and as I was paying for them I heard a familiar voice.

'Well hello you two! Didn't know you were coming tonight.'

'Hello Georgina,' I said. 'We just got the tickets yesterday, bit of a last minute decision.'

She hugged first me and then Lorraine.

'Me too. I heard a feature on Radio Newcastle and decided to come.'

'What's happening over there?' Lorraine asked.

At the other side of the hall a crowd of people waited near a table.

'It's him, Jan de Vries, he's signing books,' Georgina said. 'Why don't you go over and have yours signed?'

'Ooh yes, I will,' I said excitedly.

'Wait for me,' Lorraine said. 'I'll just buy a book so I can get it signed too.'

By the time she had chosen and paid for a book, the crowd had dispersed and only a couple of women stood waiting, books in hand.

'Lorraine, look!' I said as I saw the man sitting at the table. 'Have you seen who it is?'

'Oh no!' Lorraine said and we laughed in embarrassment.

'We only talked at him for half an hour telling him how good his own products were!' I said.

We said hello to Jan de Vries and of course he remembered us from earlier in the day. We explained that although we loved his writing and his products we'd never actually seen a photograph of him and had not realised that we were telling him all about his own books and products.

He was charming. He laughed with us and said he was pleased that we rated his books and remedies so highly and thanked us for stocking them and for being so knowledgeable about them.

'Such a lovely man,' Lorraine said as we joined Georgina who had found three vacant seats near the front and had spread herself over them to save them for us. We told her he'd been in the shop that day and about the conversation we'd had with him.

'I believe he has links with a health clinic near the High Street. He must have heard how amazing your shop is and paid a visit to check it out,' she said with a wink.

I knew she was teasing but I didn't care. I was just so happy that the man himself had been to our beloved little shop.

The talk was fascinating. We learned lots of things about keeping healthy and treating ailments naturally by including, and sometimes avoiding, certain foods and by using herbal teas and tinctures. We were so engrossed that the time flew by and before we knew it, it was time for the question and answer session and then it was over.

Jan de Vries wished us all health and happiness and then stood by the door to thank each person personally as they left. He shook hands with Lorraine and I and wished us well with the shop and we left buzzing with enthusiasm for our health business.

Not long afterwards, we were visited at the shop by a local doctor who was a great friend of Jan de Vries. He said he had come to look at our range of foods and products so that he could recommend them to his patients.

He had a very different outlook to old Doctor Pattingale, with whom Lorraine and I were registered, and who had attended to us since birth. I avoided visiting him unless absolutely necessary since I'd been to see him for advice about severe period pains when I was about fourteen and he'd told me in his slow, grating voice:

'The only remedy for that problem, my dear, is to become pregnant or wait for the menopause. Therefore, considering your tender age I suggest you go home and accept your fate without complaint, just as women throughout history have done.'

As I skulked out of the surgery in embarrassment, he'd added the dismissive comment:

'I'm sure it's not half as bad as women would have us believe.'

Doctor Kapoor was very different. He told us he believed that all doctors should be trained in both orthodox and natural medicine, and that many drugs were prescribed unnecessarily.

'Far too many people come to see me and expect me to heal them with some magic pill or other,' he said. 'I tell them, it is your body, your health and you must take responsibility. You think you can eat and drink to excess and never exercise your body then take a drug to put everything right? No, I say. You must change your ways. You must look after this amazing creation that is you, and cherish it.'

He looked at our range of stock.

'Echinacea, excellent. Black Cohosh. Ginkgo Biloba. Milk Thistle - wonderful for the liver. Ah, Valerian, such a good tonic for stress and nervous disorders.'

He hurried around the shop, hurriedly making notes in the back of a small notebook he took from his pocket.

After his visit we often had customers who would come in with the name of a product written on a scrap of paper, informing us that Dr Kapoor had sent them with a 'prescription.' It seemed that he gave his patients a choice of treatments and many chose to come to us for herbal products and also to stock up on natural foods that had been recommended for their condition. We gave him a pile of our business cards to give to his patients after writing his 'prescription' on the back.

It was a great boon for our business to be recommended by a popular local doctor, especially as he regularly appeared on local radio talking about health and often mentioning our shop and giving our location.

Lorraine and I often wondered if Jan de Vries had recommended us to him, and thought perhaps if we'd recognised the great man in the shop that day, perhaps the conversation would have been different, and may not have incited the same series of events. Who knew?

I still have my books by Jan de Vries and refer to them regularly.

Years later, I watched him on a morning television programme where he had a regular slot discussing natural health issues with Gloria Hunniford and even through the screen, his presence and warmth shone.

CHAPTER THIRTY-ONE

'I really enjoyed the talk last night,' I said as I shredded lettuce.

Lorraine was whizzing up a batch of hummus in the food blender and Nadine was putting the fresh bread delivery onto the shelves behind the counter.

'Me too,' Lorraine said. 'Jan de Vries was brilliant. Fascinating talk.'

'I wish I'd gone with you now,' Nadine said. 'Sounds like I missed out.'

'It was really interesting,' Lorraine said. 'And it was nice to get together with like-minded people. You know, ones who don't look at you as though you were an alien when you say you have a health food shop.'

'I've been thinking of going to those meetings Georgina goes to, you know, The Inspiration Group or something it's called,' I said.

'Me too,' Nadine said. 'Apparently there was a real Buddhist monk from Tibet giving a talk last month.'

'I'll go if it's Buddhism, but not if it's one of those bizarre therapies Georgina sometimes goes on about,' Lorraine said.

'They're not really 'bizarre', I said. 'It's just that they're new ideas to us.'

A lot of things that I'd previously ridiculed, I now firmly believed in, so I tried to be open minded about new ideas and practices.

'Look at all the things we're doing now that we would have taken the mick out of a while ago,' I said. 'Using homeopathic medicine, eating tofu, doing yoga…'

'Yeah, but we're not running around the woods naked, pretending we're wolves,' Lorraine said.

'What? Who's been doing that? Georgina?'

'No. Even Georgina drew the line at that one. But it was one of the Inspiration Group's events. They all met at Plessey Woods in the middle of the night a few months ago.'

'And what's that supposed to do for you?' Nadine asked.

'I'm not sure,' Lorraine said. 'Something about connecting with your spirit animal.'

'Blimey, I bet some of them resembled brass monkeys more than wolves,' Nadine said.

'Well I'm happy to give that one a miss,' I said. 'But I wouldn't mind giving the Buddhist one a go, or maybe something else.'

After we'd prepared the sandwich fillings and salads, I took the polish and vacuum cleaner into the therapy room as Maureen was due in at ten thirty.

She was fully booked again. I'd had reservations about allowing a medium to use our therapy room as I thought we'd have objections but she was extremely popular and people came from all over the north to see her.

We did have a customer who carried out a one-woman demonstration outside of the shop one Tuesday afternoon, but we just ignored her. She marched back and forth for a while, carrying a home-made banner that read 'Repent All Ye That Cavort With The Devil', then left when it began to rain. It didn't really worry us that we may have lost her custom as none of us recognised her anyway.

I always liked to make sure the therapy room was sparkling clean and had a scented candle burning and a vase of fresh flowers when it was used. Being such a tiny room, it took minutes to clean, but as I switched off the vacuum cleaner, I recognised the familiar drone of Val's voice so I switched it on again and sat on the therapy couch until I judged she had gone.

Lorraine and I often hid in the back of the shop if we didn't want to deal with a particular customer and would try all sorts of tricks to avoid anyone we didn't want to see.

We often did it with sales reps. As soon as we detected that we were not going to be interested in the products on offer, our trick was to call the other person into the shop then find an excuse to disappear.

'That woman!' Lorraine said when I returned to the shop front after peeping around the door to check that Val had left. 'I'm seriously thinking about banning her from the shop.'

'Who?' I asked innocently.

'That bloody Val. I'm getting so close to telling her she's barred.'

'You can't do that!' I said.

'Oh can't I?'

'What's she done now?'

'Well since I put that plaster on her foot, after you'd so kindly offered on my behalf, she now seems to think I'm her personal nurse.'

'What do you mean?'

'She came in yesterday with some eye drops she wanted me to put in for her, which I agreed to do, even though I didn't want to. She sat in the chair in the front of the shop and as I put the drops in like she'd told me, she screamed like a banshee making an exhibition of herself saying that I'd nearly blinded her.'

'Oh dear.'

'When she'd finished that performance she then brought out an elasticated bandage and instructed me on how to apply it to her knee.'

I laughed as I imagined the scenario. Lorraine didn't laugh with me.

'Of course I did that wrong too,' she said.

'I'm surprised you even tried, I thought you'd tell her to get lost.'

'Yes well that's easier said than done. I was trying to be nice to her.'

I looked at Lorraine and raised my eyebrows and she came clean.

'I had to be nice to her, there were loads of customers in the shop. It would have looked really bad if I'd told her to get lost.'

'So what did she want you to do just now?' I asked.

'Oh she only wants me to go around to her house and wash her head with head-lice shampoo.'

'She's got head lice?' I asked, appalled.

'Apparently so. According to her they're rife at the moment, spreading like wildfire.'

'Ugh,' I said, immediately scratching my head.

'And she said that they're mutating into super-species that are resistant to every chemical on earth and they will breed larger and larger until eventually they are the size of toads, jumping about on your head.

'That sounds a bit far-fetched.'

'Far-fetched? If I didn't know better I'd think she'd been smoking the happy-baccy.'

'Maybe she has if she thinks she has toads jumping about on her head.'

I looked at Lorraine as we both scratched our heads.

'Maybe we should stock up on tea-tree shampoo, just in case there's a grain of truth in her story?' I suggested.

'I'll go and ring Karma and put in an order,' she said.

Later I asked Georgina about the Inspiration Group meetings.

'The meetings are held on the first Tuesday of every month in the Community Centre just off the High Street,' she said. 'I don't go every month, it depends what the event is.'

'What sort of stuff do they do?' Nadine asked.

'All sorts,' Georgina said. 'Presentations about things like natural health and spiritual stuff. Sometimes there are art activities or exercise classes for yoga and Pilates. There was a belly dancing class a while ago, which was fun. And there's a Buddhist monk who visits. He gave a talk on meditation and mindfulness last time. He did a guided meditation, it was brilliant.'

'That sounds good,' I said, and Nadine and Lorraine agreed, enthusiastically. Lorraine looked at the calendar.

'So the next one must be next Tuesday then?'

'Yes but I'm not going to that one,' Georgina said. 'It's about angels.'

'That sounds interesting,' I said.

I'd always believed in angels since I was a little girl.

'I love angels.'

'So do I, to hang on my Christmas tree,' Georgina said. 'But this is a woman who claims she can communicate with angels.'

'Ooh I think I might go to that,' Nadine said. 'I talk to angels all the time.'

'I'll come with you,' I said. 'It sounds great.'

Georgina tutted and shook her head.

'Well, I'm not going,' she said.

'Why don't you want to go?' I asked her.

'I just can't bring myself to believe that there are invisible winged beings sitting on clouds waiting around for an earthling to request their help.'

'I don't think it works quite like that,' I said.

'So how does it work then?'

'I've no idea,' I said. 'It's just something I've always believed in. Whenever I ask an angel for help, I always get it.'

'What sort of help?'

'All kinds of things. Finding something I've lost or suddenly finding the solution to a problem…Or when one of my cats is missing and returns safely…just little things like that.'

'And you accredit that to an angel answering your request? Not to some other explanation, such as remembering where you left something, or the cat wandering home because he's hungry?'

Georgina had a way of making me feel a bit ridiculous sometimes.

'Well, yes I do,' I admitted.

'So do I,' Nadine said. 'And I look for white feathers.'

'Yeah, so do I,' I said, glad that Nadine was admitting to this too. 'White feathers are a message from an angel.'

'And not from a bird?'

'Well they might be from a bird, I'm not saying they are like from an angel wing or anything…' I said, trying to explain something that I had no explanation for.

'Where the feathers are from is irrelevant. The angels place them there for you to see,' Nadine said.

'Right. So when they're not sitting on a cloud plucking a harp, they're plucking birds and dropping feathers about as 'signs'.

'Well, sort of,' Nadine said.

'Stop taking the mick Georgina, you believe in loads of things that people could find ridiculous,' I said.

'It's just this whole concept of invisible celestial beings floating about on clouds with nothing else to do but wait for requests. I just can't bring myself to believe any of it.'

'Well I do and I'm going,' Nadine said.

'And so am I,' I said.

CHAPTER THIRTY-TWO

The invasion of the killer head lice was serious enough to make the local news.

Apparently schools in the area had seen a huge increase in the number of pupils with infestations and scientists were warning that the over-use of chemical treatments had indeed caused a new breed of super-resistant lice, although there was no mention of them being toad-sized.

There were also concerns about exposing children to potentially toxic treatments. The general advice was to avoid insecticides where possible, using instead olive or almond oil to coat the hair, then a fine-toothed comb to remove eggs and adult lice. The hair should be then shampooed to remove the oil. This was to be repeated daily until it was certain that the hair was clear, as missing just a few could set off a new infestation.

We stocked up on natural shampoos and conditioners and also olive and almond oil. We also ordered extra quantities of tea tree, lavender and neem essential oils which could be combined with the chosen base oil to act as a preventative.

'I itch every time I think about it,' Nadine said, as she unpacked a box of tea tree and neem shampoos and conditioners. She put down the bottles so that she could rake through her hair, scratching her scalp viciously.

'I mean, how do you know if you have them?'

'Haven't you ever had them before?' I asked. Nadine looked at me as though I'd asked if she'd ever murdered her granny.

'No I haven't,' she said adamantly. 'Have you?'

'Yes,' I said and Nadine looked at me in horror as she took a step back.

'Not now! I mean when I was at school. Well I don't think I've got them now,' I said although I was beginning to wonder. I seemed to be scratching a lot.

'Don't look like that,' I said. 'Lots of kids get them. It doesn't mean you're dirty, anyone can catch them.'

Lorraine joined us as we stood scratching and scouring at our heads.

'I'm just saying to Nadine, I had head lice when we were young.'

'Ugh, yeah,' Lorraine said. 'I remember our Mam used to check our hair every week, and then this one time, she found one on you and spent all night combing our hair with vinegar.'

The three of us were scratching now. 'And then she cut all our hair off, do you remember?'

'Yeah,' I laughed. 'It was so obvious, going into to school with your hair chopped short. Mind you, loads of the girls were the same. Everyone knew who'd had head lice because they came to school with their hair cut up to their ears!'

'At least she didn't shave our heads, that's what used to happen to the boys,' Lorraine said.

Nadine looked absolutely repulsed. Lorraine laughed at her.

'It's not that bad, loads of kids get them,' she said.

'I've told her that,' I said, but Nadine was horrified.

'What do they look like? Have I got them? How can I tell?' she asked, then screamed as a fly buzzed past her head.

Lorraine and I laughed loudly.

'Don't be so daft,' Lorraine said. 'That's a fly. Head lice are much smaller than that.'

She picked up a bag of sesame seeds.

'They're about the size of these seeds.'

Nadine shuddered.

'I'll never eat those again,' she vowed.

'And they tend to take on the colour of the hair,' Lorraine continued.

'So if I have them they'll be blond with grey legs and a black stripe down their backs?' Nadine said.

Lorraine and I laughed thinking she was joking but quickly stopped when we realised she wasn't. She was really anxious and looked close to tears.

'I'll check your hair for you if you like,' I said. 'Don't worry, I'm sure you'll be clear. It's just all the talk making us itch.'

'I'm going to fill a spray bottle with water and add some tea tree oil then we can spray our hair with it through the day to make sure we don't catch any from the customers,' she said. 'We need to warn people. We all need to stick together and fight this.'

'It's just a few head lice not the bliddy Zombie Apocalypse,' Lorraine said.

'I think we should do a window display too. The children have just gone back to school so it would be a good time for parents to check their heads,' I said.

'I'd like to do that,' Nadine said. 'Is that ok?'

She looked at me but I didn't answer.

'Chris?'

I usually changed the displays each month, I loved doing it. I would spend ages collecting things to use and planning out my designs.

If I say it myself, my window displays were spectacular.

One of my winter displays was a huge snowman made from pieces of polystyrene packaging, complete with hat and scarf and a real carrot nose. I cut hundreds of snowflakes from white paper and hung them from threads from the ceiling above him along with twinkling white fairy lights to make him look like he was in a snowstorm. On the shelves behind him I displayed all our cold and flu remedies, vitamin C, zinc, Echinacea and a selection of warming essential oils and bath oils.

Sometimes I'd display foods and recipes from a particular country, using props and artefacts to complete the look.

I designed displays for Vegetarian Week, Valentine Day, Halloween…anything I could link a display to, I did it.

My most famous and most photographed (not that I like to brag) was the one I put together after I'd seen a Teddy Bear shop in the Lake District that had window displays depicting various scenes with teddy bears using scaled down props. I decided to copy the idea and made a teddy version of our shop.

Peter made a miniature wooden counter and shelves, and I spent many happy hours filling and labelling tiny jars with herbs and spices, and making little versions of our packs of lentils, beans and dried fruits to fill the shelves. Peter and I even made tiny boxes of herb teas, veggie-sausage mix and cereals, copying the designs on the packs.

It became quite addictive to see how many of the shops features we could replicate in miniature; crates of 'organic' vegetables, a basket of eggs, loaves of bread, a pile of brown paper grocery bags – we even had a tiny version of Nadine's brush that she used to sweep the shop floor. Two teddies were customers, and a rabbit dressed in a Nutmeg apron stood behind the counter.

The local children loved it. They would stop to look on the way home from school and so I would add or move things, or change the position of the 'customers' to see if they would notice.

'Of course you can do a window display if you want to, can't she Chris?' Lorraine said.

To be honest, it was a bit of a struggle for me to agree to someone else designing a display and I did toy with the idea of refusing, but not wishing to look churlish I reluctantly agreed.

'Yeah, I suppose so,' I said ungraciously. 'But make sure it's up to our usual standard. And it will have to come out at the beginning of November for the Christmas display.'

Lorraine and I served customers and priced new stock while Nadine climbed into the huge window space behind the shelves to assemble her display. She sang to her herself as she worked, calling out from time to time for us to pass her a pair of scissors or the sticky tape or some other requisite.

'It's after two,' I told her. 'Time you were going.'

'I'll just finish this,' she said. 'I just need to stick up my poster then I'm done.' A couple of minutes later she squeezed past the shelving unit looking very pleased with herself.

'Right,' she said. 'I want you to go outside and have a look. You can tell me what you think.'

Lorraine and I left the shop and walked to the front window. Nadine peered over the shelves watching us from inside, waiting for a reaction. Aware that she was watching, Lorraine smiled widely whilst muttering 'Oh my word.'

I too grinned inanely as I looked at the neatly arrayed bottles with a huge hand written sign above them reading:

'GET YOUR DICKIE SHAMPOO HERE.'

CHAPTER THIRTY-THREE

It was that lovely time in early autumn when the nights are starting to draw in but the weather is still mild enough to enjoy being out of doors.

I love autumn. I love the abundance of fresh ingredients it brings, pumpkins, apples, pears and berries and I relish stocking up my freezer and cupboards with home-made soups, jams and chutneys.

Trees begin to let go of their leaves, dropping wisps of orange and gold that flutter to the ground, sunlight becomes more golden and the air cooler, perfect for long invigorating walks. Thoughts of Christmas begin to stir, and cosy nights in near the fire are still new and attractive.

I was looking forward to the Inspiration Group meeting. Nadine and I had talked Lorraine into coming with us but Georgina would not change her mind.

It was bright but raining as we walked through the park to the Community Centre. Gentle rain that heightened the aroma of damp earth and leaves. A bonfire was burning near the park keeper's hut, filling the air with a smoky fragrance and a huge rainbow stretched across the sky.

'I'm really looking forward to this,' Nadine said. 'I hope it's good.'

'Me too,' I said.

Lorraine didn't look so sure.

'I just hope it's going to be straightforward and not ridiculous,' she said.

'Ridiculous?' Nadine said. 'Angels aren't ridiculous,'

'Some of the people at these sort of meetings are though.'

'That's a bit sweeping,' I said.

'You know what I mean,' Lorraine said. 'There's a line between having an open mind and being so gullible that you believe everything you're told.'

At the community centre, a woman dressed in what looked like a vividly patterned duvet cover greeted us with a welcoming, if somewhat toothy, smile. She introduced herself as Manda and told us that the aim of the group was to bring inspiration and light to as many people as possible. She threw her hands about as she spoke, giving off clouds of patchouli and causing the rows of bangles on her wrists to clatter as the colourful sleeves of her kaftan flapped wildly.

'What we want is to bring like-minded people together in a safe environment where we can indulge in our beliefs without scepticism or ridicule,' she gushed.

'Maybe you should just leave now,' I whispered to Lorraine.

Lorraine looked cynical but managed to force a smile as Manda directed us to a nearby table where drinks were being served.

'Help yourself to refreshments, my friends, then make your way into the main hall.'

She gave us another tombstone smile, before turning to enthusiastically greet the next arrivals.

Lorraine opened her mouth to speak.

'Shush,' I said. 'She was very nice.'

'What makes you think I was going say anything derogatory?'

'We know what you're like,' Nadine said as we picked up cups and read the labels on the large thermos jugs.

I was dying for a cup of straightforward, no-nonsense builder's tea but as there was none on offer I plumped for green tea. Nadine chose peppermint and Lorraine grumbled a bit that there was no 'proper coffee' and made do with a chicory and hazelnut substitute.

'There are not many people here,' I said

'I'm surprised that there are men here,' Nadine said. 'I thought it would be all women.'

'Actually most of the people here look quite normal,' Lorraine said, surprised.

Next to the refreshment table was a display of books and items for sale with a sign stating that a percentage of the profits would be donated to the Children's Department at the Freeman Hospital.

'I'll have to buy something, it's for charity,' I said, examining crystal angel keyrings and jewellery.

'As if we ever needed a reason to spend!' Lorraine said.

We chose a different book each with the intention of swapping when we'd read them, and we also bought keyrings and tiny angel lapel pins.

The meeting was being held in an adjacent room and as we walked in, I was disappointed to see the circular arrangement of chairs. I was hoping to hide at the back in case I got the giggles.

We found seats next to a couple of women who I recognised as customers, and after the usual obligatory comments about the weather the older woman, Elaine, said,

'I must congratulate you on your window display, it's wonderful.'

'The scented-candle one?' I asked, referring to a selection of new candles and oil burners I'd arranged in the small side-window.'

'No, the head lice one. It's brilliant. How we laughed! Didn't we Margaret?'

'Oh yes, we loved it!' Margaret agreed.

'Really?' I asked and Nadine beamed.

'That's one of my designs,' she said proudly.

'It's great. It eliminates any shame people may feel about having head lice. After all, anyone can catch head lice,' Elaine said.

'You mean dickies Elaine, ha ha,' Margaret said.

'Yes, ha ha, dickies,' Elaine said.

'Dickies? Oh yes, you mean the poster?' I said.

'Such a good old Geordie word, hadn't heard it since I was at school! Dickies!' said Margaret.

'I love the way you used the word 'dickies' to conjure a feel of childhood nostalgia and also to show a sense of humour,' Elaine said to Nadine.

'Dickies?' Nadine said. 'I thought that's what everyone called head lice.'

'Ha ha, you're so funny!' Margaret said. 'Dickies!'

'Dickies, hee hee' Elaine laughed.

I wondered how many more times we could say 'dickies' and still find it amusing.

'Dickies! Ha, ha,' Lorraine said. 'It does sound funny.'

Blimey, even Lorraine was joining in now.

Fortunately, it was time for the meeting to begin so the word was temporarily forgotten although as I tried to discretely scratch my head, I noticed the others doing the same.

There were about thirty people seated in the circle, the odd empty chair had been used to hold discarded coats.

207

The 'Angel Lady', who was appropriately named Joy, began the meeting with a short talk about the role of angels as messengers and protectors in many different religions. She described how she connected and communicated with angels and told us that we too could do this to enrich our lives. She was very pragmatic and believable and I became totally engrossed.

I can't ever remember being told I had a guardian angel, I'd always just felt that I had. When I was a little girl I'd ask my angel for help - usually for the starving children in Africa who would be glad of the dinners I left uneaten, and for mistreated animals that I'd cry over.

I still talked to angels and asked for help although the conversations had lost the reverence of my younger self and were more familiar, as though having a chat with an old friend. For obvious reasons, this was something I tended to keep to myself, but now Joy made me feel as though this was a normal part of life and I felt maybe it wasn't something to feel silly about after all.

She spoke with humour and enthusiasm, amusing us with stories of her experiences and the time flew by.

There was a break for refreshments and Nadine and I were buzzing as Manda directed us to a queue for herbal teas and flapjacks

'I'm really enjoying this, what a lovely speaker,' Nadine said.

'Me too,' I said. 'I'm going to buy the rest of her books so I have my own copies. I can't wait to read them now.'

Lorraine showed less enthusiasm.

'I'm keeping an open mind,' she said.

Margaret and Elaine had loved it too.

'I've heard Joy speak here before,' Elaine said. 'She's so down-to-earth. Some of these speakers can be a bit unconventional, shall we say.'

'Happy-clappy people, I call them,' Margaret said. 'Some of them are not on this planet.'

'That's what we were concerned about,' I said. 'We thought it might be a bit weird but as you say, she's very credible.'

'Are all the meetings as good as this?' Nadine asked.

'Mostly,' Margaret said. 'Although there have been a few peculiar ones. I suppose it just depends on what you like.'

We made our way back to our seats, carrying hot drinks and plates of flapjacks.

'We came to a talk about pixies a while back,' Elaine said. 'We'd previously been to a talk about the Cottingley Fairies, you know, about the two young girls in the nineteen-twenties who managed to convince a lot of people that they'd photographed real fairies?'

'Oh yes,' I said. 'I know the case you mean.'

'There was a documentary on television about it not long ago,' Nadine said. 'It was fascinating.'

'So was the talk,' Margaret said. 'So when we heard that there was a speaker coming to talk about fairies and pixies we thought it would be similar.'

'And wasn't it?'

'No. It started off ok. The speaker introduced himself and the first thing he said was that there was a lot of confusion as to what was folklore and what were facts. He said he wanted to 'keep it real' and if we had come to hear a lot of silly nonsense about fairies and pixies we would be disappointed.'

She looked at Elaine and they both laughed as they remembered.

'So did he 'keep it real'?' Lorraine asked.

'He said his first encounter with a pixie was in Devon in the 1960s. He was walking by a stream and saw the little fellow fishing.'

'From what I've heard lots of people saw strange things in the sixties!' Lorraine said.

'Apparently, no self-respecting pixie should ever be so careless as to be discovered by a human and the poor pixie was so dismayed at being discovered that he offered him a handmade pixie suit.'

'So he definitely 'kept it real' then!' I said.

'It gets better,' Margaret said. 'He then left the room to put on that very pixie suit and after we'd waited for ten minutes in anticipation, he returned wearing his pants and vest. Oh, and his socks.'

'He didn't!' I said as we all laughed.

'He did,' Elaine said. 'It was hysterical. You could see everyone was trying not to laugh.'

'So he was making out that his underwear had been hand made by a pixie?' Nadine asked.

'No. He reckoned he was wearing the pixie suit but it was invisible so only he could see it!'

We all laughed and I was relieved that Margaret and Elaine felt the same as I did.

'I'm so glad it's not like that tonight,' I said to Lorraine.

'Well some would say it is,' Lorraine said. 'It just depends on your beliefs. I mean, you're laughing at a man who believes he was given an invisible suit by a pixie, and yet believe that there is an angel specially assigned to your life who helps whenever you ask.'

'So you think the idea of the existence of angels is as ridiculous as a belief in pixies hand-making invisible clothing?'

'No, I'm not saying that. I just mean we are all guilty of ridiculing the things other people believe in, yet most of us have faith in something or other that can't be fully explained.'

'Hmm. I see what you're getting at,' I said. 'Whether it's the existence of God, or of alien life or even something simple such as lucky symbols and rituals I guess we all have our levels of belief.'

'Exactly. Although I have to say angelic existence sounds so much more plausible to me than a man in an invisible pixie suit.'

'Well I think it sounds really interesting,' Nadine said. 'I'd loved to have seen it.' Lorraine and I turned to look at her, questioningly.

'The invisible pixie suit,' she said. 'I wish I'd been to the meeting. I wonder what it looked like.'

The second half of the talk included a guided meditation by Joy who asked us to request a sign from the angels as a confirmation of their presence. She said we would feel this as a light breeze or a gentle touch on our face.

'I felt it, I swear I did!' I said afterwards. 'I felt something light like a feather brush my face.'

'Me too,' Nadine said, excitedly. She turned to Lorraine. 'Didn't you feel anything?'

Lorraine was giving nothing away.

'The breeze is from the window,' she said. 'And Joy probably paid someone to run about with a feather on a long stick!' she said.

'Is that not ridiculing our beliefs?' I said, as we all laughed at the thought of it.

'I just said we're all guilty of ridiculing other people's beliefs, I didn't say I was going to stop ridiculing yours!' Lorraine laughed.

'I suppose I'd just love to have proof that angels really do exist,' I said. 'I just really want it all to be true.'

'But that's what faith is all about,' Lorraine said. 'Belief without proof.'

'Well I've had proof tonight,' Nadine said. 'An angel brushed my face with a feather from its wing, I know it!'

Lorraine smirked.

'As I said before, there's a fine line between having an open mind and being gullible.'

After the talk, everyone seemed reluctant to leave. Joy stayed to answer questions and people chatted and laughed in groups.

'What a lovely atmosphere there is here,' Nadine said.

'I know,' I said. 'Everyone is so friendly. I think I've spoken to everyone here.'

A few people had recognised us from the shop and had mentioned how they loved what we were doing. Others had said they'd make sure to call in.

I'd met a woman who had published a wholefood cookery book that I intended to buy the next time I was in town, and I'd had an interesting conversation with a couple who ran a community garden for local people to grow and share produce.

Everyone was open and down-to-earth and I'd really enjoyed chatting and meeting new people, although I think it was still a little fanciful for Lorraine.

'Have you enjoyed it?' I asked her.

'Yes, it's been a really good night. Some of it is still a bit far-fetched for me, but I have enjoyed it.'

'It's always a lovely night,' Elaine said. 'I always go home feeling really uplifted after I've been to one of these meetings.'

'That's how I feel,' I said. 'I've loved it.'

'Me too,' Nadine said. 'I'm definitely coming next month.'

'Any idea what's arranged for next time?' Lorraine asked.

'There's a list on the newsletter,' Margaret said. 'Didn't you pick one up at the door?' She pulled a folded sheet of paper from her bag.

'It says 'A talk and slide show by the celebrated artist Haruto Matsumoto, whose works in oils and acrylics explore the theme of the dragon. Prints and greetings cards featuring his work will be on sale.'

'I'm up for that,' Nadine said. 'Fancy it?'

'Yes, I'll come with you,' I said.

Lorraine too said that she would come along.

'What about you two?' I asked Elaine and Margaret. 'Will you be coming?'

I was hoping we could meet up with them again. It would be nice to have a down-to-earth, level-headed group to attend and discuss the sessions with.

'Sounds good,' Elaine said. 'What about you Margaret? I know how you love anything to do with dragons.'

'I'll certainly come along,' Margaret said. 'I just hope it's a good sensible session. I do love anything to do with dragons and I'd hate it to be spoilt by happy-clappy types.'

She leaned towards us and said gravely,

'I have an affinity with dragons, you see, because I was sacrificed to the Dragon of Prosperity in a previous life.'

CHAPTER THIRTY-FOUR

'But, I mean, dragons aren't real,' I said.

'Oh, is she still going on about that!' Lorraine said to Nadine as they lifted the trays containing the morning's fresh bread onto the counter.

Nadine was as perplexed about Margaret's comment as I was.

'I think they must be real. If Margaret was sacrificed to one then they must have existed.' Nadine said.

I emptied bags of coins into the till as Lorraine and Nadine filled the bread shelves.

'But they didn't,' I said. 'We know they didn't.'

'How do you know?'

I shrugged.

'There would be evidence of them having existed.'

'Maybe she meant in another dimension or space,' Nadine said.

'Oh for God's sake,' Lorraine said. 'You two are off your trollies.'

'I'm just trying to look at it with an open-mind,' I said.

'Well don't bother,' Lorraine said. 'She's as balmy as that speaker she was telling us about and so are you if you believe her.'

'You don't need to be so judgemental,' I said.

'Well, honestly. Human sacrifices to dragons and invisible pixie suits. Please!'

'Well it all just confuses me,' I said. 'Angels, pixies, fairies...now dragons. Just what are we supposed to believe in?'

'You can believe in whatever you like. I just wish you'd stop going on about it.'

'Well I believe in dragons now,' Nadine said, at which Lorraine snorted.

'You believe anything anyone tells you!' she said.

'And you believe nothing!' I said, defending Nadine.

'At least we both have an opinion,' Lorraine said. 'You just dither about not knowing what to believe in and boring everyone to death with other people's silly theories.'

Nadine, sensing that one of our explosive rows was brewing said suddenly:

'I'm thinking about getting married.'

Lorraine and I turned to her in surprise.

'Wow! I didn't know you and Brian were that serious,' Lorraine said.

'We're not. I'm just sort of thinking about it…'

I laughed realising that she'd said the first thing that came into her head to avoid one of the rare but fiery arguments that she hated.

'In another dimension or space?' I asked and she laughed, knowing I'd caught her out.

Lorraine climbed onto the window ledge to pull up the huge blinds that covered the shop windows.

'Time to leave the Twilight Zone and return to the real world,' she said, and I turned the sign on the door to 'open' to start our day.

Georgina arrived with Nige in tow. I hoped she wouldn't ask about the Inspiration Group meeting as it would be sure to re-start an argument so I kept the conversation away from angels, fairies, pixies, and dragons and instead asked Nige when he was going to have a reading with Maureen.

'You've been saying for ages you want to have one,' Lorraine said.

'Yeah I know but I missed the free ones,' he said.

'You're such a tightarse,' Georgina said. 'If you want a reading, just book one.'

It was true that Nige didn't like spending money. He rarely if ever bought anything from us and he was always complaining about the cost of things.

'How much will she charge?' he grumbled.

'Look, she's in tomorrow, her last appointment is three-thirty, why don't I ask if she can see you at four-thirty and see if she'll give you a discount.'

'Ok,' Nige said ungraciously. 'I hope it's worth it.'

'Hey, we're not forcing you,' I said.

'No, I know, I know. I'll do it.'

Later that morning we had a visit from Jim Dixon.

'Will I be seeing you both next week in Brighton?' he asked.

'To be honest Jim, we'd forgotten about it,' I said. 'I did mean to ring but kept getting distracted, do you think it's too late now?'

'You'll get tickets for the show but I don't know about accommodation. The special price rooms will be gone and as well as the Health Fair there's a big political conference and an international rugby match so a lot of places will be fully booked. I'd still give it a try though, but don't leave it any longer.'

'We'll get onto it after lunch,' Lorraine said.

Tasks like booking a hotel were more time consuming in the days before the internet.

'How do we find a hotel in Brighton?' Lorraine said. 'Where do we start?'

'Why don't we nip to the travel agents up the bank and see if they can help?' I suggested. 'You go if you like, I'll watch the shop.'

Lorraine was away ages and the shop was quite busy so I was glad when she eventually returned.

'Any luck?' I asked. She shook her head. 'They only deal with the big hotels, they had no information about smaller independent places or bed and breakfasts. Everywhere they tried was fully booked.'

'So what now?'

'They suggested ringing the Brighton Tourist Office, they looked up the number for me. I'll get straight onto it if that's ok.'

'Yeah. Put the kettle on before you start, it's been really busy in here, I'm parched.'

The Brighton Tourist Office said they would fax through a list of local hotels, so as we didn't have a fax machine, Lorraine ran down the bank to the printers to ask if they could send it there, ran back to the shop to telephone the Tourist Office with the number and then ran back to the printers to wait for the fax. She returned with the list and went into the office to start making calls.

'I think I've tried every hotel in the whole of Brighton,' she said half an hour later. 'Everywhere is full. Shall we just give up?'

'No, keep trying,' I said. 'I'm really keen to go now.'

I took the sheets of paper from her and looked down the hotels advertised. They had all been crossed out in black biro as she'd worked her way down the list.

'What about these numbers at the bottom under B and Bs? Have you tried those?'

She went back into the office to try again while I stayed in the shop front, serving late customers calling in on their way home from work, and tidying the shop.

I had cleaned the kitchen and was sweeping the shop floor when I heard her call to me.

'Chris, there's a place here with a twin room available, shall I book it? It's a bit of a walk to the Health Fair but we could get a taxi if necessary.'

'Yeah just book it,' I said excitedly.

I had my mind so set on going now that I'd even considered looking for a campsite and borrowing a tent.

I heard her confirming the booking then she came through to the shop front.

'Done!' she said. 'It's a Bed and Breakfast place. They don't do evening meals but that's no problem we can eat out. Too late to send a deposit so we just have to pay the full amount when we get there.'

'Ok,' I said. 'How much?'

'Sixteen pounds.'

'Each? That's reasonable.'

'No that's for the two of us.'

'Sixteen for both of us? You sure?'

'It does sound cheap doesn't it? I wonder if he said sixty and I misheard.'

'Ah well, we'll find out when we get there. At least we're sorted.

The next morning I gave the therapy room a quick clean ready for Maureen and as usual she arrived complaining, this time about the road works further along the road where new houses were being built.

'I've been stuck in that traffic for ages, there's cones everywhere. Why they need so many I don't know.'

'Gawd here she is, the happy medium,' Georgina said.

Maureen ignored her and began carrying her bags containing her props and wig, and of course Billy, into the therapy room.

'Now, before I start, a cup of tea would just go down lovely,' she said. I went to put the kettle on as she unpacked her bag, laying her black wig and her clothes on the therapy couch.

I really don't know why she bothered with the costume and all the drama. Most of her best insights and predictions had come when she'd been out of character having a cup of tea with us before she left. It was during these times that she'd given accurate facts about our Grandad and other family members who had passed on, and had given predictions that had come true.

But as she said, her 'punters' seemed to like the show she put on and she was always very careful not to let them see her without her 'Mariana' get-up. Mind you, they probably wouldn't have recognised her anyway.

I was interest to see what Nige would make of Mariana as he'd only met Maureen.

'Don't forget I'm coming in later for my reading,' he said when he arrived with our mail. 'I hope it's good news that I'll be hearing.'

'What till you see the plight of her,' Georgina began but I interrupted her.

'Don't spoil it for him,' I said.

'Why, what does she wear, like?' Nige asked.

'Wait and see,' I said.

'Really weird stuff,' Georgina said.

'Like you then?' Nige said to her.

'Actually my look is artistic and stylist,' Georgina said, and we all looked at her outfit of black leggings and Doc Martens worn with a vintage men's shirt that was patterned with orange and pink swirls.

'I had a shirt a bit like that in the seventies,' Nige said. 'I used to wear it with a yellow kipper tie.'

'Ha ha, I bet you looked great!' Nadine said as Nige demonstrated his disco dancing skills.

'I bet you didn't,' Georgina said at which Nige took offence.

'Well at least I wore mine in the seventies instead of waiting until it was twenty years out of fashion.'

'I'm wearing mine ironically,' Georgina said.

217

'What's the difference?' Nadine asked. 'I mean, I'm not being funny but how are people supposed to know whether you are just *wearing* it or wearing it ironically?'

'You mean you can't tell?' Georgina said.

'No,' Nige said. 'You just look like you're wearing a naff old shirt to me,' and we all laughed.

'It's vintage,' Georgina said.

'If you have to tell people that you're wearing it ironically, they will just think you're wearing a naff old shirt before you tell them though. Won't they?' Nadine said, confused.

'It's quite simple.' Lorraine said. 'It looks naff until you say 'I'm wearing it ironically' and then it looks stylish.'

'In the same way that an old shirt is just an old shirt unless you tell people it's vintage and then it becomes chic,' Nige said.

'Honestly, you lot are so unenlightened,' Georgina said. 'It's about style and being individual. Putting pieces together to create a boho look.'

'That's where we've gone wrong,' Nige said. 'We've being going for the hobo look.'

Nige returned for his four-thirty appointment with Maureen. Peter arrived soon after and caught me listening at the door.

'Come away from there,' he said. 'It's supposed to be private.'

'I can't hear anything anyway,' I said.

'Who is in there?'

'Nige. He's in there with Maureen, contacting his departed pals and hearing predictions for his future.'

Peter swept the floors and tidied the shelves while I served the last customers of the day. I was writing the day's cheques into the banking book when Nige came out of the therapy room.

'Oh my Lord that was amazing!' he said. 'She was totally transformed, taken over by a spirit. I couldn't believe it was the same woman.'

I laughed to myself thinking how predictable that Nige should be impressed by the drama side of it.

'So what did she tell you?' I asked.

'Loads of stuff,' he said. 'I'd thought twenty pounds was a bit much but actually it was worth every penny.'

'Tell me what she said.'

Nige clapped his hands together with excitement.

'She told me that I worked for the Post Office, I live in a house nearby and I'm not afraid of showing my feminine side.'

'Nige, I could have told you that,' Peter said. 'And I would have done it for a tenner.'

CHAPTER THIRTY-FIVE

We took a taxi into Newcastle, our train was at eleven, and we'd booked early appointments at a chic hair salon, not far from the station.

Lorraine wore a long skirt and jacket in taupe with a cream blouse and I wore a pencil skirt and short fitted jacket in soft grey with a pale pink blouse. We were both impeccably made-up and wore our best jewellery.

'I'm really going to enjoy this,' I said as the taxi dropped us at the salon.

'Me too. We deserve it, we've worked really hard since the shop opened. It's going to be a fab trip.'

The hairdresser cut my hair into layers and styled it into soft curls. When she'd finished she held a mirror behind my head and I smiled with delight. It cost more than I'd ever spent on my hair before, but it looked great and it's not often I can say that.

Lorraine's hair had been shaped at the front to flatter her face and really suited her.

We admired each other, and ourselves, before leaving to walk to the station, our high heels clicking as we pulled along our new wheeled suitcases.

'I feel great,' Lorraine said. 'We should do this more often.'

'You look great,' I said, and she took the cue.

'You look great too.'

At the station we sat outside one of the cafes and drank coffee while we waited for our train. I noticed we were getting quite a few admiring glances from some of the businessmen passing by on the way to their platforms.

'Did you see that man looking at me?' I said to Lorraine. 'It must be my new hair.'

'Fat heed,' Lorraine said, but I could tell that she too was pleased at the attention we were getting.

Our train journey was uneventful. We chatted and relaxed as the window flashed with the colours of the world outside rushing by.

We had a cup of tea and an overpriced sandwich and we read magazines about celebrities I'd never heard of doing things I wasn't interested in.

At King's Cross we took the tube to Victoria.

I was expecting the tube to be like the Metro in Newcastle but it was older, noisier and dirtier. The people were different too.

There was a rush to get onto the train so we stood back and waited, getting on last. As we carried our cases into a carriage, I said hello, giving smiles of acknowledgement to the people close by, but they did not respond.

There were two vacant seats so I took one between a woman clutching a large bag to her chest and a man with a chocolate Labrador at his feet. Lorraine sat further down the carriage next to an elderly man.

'Lovely day,' I said to the woman on my right, and she clutched her bag closer to her chest.

'We're off to Brighton to visit the Health Fair.'

No response.

'I'm saying, we're off to Brighton for a Health Fair.'

The woman shuffled along the seat away from me. I looked at the row of people opposite and smiled but they all seemed to be avoiding eye contact.

The Labrador looked up at me and I leaned to pat his head.

'Georgeous dog,' I said to the man. 'So well behaved too.'

The man pulled the dog away from me but did not speak.

My embarrassment at being ignored somehow made me carry on.

'They're my husband's favourite, chocolate labs.'

Silence.

I looked around the carriage.

'I have two cats at home,' I announced.

The woman with the bag got up and moved to the next carriage. I noticed that the man directly opposite was watching but as soon as I looked at him he averted his eyes.

What was wrong with these people? If this had been the Newcastle Metro there'd have been a full scale discussion in progress by now. Everyone appeared to be shrinking away from me, as much as was possible in these close seats, and no-one appeared to be able to look me in the eye.

I began to wonder if I'd suddenly developed signs of a tropical disease without realising. I smoothed my palm across my face to check, half expecting to feel it covered with bulbous boils but it was as normal.

I kept my head down and looked at the dog for the rest of the journey.

The train from Victoria got in at Brighton at four-fifteen and we left the station and walked towards the seafront, following the directions we'd been given.

Brighton was buzzing with an invigorating energy. I would have loved to have lingered awhile just to soak up the atmosphere and perhaps browse around some of the shops that offered all kinds of art and crafts, jewellery and fashion, but I knew we needed to find our bed and breakfast first before we could explore.

The sky was overcast and the sea grey and hostile, but I was glad of the cool fresh breeze after the stuffy heated air of the train. It was good to stretch my legs and I felt uplifted by both the vibe of the place and the sea air.

We walked along, cases trundling behind us as we passed grand houses with carefully designed gardens, hotels, wine bars and restaurants. We were both hungry and the aromas of cooking food were very tempting.

'I'm starving,' I said as a particularly strong blast of garlic and peppers hit us. 'Shall we stop somewhere to eat?'

'It's still a bit early. It would be nice to have a shower and get changed then come back out,' Lorraine said.

'Yeah, let's do that,' I said. 'We'll make a night of it.'

Frequently we'd stop to view a menu, agreeing to return for our evening meal if it was not too far to walk back.

'We could always get a taxi,' Lorraine suggested after we'd read a particularly delicious menu at a restaurant promising food that would 'nourish the soul'. We kept it in mind, along with several others and continued walking.

We came to The Grand Hotel and stopped to look. The heavy sky gave added drama to the majestic Victorian façade with its tiers of balconies rising into the grey backdrop.

'That's the hotel that was bombed isn't it?' Lorraine said, as we crossed the road towards it, away from the sea.

'Yeah. Nineteen-eighty four I think it was.'

'Such a beautiful building.' As we stood admiring the ornate balconies, the temperature dropped a little and the wind picked up.

'We'd better hurry,' I said. 'I think it's going to rain.'

We picked up our pace and carried on.

Soon we had left the sea behind and were in a more residential area. I'd had enough fresh air now and was beginning to feel cold in my light jacket. It began to drizzle and my shoes were rubbing at my heel.

'I didn't think it was this far,' I complained. 'My feet are starting to hurt. I think I'm getting a blister.'

'My hair will be as flat as a fart with this damp,' Lorraine said.

'Mine will start to frizz.'

'I've got a brolly in my bag.'

We stopped to put up her umbrella but it was difficult to hold it in a position that gave shelter to us both. Our cases and handbags were cumbersome and we battled on, bumping against each other as we struggled to stay beneath the cover of the umbrella, until passing a corner, a gust of wind blew it inside out, bending the spokes and rendering it useless.

'How much further do you think it is?' I asked. 'We've come miles.'

Lorraine shoved her broken umbrella in a litter bin and we checked the paper with the directions scribbled on it, and saw that we still had quite a distance to go. We hadn't passed a hotel or a restaurant for ages, although there was a run-down pub on every other corner.

'Are we even still in Brighton?' I asked.

'I don't know but I wish we'd got a taxi now.'

There was a sudden loud scraping noise and Lorraine lost her grip on her case and it toppled over onto the pavement, landing in a puddle.

'Shit,' she said. 'I think the wheel's broken.'

We struggled to get it upright and continued our journey carrying her case between us as I pulled my case behind me.

The further we walked, the more run-down our surroundings became; the houses smaller and shabbier, the pavements littered and buildings defaced with graffiti.

My heel was really hurting and felt wet as though it was bleeding, although it could have just been water as I had stumbled through a few puddles. We jostled Lorraine's case between us complaining about the rain and about our ruined hairstyles.

'I can't walk any further,' I said, putting down my end of the suitcase. 'My feet are too sore.'

'Well you'll have to,' Lorraine said snappily. 'Unless you're going to bed down on the pavement for the night.'

I limped along as we argued our way through the streets, checking their names as we passed in hope of seeing the one that would lead us to our bed and breakfast.

'I'm going in here,' I said, as we came to a pub. 'I need to sit down.'

I dropped her case and hobbled towards the run-down Ship Inn. I pushed my way through two sets of doors into a smoke filled lounge, Lorraine grumbling as she followed behind yanking her case with her.

I immediately regretted my rash action as the place suddenly fell silent and several groups of elderly men turned from their pints of beer to look at us. All eyes followed us as we made our way to the bar where we ordered drinks and carried them to a table where we perched on a rather sticky bench.

The men resumed their supping in silence, watching us suspiciously as we gulped a few mouthfuls of wine before leaving our half-full glasses on the table and lugging the cases back out of the door.

'Well that was refreshing – not,' Lorraine said argumentatively. But I was too weary to bite. I was cold, tired, hungry and fed up. All I wanted was to find the house we were staying in and have a hot shower and a cup of tea.

As we turned a corner I pointed to the street name.

'This is it!' I said. 'We're here.'

It was not what I was hoping for. The houses looked neglected, many with discarded furniture and rubbish in the garden, and some were boarded up and vandalised. We carried Lorraine's case, which seemed to get heavier with time, as we made our way along the pavement, stepping over the occasional pile of dog poop and at one point, squeezing by an upturned pram, thankfully devoid of a baby.

We counted the door numbers as we walked, until we finally arrived at our home for the night.

'Oh no. Please tell me this is not the place,' I said.

'It can't be. It's a dump.'

'It doesn't even have a B and B sign.'

'We must have got it wrong.'

I checked the address on the paper for what seemed like the millionth time.

'It is,' I said. 'This is it. This is where we are staying.'

CHAPTER THIRTY-SIX

We walked up the path, over discarded house bricks, pizza boxes and lager cans. A piece of hardboard had been nailed to the door, covering everything including the letterbox. A roughly sawn square hole cut into it allowed access to the Yale keyhole. A hand written notice stapled onto the board, informed us in water-stained letters that we needed to collect the key from the pub we'd just left.

'Oh great. We're going to have to walk back to that horrible pub,' I said.

'You wait here,' Lorraine said. 'I'll go and get the key.'

'You sure?' I asked, and I was relieved when she nodded and set off, as the last thing I wanted to do was to struggle back down the street to face the hostile faces of the drinkers in The Ship Inn.

I balanced Lorraine's broken case against mine and clutched my handbag to my chest as I stood guarding them, although the street was deserted and eerily quiet.

I looked up at the house in which we were to stay the night.

Water trickled from a cracked overhead gutter, forming a spreading pool on the path. Weeds sprouted from crevices in the brickwork and the windows - several cracked and all dirty - were framed by peeling paint.

My heart sank and I wanted to cry. My nose was running and I sniffed as I searched in my bag for a tissue.

The drizzle had penetrated my jacket and blouse, the fabric lay damp against my skin and I could feel that my newly styled hair was now frizzed to twice the size.

I waited, feeling more miserable by the minute as the rain became heavier, and I began to wish I'd made the effort to walk back up the street with Lorraine. I felt very conspicuous, standing alone, soaked to the skin with two suitcases, even though there was no-one in sight.

I heard someone approaching and turned to see Lorraine. As she got closer the rain suddenly put on an extra spurt and by the time she'd run the last few yards, her hair was flat to her head and her make-up in two black streaks beneath her eyes. She held up her hand and I saw a key dangling from her fingers.

'Room number eight,' she said. 'Right at the top, in the attics.'

We looked at each other then moved toward the door. Neither of us spoke until Lorraine, having inserted the key into the lock, turned it and pushed the door open.

'Oh my God,' she said, and one of the tears I'd been holding back escaped, joining the drops of rain on my face, as an odour of rancid cooking oil, mildewed carpets and urine emerged from the house.

'We can't stay here, we can't...' I said, beginning to panic.

Lorraine touched my arm.

'Don't get upset,' she said. 'Let's just go in out of this rain and think about what we're going to do.'

I choked back a sob and we picked up our cases and stepped over the threshold.

A door marked 'kitchen' stood directly to our left, and further down the corridor were three doors with the numbers one, two and three painted on them consecutively.

A flight of stairs lay to our right and taking care not to trip over ripped edges of carpet, we made our way up passing a bathroom on the landing and then rooms four, five and six.

Unfamiliar sounds leached from behind the numbered doors; racing commentary from a radio, voices arguing in a foreign language, a laboured, hacking cough.

We climbed a second flight of stairs up to the attic rooms. At the top side by side, were rooms seven and eight. The ceiling was low and we huddled with our cases on the cramped landing. The sound of a television set at full volume blasted from room seven, the voices distorted and booming.

'Here it is, number eight,' Lorraine said. 'I only have one key, it must open this door as well as the front door.'

'It looks open,' I said, giving it a push, at which it swung open revealing a large but shabbily furnished room.

We staggered in and put down our cases.

'This isn't a Guest House,' Lorraine said. 'It's a dump.'

There were two single beds with mismatched headboards, one with a yellow nylon bedcover and one with blue, set against the wall opposite the fireplace that held an old-fashioned, disconnected gas fire. Next to it, for some unknown reason, stood a rusty coal bucket and companion set.

A huge Victorian chest of drawers, which at one point in its life had probably been highly polished and cherished, stood against the wall nearest the door, its drawers dull and split and riddled with worm holes.

The alcove to the right of the fireplace held a cracked washbasin, and had near it a circular plastic tea trolley – the type that made a brief appearance in the 1970s – holding a kettle and cups.

The alcove on the left housed a monstrous wardrobe.

Odd bits of defective furniture filled the rest of the room and a worn swirly-patterned carpet covered the floor.

'What are we going to do?' I said. 'There's no way we can sleep here.'

'Let's have a cup of tea and decide what to do for the best,' Lorraine said.

I walked to the plastic tea trolley and picked up the kettle that stood on a battered tin tray along with two chipped mugs and a saucer holding a few teabags and sugar sachets. There was no milk.

'Actually, I'll pass on the tea,' I said as removing the lid I saw the furred up element and stale water inside. 'This is awful. Surely people don't really stay here? We wouldn't.'

'I think we may have to,' Lorraine said. 'I don't know where else we can go.'

'We can't stay here, it's minging.'

'There's nowhere else. You know how we struggled to get this booking, everywhere is full.'

I looked at her, slowly absorbing the truth that we were here for the night and that later I would be sleeping in one of those grubby nylon covered beds. My stomach sank and the last remaining drop of enthusiasm and excitement that had filled me earlier dripped away with the drops of rain that were still falling from my hair.

I walked to the attic window and pulled back the torn, yellowed net curtain. Beyond the sash window was a metal staircase, the steps of which were littered with take-away food boxes, leading down to a small damp yard where a group of dustbins stood in the shade of the walls. From this height I could see into the adjacent yards, and beyond to the backs of the houses opposite. I scanned the scene, looking for one redeeming feature amongst the higgledy row of back yards strewn with broken glass and rubble, up to the decaying walls of the facing buildings with their shabby window frames and crumbling chimneys.

My eye caught sight of a plant clinging to a recess created by a missing brick, its delicate white flowers cascading downwards as they moved gently in the breeze. I don't know why but the sight heartened me greatly and I turned to face Lorraine.

'We'll be ok for one night,' I said, and I realised she was just as anxious but was putting a brave face on things, probably to protect me.

'Yeah, we'll be fine,' she said.

'It will be an adventure.'

'Quite funny really.'

'Yes, just wait till we get back and tell the others!'

'They'll die laughing, ha ha!'

'Ha, ha, ha.'

'Ha, ha.'

Our false bravado stopped as abruptly as it had begun as we caught the desperation in each other's eyes and we both sobbed.

'It's awful!'

'I wish we hadn't come!'

'I just want to go home!'

'We'll catch fleas!'

'We'll be murdered in our beds!'

Lorraine handed me a tissue and we blew our noses and calmed ourselves down.

'I'm so cold and wet.' I said.

Oh to be at home in a hot, scented bath with a glass of Merlot and a magazine.

'I'd love a hot bath right now,' I said.

'We can go and check out the bathroom if you like?'

'No. I don't think my nerves are up to it at the minute.'

'Come on let's get out of here,' Lorraine said. 'We don't need to stay here all evening.'

'Yeah. Let's go and find something to eat or a pub to sit in until bedtime or something,' I said.

We pushed our cases behind the second bed, picked up our handbags and still wet and bedraggled, left the house.

CHAPTER THIRTY-SEVEN

'Left or right?' Lorraine asked as we stepped out of the path.
'Left.'

There was no point in turning right and retracing our steps. The restaurants I'd be happy to eat in were miles back towards Brighton, so we walked away from the sea, hoping to find a shopping area with maybe a restaurant or two.

A mist had crept in from the sea obscuring the way ahead and as we walked through the rain each few steps revealed another depressing sight.

An old stained mattress thrown into a garden. An upturned dustbin with its contents spread across the pavement. The remaining shell of a burnt-out car.

After walking for a couple of blocks, we came to a junction, and crossing the road, turned a corner onto a row of shops.

'Not really what I'd hoped for,' Lorraine said.

The first shop was boarded up, the blocked windows covered in graffiti. There followed a betting shop and a discount liquor shop, both grimy and run-down.

An unkempt man carrying a carrier bag of clanking bottles came out of the nearest shop and pushed past us, causing Lorraine to stumble.

'Ignorant auld git,' she said, and I hoped he hadn't heard.

I'd felt uneasy in the deserted street earlier and had hoped to see people about. Now there were more people around I felt increasingly uncomfortable.

A group of young lads, drinking and swearing passed by on the other side of the street. One of them threw a bottle which smashed in the road, and they laughed as I jumped in fright.

Lorraine took my arm and we continued past another empty shop, where a girl sat smoking a joint in the doorway.

'Look, there's a phone box,' I said, as I saw the familiar red shape on the corner, comforting and solid; a recognisable feature in this alien place. 'I'm going to call Peter.'

I hurried over to it, Lorraine following behind.

'I think someone has used this as a toilet,' Lorraine said.

I tried to breathe through my mouth. I dialled my home number and we stood close trying not to touch the walls of the kiosk as I waited for Peter to pick up.

'I'm just going to let him know we've arrived safely. I'm not going to tell him about where we're staying because he'll just worry.'

'I agree,' Lorraine said. 'There's nothing he can do and he'll probably fret all night worrying about you. We can tell him all about it when we get back.'

At the sound of the pips I pushed in my coins and as I did I happened to look up at the wall behind the telephone. Lorraine must have looked at the same time because I heard her gasp of disgust and she squeezed herself closer to me as we looked at the cluster of leaflets advertising sex for sale. Some of the ads were hand written, some printed. Many had photographs and most had details of the services offered, described in coarse language.

'Hello…hello?' Peter's voice questioned, as Lorraine and I stared at the ads, unable to look away, yet not really wanting to read what women were willing to do with strangers for money. I had no idea of what some of the acronyms meant, committing them to memory so that I could ask Lorraine later.

'Peter?'

'Hello, you.'

Two words in Peter's gentle and loving voice. It was enough to tip the balance.

'Peter!' I sobbed. 'It's horrible! It's a doss house…the beds are dirty…there's prostitutes in the phone box…'

'I thought you weren't going to tell him,' Lorraine said, but I was on a roll now.

'The kettle is mouldy…I want to come home…it smells…the beds are manky…'

'Is there a train back to Newcastle tonight? Do you want me to come and get you? I could leave Rosie with your Mam and drive down. If I set off now I should be there at around midnight…'

The concern in his voice brought me to my senses. I sniffed and took a deep breath.

'No, no, sorry, I'm fine, we're fine. I'm just a bit tired…'

'You sure?'

'Yes, sorry. It was just hearing your voice, I'm just missing you so much.'

'Ah,' he said and I could hear the smile in his voice. 'Miss you too, but it's just one night. You'll be back tomorrow.'

I heard Rosie giggling deliciously in the background.

'She's laughing at the cats playing with one of her toys,' Peter told me and I ached to be with them, warm and dry with my little family at home instead of shivering in a pee-reeking phone box where prostitutes touted for business.

After I'd reassured him that we would be fine for the night, I reluctantly hung up and we went back out into the rain.

'Ugh. I feel like I need to jump in a sheep-dip after being in there,' I said.

'Look, there's a takeaway,' Lorraine said. 'Shall we just get a pizza and take it back? I don't think we're going to stumble across a nice little Italian Restaurant, do you?'

We admitted defeat and ordered a pizza to share and two take-away teas.

'I didn't think women really advertised in phone boxes,' I said as we waited for our order.

'Me neither,' Lorraine said. 'I always thought it was just a stupid joke.'

'I've never seen it in Newcastle, have you?'

'Never. Mind, I'm not saying it doesn't go on. They must just advertise in different ways.'

'What sort of men would answer those ads though?' I asked.

Just as I spoke, a thin, balding man in a grubby raincoat entered the shop, eyeing us over as he walked to the counter. Lorraine nudged me and nodded at him and we giggled as we collected our pizza and left.

'At least we've got plenty to tell everyone when we get back,' I said to Lorraine as we left the shop.

I was starting to feel a bit better now. The thought of a hot cup of tea was comforting and the smell of freshly cooked pizza made me realise how hungry I was.

'Look,' Lorraine said. 'Seems we aren't the only ones who don't like those ads.'

A girl stood in the dimly-lit phone box, her hooded coat hiding her face as she ripped down the posters we'd seen earlier. She came out of the kiosk as we passed and looked at Lorraine and me with alarm in her face. I smiled at her, anxious that she should not feel scared by us.

'We saw those earlier,' Lorraine said. 'I'm glad you've taken them down.'

The girl looked relieved.

'Oh, so they're not yours then?' she asked but before we could confirm that they most certainly were not, she said:

'This is my effin area and someone keeps putting their effin numbers up. It's my best box this one, and I'm not letting no-one muscle in on it. And you can spread the word that if Big Ron finds out who's on our patch there'll be effin hell on.'

'Right,' Lorraine said. 'Big Ron. Ok.'

'Good,' the girl said, and she went back to replace the ads with ones of her own.

'Hey!' she shouted after us as we walked on. 'If you want I can introduce you to Big Ron? He's always effin looking for girls.'

'No thanks,' I called back. 'We're just passing through.'

I took Lorraine's arm and we quickened our pace.

'Can you believe that? We've just been offered jobs as prostitutes.'

I balanced on the thin line between hilarity and hysteria. Lorraine looked at me and shook her head. For once she was speechless.

I looked at her rain-soaked face, the stubborn black make-up smears beneath her eyes and her hair looking like the proverbial pancake, flat and drooping over her ears as though casually tossed there. I knew mine would be the opposite, I could feel it, frizzed and voluminous.

'I tell you what. You wouldn't get many calls if I put up a photo of you looking as you do at the moment,' I told her.

'You'd would get loads. That's if there are any depraved men out there with a fetish for Diana Ross dressed as a ghoul,' she said and we fell into excessive laughter that substituted for angst.

Back at the house, Lorraine pointed at a 'No Food Allowed in Rooms' sign pinned near the kitchen door.

'Bugger that,' I said. 'Anyway, there's no-one here to check.'

I started up the first few steps only to stop and descend as we heard heavy footsteps coming down. It was a hefty man in a big overcoat, the smell of which made my nose curl as he came closer.

'Excuse me,' Lorraine said to him and he stopped suddenly, staring out from a mass of grey hair and beard as though he was shocked to have been spoken to. When he didn't speak, Lorraine asked him:

'Would you know if it's ok to take hot food into the rooms?'

He looked at us for a couple of seconds, his bloodshot eyes taking in first Lorraine and then myself.

'YE CAN DAE WHAT THE FOOK YE LIKE,' he bellowed, as he wrenched open the door and slammed it violently behind him, leaving Lorraine and me to scuttle upstairs like two scared mice.

Back upstairs the depressing reality hit us again.

'I sort of thought maybe we'd imagined how bad it was,' I said.

'It's even worse now the sun has gone down,' Lorraine said.

We switched on the bedside lamps. One gave a sickly green light, due to its faded olive coloured shade and the other was missing a light bulb. The attempt to cosy up the room had made it feel gloomier than ever.

The door would not close properly. At some time in the past it had been forced open and the Yale lock was broken.

'I don't feel safe with the door like that,' Lorraine said and so we decided to drag the huge chest of drawers in front of it. We heaved and panted as it slowly inched towards the door, dragging the carpet into a bulge.

'This reminds me of the time we moved that big fridge in the shop. Do you remember?' Lorraine panted.

'Yeah, the one we got stuck in the doorway. Let's hope we don't do the same with this or we'll have to climb down the fire-escape.'

I put my back against the chest of drawers.

'One more push should do it.'

A last effort from both of us brought it into position.

'No-one could get in now,' I said, trying not to look at the filthy wall and skirting it had uncovered. 'Right, let's get these wet things off.'

I found some wire hangers and we hung our wet things on the side of the monstrous wardrobe in the alcove.

We sat in pyjamas, on the single beds facing each other and picked at the pizza although neither of us had much appetite. I drank my tepid tea, and as Lorraine didn't want hers I drank that too.

We tried to keep cheery, talking about what we might find at the Health Show and who might be there, but it was very forced. The time seemed to slow down and glancing at my watch I couldn't believe it was only ten past nine.

'I reckon the quicker we go to sleep the quicker the morning will come,' I said.

'Like Dad used to tell us to do on Christmas Eve?' Lorraine said, and we laughed, remembering how excited we'd be, hanging up stockings and jumping about unable to sleep.

Our Dad had endless patience and would repeatedly tuck us into our beds in the room we shared, telling us that Santa Claus couldn't come until we were asleep. We'd push our luck, messing about and calling for him to bring us a drink of water, or come and tuck us in again until our Mam would come in and tell us in no uncertain terms to be quiet and get to sleep or we'd get nothing.

I looked at the two uninviting beds, unable to decide which looked worse, the one with the insipid yellow nylon cover or the one with the faded blue. Both had stains that I did not allow my mind to contemplate.

'Which bed do you want?' I asked.

'Neither really. There's not much difference, they both look manky. You choose.'

The yellow covered bed was closest, so I pulled back the nylon cover to reveal beneath, nylon sheets spotted with cigarette burns.

'I thought nylon bedding died out in about 1974,' I said, looking at them in disgust.

'Oh man!' Lorraine said. 'Look at that!'

An old pair of underpants lay in her bed.

'Ugh! Are they clean?' I asked.

'Do you think I'm going to check, like? Aw that's disgusting. These beds haven't even been changed since the last time they were slept in.'

I don't know why we were surprised by that.

'That's revolting. I'm not sleeping in those sheets, I'm just going to lie on the top,' I said.

'I can't lie on a bed with filthy old underpants in it!' Lorraine said.

I looked around the room for a suitable implement and picked up the misshapen pair of ornamental coal tongs that hung on the fireside companion set.

'Open the window,' I commanded, and in one swift movement I hooked up the pants and slung them out of the window. 'And I'm not putting my head on that!' I said and jabbed the pillow with the tongs until it fell to the floor.

Lorraine nodded to her pillow and I did the same with that.

'Are you going to clean your teeth in the bathroom or in that?' Lorraine asked, pointing at the grubby sink in the alcove. We hadn't even looked at the bathroom. I could only imagine what sort of state that would be in.

'In here,' I decided. So we washed in cold water and cleaned our teeth then wrapped ourselves in our bath towels because we didn't want to lie on the bedcovers. We lay in the sickly glow of the lamp facing each other across the gap between the beds.

'Night, then.' Lorraine said.

'Night,' I answered and she turned off the light, leaving my eyes to slowly adjust, bringing unfamiliar dark shapes into focus.

CHAPTER THIRTY-EIGHT

'Lorraine! You awake?' I whispered.

I looked through the darkness trying to see if she was sleeping.

'I need to go to the bathroom. You'll have to help me move the chest and then come with me.'

'Yeah ok.' Lorraine's voice, tired and expressionless, came out of the darkness and I guessed that like me, she'd been lying staring into the blackness, listening to the background sounds of thuds and doors banging, trying to entice the oblivion of sleep.

She swung her legs and sat up, yawning, and we stumbled our way across the room in the dark to struggle with the chest of drawers for a while, until we thought to switch on the lamp.

'A couple of inches more and I'll be able to open the door enough to squeeze out,' I said.

We picked up our handbags just in case a thief was hiding on the stairs waiting to take advantage of our absence.

I hesitated at the door. The sound of the television was clearer out here and I could make out the sound of gunshots and drawled voices interspersed with sudden blasts of dramatic music. There was no-one in sight on the stairs although I could hear coughing and muffled voices from the floor below.

'What if we bump into that big beardy Scotsman?'

'We'll tell him to go and fook off.'

We made our way down the stairs to the bathroom as stealthily as we could. The corridors were surprisingly empty considering the constant footsteps and drunken voices we'd heard from our room.

We took turns to hover above the stained, seat-less lavatory as the other kept guard and then returned tentatively along the corridor, tense with fear that we might encounter one of the faceless occupants.

Back in the relative safety of our room, we replaced the chest of drawers and once again, wrapped ourselves in bath towels and lay on our beds to wait for sleep.

I closed my eyes and tried to imagine myself in my own bed at home, but it was difficult. I could not block out the constant drone of next door's television and Peter's warm body was not there to snuggle into. I shook thoughts of Peter from my mind, knowing it would make me feel worse to dwell on the fact that he was miles away.

I turned onto my side and lay listening to the increasingly familiar soundtrack of the house. Footsteps, doors banging, voices, thuds, footsteps, voices, doors banging…on and on like some endless nightmare. I wondered what these people were doing in the middle of the night. Why they were banging doors and running up and down stairs? I began to think that perhaps the businesses advertising in the local phone box operated from here. I turned onto my back, trying to deter my imagination from running off in the direction that it was heading.

The bed was very uncomfortable. My back ached and the blisters on my feet were painful. I shuffled about trying to find a more restful position. I'd have preferred an over-hard mattress to this sagging, lumpiness. As I moved my body, I felt a pressure in my bladder.

'Lorraine!' I hissed. 'I need to go back to the bathroom.'

And so began the pattern of the night.

We'd heave the chest away from the door, gather our handbags and make our way down to the filthy lavatory. Back in the bedroom, I'd once again lie in the dark in a state of semi-sleep until a particularly loud thump or voice would jolt me into consciousness and I'd feel the need to pee again.

'You can't possibly need to go again,' Lorraine said after the third or fourth time. 'You've just been and anyway, you only had two cups of cold tea.'

'I do, I need to go,' I whinged like a naughty child.

'It's psychological. You know what a palaver it is to get out of the room, so every time you try to relax you think how awkward it would be. Getting up, moving the chest, creeping downstairs, and then you think you really need to go and you think…oh man!'

'What?'

'I need to go now.'

I must have eventually succumbed to sleep as I was awakened by a glittering light playing on my closed eyelids. Opening my eyes I saw a thin shaft of sunlight coming through the window, a single beam of luminosity that cut through the dark, hitting the cracked mirror and throwing flickers of light across the shaded room.

I stretched and pulled myself up. My body ached and my eyes were gritty. I felt as though I hardly slept a wink. Which of course I hadn't.

I walked stiffly to the window. A cloudless blue sky spread endlessly above the vista of backyards and run-down buildings, and the sight warmed my soul. Morning had arrived, our night here was over.

I looked at my watch. Seven a.m.

Lorraine lay wrapped in her bath towel, legs tucked up and arms wrapped around her body. I wondered if I should wake her or leave her to sleep a little longer.

I stood at the window awhile pondering on how the morning sunshine had taken away the menace of the place, everything looked better, less sinister.

My little plant had turned its flowers to the sun, although the yards below still lay in shadow. I wondered if the shafts of sunshine ever reached far enough down to warm them, or if these fleeting rays high above were as close as they ever got.

I looked down the metal staircase and saw the underpants I'd thrown last night hanging over a step, next to a take-away box. On impulse I pushed up the sash window and flung out our pizza box, watching it bounce down the steps until it finally came to rest next to a couple of beer cans. Not really the kind of thing I'd usually do but I was feeling rebellious this morning.

Lorraine woke as I was fiddling with the wheel of her case. I could see that a small stone was wedged in the hub of the wheel arch causing the wheel to lock, and I managed to dislodge it with the handle of a teaspoon.

'Morning,' she croaked.

'Morning. I've managed to fix the wheel on your case. How did you sleep?'

'Like shite.' She sat up and stretched. 'I feel like I've been lying on a sack of spuds.'

The house was quiet, the activity of the night seemed to have settled down to the occasional door slam and of course the sound of Room Seven's telly.

'That bloody telly's been on all night,' Lorraine complained. 'I wonder if there's actually anyone in there or if it's just been left on by accident.'

'Maybe someone died in there watching it and hasn't been discovered yet,' I said, giggling.

'Wouldn't surprise me a bit,' Lorraine laughed.

Funny how a bit of morning sunshine changes perception. The night before, speaking of a dead body sat in front of a blaring television would have scared us senseless.

After we'd washed and dressed, we did the best we could to put each other's hair in some sort of style using Lorraine's electric styling tongs and lots of hairspray.

As we applied make up, sounds of the house waking up, as well as the smell of eggs and bacon, drifted up to us. The cooking smell was obviously a sign for the occupants to trundle down to breakfast judging by the increase in door slams and footsteps.

I knew without either of us saying that we would not be eating here.

'We'll have to walk back to Brighton and find somewhere for breakfast,' I said. 'I'm so hungry, even that greasy bacon is beginning to smell appetising.'

'I think we should get out of here as quickly as possible,' Lorraine said, putting the last of her things away in her case and zipping it up.

We pushed the chest of drawers across the lumpy carpet for the last time and I carefully opened the door and peered out.

'Anyone around?' Lorraine asked.

'No, but there seems to be a lot of action in the kitchen. The owner must have arrived to cook breakfast.'

'We should get reduction for not eating breakfast here.'

'We should get a reduction for staying the night.'

'Actually, he should pay us for staying.'

'Do you think we should tell him what we think of the place?'

'Oh yes,' Lorraine said, and I could tell by her face she had plenty to tell and would do so.

'What if he gets nasty? The weird beard man might be one of pals. I wouldn't like to annoy him.'

Lorraine straightened her shoulders and her face took on what I recognised as her don't-mess-with-me expression.

'Right,' she said. She narrowed her eyes and lowered her voice. 'This is the plan. We descend the stairs. We open the front door and place our cases in the path where you will wait with them.'

She was like Alec Guinness instructing the Ladykillers on their next action.

'I will go into the kitchen and confront him. You be ready to run. If he looks threatening, I'll shout 'run' and we'll scarper.'

'Ok,' I said, a little scared but also a little exhilarated.

As we moved down the stairs the smell of breakfast became less appetising as a smoky blue haze brought the smell of hot grease to us.

I opened the front door quietly, relishing the sea-scented fresh air, and took up my position.

The kitchen door was open and I could see Weird-Beard-Man, sitting with his back to me, still wearing his overcoat. A radio was playing - I was not happy to hear Bill Withers singing about waking to a lovely day. It was one of my favourite songs and I did not want it to be forever connected in my mind with this place.

There were no voices, no conversation, just the scraping of cutlery on plates and the hacking cough that we'd heard for most of the night.

'Here goes,' Lorraine whispered and in she went.

I heard a man's voice greet her with a cheery 'Good morning.'

It was not the kind of voice I'd expected, being reedy and rather effeminate.

'Morning,' Lorraine answered gruffly, and I heard her intake of breath, ready to launch her grievances.

'Bacon, eggs, sausages?'

I tried to squint through the hinged side of the door to see the man who I now imagined to be slightly built and meek rather than the menacing bearded giant I'd expected.

'No thank you...' Lorraine started.

'Black pudding, white pudding? It's all cooked and ready.'

'We won't be staying for breakfast...'

'Kippers?'

'I said no, thank you, we won't be eating here...'

'Cereal? Toast? No? Can't tempt you then?'

'Look here, we won't be staying for breakfast and we won't be coming back. In fact, I shall be complaining to the tourist office who suggested we should stay here. I have never in my life stayed anywhere as horrendous as this. The place is filthy, the facilities are inadequate and as for the noise, well! Televisions blaring all night, people running up and down stairs, shouting, doors slamming, it is absolutely disgraceful. I don't know how you have the audacity to charge people to stay here. I would rather sleep in a pigsty.'

There was a pause, the cutlery ceased its scraping, while Bill Withers, oblivious of the tension, continued to sing of the lovely day.

I grasped the handles of the cases, poising myself ready to run.

'I totally agree,' our host said. 'It's disgusting.'

I could almost hear the wind seeping from Lorraine's sails and wondered what she would say next, but before she could speak, the cheery voice spoke again.

'That's why I moved out. I used to live in Room One. Couldn't get a wink of sleep. Never again. Wouldn't stay here if I was paid.'

'Well!' Lorraine said, seemingly lost for words. 'There's your money.'

'Thank you very much. Sure you don't want a cuppa before you leave? Bacon sandwich?'

'Goodbye!'

'Well that told him,' she said as we closed the front door behind us for the last time ever, leaving Beardy-Weirdy and the coughers vying for our uneaten breakfast.

CHAPTER THIRTY-NINE

We took a shortcut through the silent streets, the only sounds being the clicking of our heels and the rattling of our case wheels.

I hobbled along, trying to walk without putting pressure on my blisters, which was nigh on impossible.

As we turned into the next street we saw a corner shop, the type that sells everything from food to coal to hardware. A man carried out a tower of stacked buckets and placed them next to the mops, brushes, nets of onions and sacks of potatoes that were spread across the pavement. I noticed that he had secured his wares by running a thin blue rope around them and tying the ends to the handle of the open shop door.

The shop smelled of sweat and dust. We found bottled water in a fridge at the back of the shop – we hadn't had a drink since the previous evening - and I bought a box of plasters. I sat on a wall outside and applied them to my blisters. My excuse for doing this in public is that I would not have been able to walk another step without them.

To my disgust Lorraine came out of the shop with a pack of ten cigarettes and a box of matches.

'Aw man! What you buying those things for?' I asked as she opened the pack, took a cigarette between her lips and lit it.

'I just need one after the night I've had,' she said, closing her eyes and blowing out a long curl of smoke.

'Me too,' I said. 'Pass one over.'

I had no intention of smoking one and had said it because I knew she wouldn't let me anyway.

'No way,' she said.

'Go on,' I said. 'Let me see how sucking on a burning stick of nicotine makes a night like last night seem better.'

'Get lost. You're not having one.'

'Why not?'

'Because I don't want you to. They're bad for you.'

'And I don't want you to. They're bad for *you*.'

We walked along, Lorraine trying to justify her lapse as I nagged her and presently we were walking along the seafront, the streets cleaner, the houses bigger and much better maintained.

It was a beautiful morning. The sea was calm, caressing the shore with gentle waves, and the sky clear and bright.

'We seem to have walked back a lot quicker than we did on our way there yesterday,' Lorraine observed.

'We know where we're headed this time. And it's not raining.'

The hotel came into sight and soon we were walking past manicured gardens, up stone steps and into the foyer.

A helpful lady at the reception desk suggested that as we were very early for the Health Show, we may like to leave our luggage in the cloakroom and have breakfast in the coffee lounge.

After depositing our cases, we sat in the powder room in front of ornate gold-framed mirrors and freshened up our make-up. I had dark circles under my eyes that Uncle Fester would have been proud of so I began to apply another layer of concealer.

'Can you hurry up with your titivating, I'm desperate for a cup of coffee,' Lorraine complained, so I quickly blended it in and we made our way to the coffee lounge.

We looked around in delight at the deep red sofas and armchairs grouped around low tables that held beautiful floral arrangements.

I felt my heels sinking into the thick carpet as we walked to seats near the ceiling-high French doors that were open to allow in the warm sea air. Cream silk curtains billowed gently, framing the view of the sea and as I sank into one of the chairs, my senses were blissfully soothed by the soft embrace of the cushions, the fragrance of the flowers and the soft, tinkling piano music.

I could quite easily have fallen into a restful sleep, except for the fact that I was ravenous.

A waiter in a black bowtie and highly polished shoes came for our order. He wasn't just wearing the bowtie and shoes of course, but it made an impression on me. I couldn't believe the contrast from the hovel we'd just left.

'This is more like it,' Lorraine said. 'To think, if we'd got our act together sooner we could have spent the night here.'

The waiter returned with a silver tray holding a pot of tea for me and one of coffee for Lorraine. There was a plate of what had been described as 'breakfast pastries'; mini-sized croissants with chocolate or lemon filling, little Danish pastries with apricots and peaches, individual strawberry and lime flans and tiny tartlets filled with crème patisserie and fresh berries. I felt like we'd wandered into Heaven.

It was one of the most pleasurable breakfasts I've ever had.

The sheer comfort of the cushions, the soothing music, the delicate fragrance of the flowers mingling with that of the freshly roasted coffee. Everything radiated an air of luxury. Polished tables, crystal vases, thick linen napkins, a silver tea strainer to hold my tea leaves.

The waiter returned, bringing more coffee and tea and offering more pastries which I'm ashamed to say we accepted and demolished.

When we could eat no more, we reclined in our chairs and Lorraine, taking up a magazine to read, offered me one. I shook my head.

As our seats faced the sea, I was hidden from view in the high backed chair and I closed my eyes and snuggled down.

I pondered on the theory that you need to experience pain to appreciate pleasure, darkness to recognise light. Would I have loved this so much if we hadn't spent the night where we had? I nodded off into a bizarre dream of croissants, grey bearded old tramps and a huge chest of drawers.

I was pulled from my dream by Lorraine nudging me gently.

'It's quarter to ten,' she said. 'We have fifteen minutes to freshen up before the show officially opens.

We were amongst the first in the queue, shuffling in to show our tickets and pick up a floor-plan and goody-bag.

'Let's go and find Jim,' I suggested. It would do us good to see a familiar face.

We located the Herbfirst stand on the plan and made our way through the rows of exhibitors, each stand having something exciting to entice me. Vegan foods and ingredients, current-trend supplements and herbal medicines, cruelty-free cosmetics and toiletries, organic cotton clothing, crystal jewellery, juicers, books…I wanted to stop at each one but I resisted.

There were therapists offering sample treatments and cookery demonstrations and I decided that once we'd seen Jim I'd plan a route around the exhibition halls, taking in every stand. I didn't want to miss a thing.

Jim was standing at the Herbfirst stand, clipboard at the ready and we were so pleased to see his familiar face and hear his lovely Scottish accent that we ran to hug him. He was delighted at how happy we were to see him, and also a little bemused.

We ordered stock from him, claiming our free cases of Echinacea, exclaiming loudly about how wonderful his products were, in hope that we would entice more customers for him.

We told him briefly of our adventures at the B and B but had to stop and calm him down as it did not look very professional for him to be standing in his smart suit, with his order book and product samples, spluttering and wiping away tears of laughter.

'Such a shame you didn't manage to get a room here,' he said. 'My room is fantastic. Huge king-size bed, Jacuzzi bath, balcony looking out to sea.'

'Aw be quiet, man,' Lorraine said.

'Really good offer too. It included free use of the gym and pool and there were complimentary drinks when we arrived.' Jim laughed as we told him we didn't want to know.

'Maybe next year,' he said.

There seemed to be a couple of people waiting to speak to him so we left him to it and headed off like two kids let loose in a sweetie shop.

We flitted about, tasting samples and talking to people, many of whom we'd spoken to over the phone but had never met. I met the girl from Karma who took our telephone order every week, and representatives from many other suppliers we used.

We placed orders and filled our (free) jute bags with the many samples we were given; herbal teas, vegan chocolate, organic breakfast cereal, apricot and sesame bars, sachets of seaweed shampoo, and our favourite – chocolate-dipped dried mango.

We were even given tiny aloe vera plants in little cardboard pots cut from old egg-boxes from the Pure Aloe Company. (I gave mine to Peter and he still has it. It is now a huge great thing that lives in a terracotta pot and over the years has had many of its offshoots re-potted and given away. I reckon there must be hundreds of people in the north-east with an aloe-vera plant that originated from my free sample.)

The hall at the top of the building had been set up for refreshments. There were food counters at the back offering all kinds of vegetarian and vegan food; curries, stirfries, pies, sandwiches, salads, burgers, wraps and soups to name but a few. We bought fruit smoothies and veggie-hotdogs, and sat at a table with a view out to sea, although we'd scoffed so many free samples, I'm surprised we found room for them.

We spent the afternoon retracing our steps, making sure we hadn't missed anything, and also looking at stands that had been too busy to see anything when we'd passed earlier.

We returned to a stand selling toiletries made with rose oil we'd visited earlier where we'd ordered a whole stand of rose-oil products for the shop and had been given free gift packs to take home. One of the factors that had influenced our purchases was the woman demonstrating the products. Her thick shining dark hair and radiant flawless complexion were enough for us to believe in their effectiveness, as she claimed to use nothing else.

She noticed us, and calling us over, offered us each a free facial treatment as she'd been too busy earlier.

I watched as Lorraine had her facial first, then I lay back enjoying the scent of the rose oil as it was massaged into my skin. I struggled to stay awake, the sleep owed to me from the previous night crept up as I relaxed. I managed to fight it off and when my treatment was finished, I drowsily opened my eyes to see a great crowd of people watching.

'Thank you,' I said as I pulled myself up.

'No. Thank you. You've brought me lots of customers.' She gave us each a bottle of rose oil to thank us and we left her with a queue of women waiting to try the treatment they'd seen us enjoying.

By four o'clock we were foot-weary and laden with goodies to take home.

'I'm sure we've seen everything at least three times,' I said. 'And we'll have to be leaving soon, it's a long walk to the station.'

We went to say goodbye to Jim and made our way back to the hotel reception area.

'Let's order a taxi and spent the last hour in the hotel bar rather than walking to the station with all these bags and our cases,' Lorraine suggested.

'Do you think we should?'

'Why not? Neither of us are driving. Let's have a cocktail to finish off our visit.'

We made our way back to the cloak room where we stashed our bags of samples and freebies with our cases, then went into the Powder Room.

'Was it just this morning that we were in here?' Lorraine said as we sat in front of the mirrors admiring our complexions after the rose oil treatment.

'Yes. And what's even more difficult to believe is the fact that we were in that bloody awful house just this morning.'

'Seems like days ago.'

'I know. I felt so wretched in that place, I thought we'd made a huge mistake coming. Yet I've really enjoyed today.'

'Me too. And I've felt as though we were part of it. You know, that we are doing what we are meant to be doing.'

'Yes, I've felt like that today. As though we're really part of the Health Trade now. Like we know what we're doing and not just muddling along anymore.'

I laughed.

'Well I'm not so sure about that,' I said. 'I'm sure we've many more potholes to fall down yet.'

We tidied our hair and applied lipstick and blusher then went into the hotel bar. It was busy but not crowded and we found a couple of high seats at the bar.

Lorraine picked up a cocktail menu and read out suggestions but I wasn't really listening. I was looking at our reflections in the mirror behind the bar.

'Hey look at us,' I said, nudging Lorraine. The tinted mirror and the soft lighting was very flattering and we tried out a few poses, crossing our legs and turning our heads as we pouted and preened.

The barman arrived as we were laughing and trying to out-do each other.

'What can I get for you, ladies?' he asked.

'We'll start with daiquiris I think,' Lorraine said.

I noticed it was the first drink on the list and I hoped she wasn't intending for us to make our way through them all.

'You choose the next one, we'll take turns,' she said, and we sat drinking cocktails as though we were two highly successful career women and not just two daft lasses from Walker.

CHAPTER FORTY

As the taxi pulled up to the station it was drizzling. We'd spent too long in the bar, and probably had one cocktail too many and just made it onto the train in time.

We found our seats, stashing our bags in the luggage rack and began the first part of our journey home.

As the train pulled out, the heavens had opened. Heavy black clouds hung in the sky as the rain lashed at the windows, running in horizontal channels, forced by the movement of the train rushing through the deluge.

From Victoria we took the tube back to King's Cross. I sat avoiding eye-contact with my fellow-passengers – I had learned that you do not speak to strangers on the Underground.

At last we boarded the train to Newcastle, the final but longest leg of our journey.

The carriage was warm and our seats comfortable and at last I could lean back and give in to the tiredness that had been waiting for relief all day. I closed my eyes and aided by the cocktails and the after-slump of the activity of the day, tumbled instantly into a deep slumber.

We must have slept for hours. I was aware that I'd surfaced occasionally, the rhythmic der-der-der-dunk of the train shifting seamlessly from my dreams to my wakefulness as I stretched and shuffled in my seat only to drift off again to the pulse of the railway.

Lorraine woke me as we were passing through York.

'We're about an hour from home. I've been to get us a cuppa, we've just got time.'

'Lovely, thanks,' I said as I took the cardboard cup and the Kitkat she held out to me.

The tea was perfect; hot and cheering. I took a sip, smiling to myself as I realised I would soon be back with Peter.

How I had missed him! Such a short time apart and yet I knew I never wanted to be parted from him again. And of course I'd missed Rosie. I couldn't wait to hold her in my arms again and feel her soft curls against my face.

'What are you smiling about?' Lorraine asked.

'Just thinking about Rosie.' I said, as I snapped my Kitkat and bit into one of the chocolatey fingers.

'I think it's been quite a success, all things considered,' Lorraine said.

'Definitely. I can't wait for all our orders to arrive. The rose oil stand will look great in the shop, I know just the place for it, near the toiletries at the back. And I'm looking forward to getting those Dead Sea toiletries. Maybe I'll make a window display of beauty products. You know, a Christmas gift idea display.'

'I loved that frozen meal company,' Lorraine said. 'Frozen meals are so often full of salt and additives but they were just like homemade and all vegetarian too.'

'Hey I've had one of my brilliant ideas,' I said, and Lorraine rolled her eyes.

'Come on then, let's have it.'

'You know how sometimes we cook dinner in the shop to take home with us? Well I think we should make huge amounts and freeze portions to sell. We could do curries and chillies and soup and lasagne…all sorts of stuff. We just need to order some foil boxes and we'll need a new chest freezer…'

'Mmm, sounds good. Actually I had a bit of a brilliant idea myself.'

'Yeah?'

'Yeah. It was the food hall that set me thinking. The food offered was nice, but we could do better.'

'You want to open a food hall?'

'No! I think we should provide a catering service. Vegetarian and vegan food for parties. We could do weddings, birthday parties, meetings…'

'Great idea! And what about party food for children on special diets?'

'Yes, and even dinner party food for people unsure what to give vegetarian guests.'

'The only problem is delivering it. My car is on its last legs. And it looks like a boxer that's been in the ring too many times. Not ideal for a catering business.'

'I'm sure the shop could pay towards a new one. After all it will be being used for business, I'm sure we can put it down as an expense. We could ask the accountant the best way to do it.'

'Great! Lorraine said. 'So that's frozen foods, catering service, new car. Anything else?' I began rooting about in my handbag.

'Do you have a pen? I need to make a list.'

'No time for that, it's nearly time to get ready to get off the train, we're home.'

We stood and retrieved our cases from the luggage rack and I looked out of the window as the train slowed as we headed from Gateshead towards the river.

As we crossed the Tyne, I looked past the Swing Bridge to the great arch of the Tyne Bridge welcoming me home. The city lights illuminated the familiar Newcastle skyline; the Quayside and The Guildhall in the foreground, and the majestic tower of the Cathedral crowning the city with its coronet shaped spire.

The train pulled into the Central Station, warmly filled with light and with people, and finally came to a stop.

The door was opened and we shuffled forward as people ahead of us descended onto the platform.

We lifted down our cases and were making our way along the platform through hordes of people, an unintelligible voice giving announcements on the tannoy, when I heard my name.

I turned to see Peter, moving through the crowd, Rosie's chubby little arms around his neck, her face glowing as she smiled at passers-by. She caught sight of me as I hurried towards them and she held out her arms, her little hands splayed like starfish as she squealed with joy.

'Mumma' she said, and I knew I was home.